brain, mind, soul

καλὸς κάγαϑός

the metaphysics of neurons

*from a rigorous discussion
of the properties of the neurons and the brain
to the mechanisms through which this grayish jelly
generates and explains the emotional life, consciousness, thought,
the sense of beauty and justice, the need for infinity
and almost all that we love to call "soul"*

published by *Amazon*
ISBN 9798345638149

This is an ambitious and playful attempt at examining how neurons and the brain work, on one side, and the properties of consciousness and emotional life, on the other, in search for the origin of that need of ours for infinity, our perception that something in us – something we love calling 'soul' – transcends ourselves and expands in space and time, beyond the limits of our body and our life.

It is a need for infinity.

Precisely. _Infinity_, not _all, or everything... Infinity._

Because 'all' implies a limit that encloses. Like a photograph, a cage, four walls to guard what is inside. Infinity, instead, is freedom; it may be difficult, hard, full of obstacles, but it is always open to navigate, discover, conquer. Infinity blooms into further infinities, in ever new directions and dimensions: countless interpretations and viewpoints, on reality, emotions, life, their variety and novelty.

The organization of our brain suggests where this longing for infinity, knowledge and freedom arises from. In fact, there are no photographs in our mind, no drawings that fix or enclose reality. Only relations are recorded in the brain, and they are used to _assemble_ an internal _model_ – not a mere depiction – of reality and life, and to keep modifying it, over and over again.

In our mind reality is but an intricate network of relations, over many planes and along many independent and orthogonal dimensions: a network that includes a constantly rebuilt image of ourselves, centered in space and TIME. Not the time we perceive, but a time that we create, invent within ourselves by _composing_ it as an intersection of experiences, sequences, threads that run, slow down, vanish and reappear.

The countless viewpoints on this network of relations constitute _our_ reality, _our_ time, _our_ life. It can be seen as the product of metaphysical consciousness, but the multiple views, and their being centered on oneself, are the crucial intrinsic features of neuronal processing.

Everything that happens to a living organism – whether it has a brain or not – is evaluated in terms of its possible relevance for survival and well-being, through either innate associative mechanisms, based on previous experiences. This may produce specific bodily responses and changes in the operating mode of the nervous system, what has been defined as the body marker of emotion.

Meanwhile, since a neural circuit is always producing some activity, if a brain is there it will necessarily be continuously active and elaborate the incoming information and the one it contains through an activity that sustains mind ring and imagination.

In the complex interplay of perception, imagination and emotion, neuronal systems perform their tasks – from mere sensory processing to attribution of meaning, from modeling reality to higher cerebral functions – by *cruising* among data, actual and possible relations, variable readings, trying to follow a thread, but capturing and being captured by continually changing overall perspectives.

This same multiplicity – and this wandering among many threads and intuitions – is the keystone and mode of *consciousness* itself, which emerges from the contribution of multiple cerebral circuitries as the capability of harmonizing the countless diverse views that pop up in our brain into a 'unitary' reading, consistent but complex and mutable as we feel our *Ego* is, infinite, multifarious and complex, capricious, *alive*.

From this activity of building a 'sense', the esthetic (ecstatic?) attitude emerges: sensitivity to multiplicity, to the harmonic convergence of many dimensions. It is our pleasure in perceiving ourselves growing and expanding in ever new, unexplored territories, in directing our gaze to catch novel abstract essentialities. And such abstract essentialities are for us as real as objects are, as real as anything else we look at, because our gaze tells us what we can feel and *live*, rather than what we can see.

But esthetics, the sense of beauty as a sensitivity to higher harmonies, also guides our behavior: a link that connects ethics and esthetics, beautiful and good: καλὸς κάγαϑός.

The soul, *anima*, appears here as the subject of this complex and deep gaze onto reality. The subject of a legendary translation of things, of facts and events; of love, commitment, work, sociality; of ideal life as well as everyday life. A translation that does not deny concreteness or truth to reality, time, life, but simply animates ('*anima*'...) them, changes them from sobs into poetry, from sounds into music.

* * *

This is a textbook of Physiology and Metaphysiology, and as such it aims at scientific correctness.

Indeed, it tries to be *extremely* scientific.

A solid rule that has always guided scientific research – never confessed but inexorable – is that among possible interpretations of experimental data the right one, the true one, the one to be defended even in the face of torture, must be the most beautiful one. Thus, we tried and pursue this path as far as possible, looking for a truth that be not only beautiful, but also approaching music and poetry, as closely as possible.

Poetry may well be an ambitious target.
But, given the topic, how could one be content with less?

* * *

<u>This is a three-level book.</u>

The main body is a discussion of what our current knowledge of the functioning of the nervous system – and its capability of learning and changing – can explain about mental functions, affects, motivation, love, esthetics, ethics, ideals and our need for something infinite that transcends us: all that is generally referred to as 'the soul'. It is written in a conversational and sometimes imaginative way, but the notions and claims it contains, though sometimes far from demonstrated, are in all cases consistent with current scientific knowledge (tentatively 'true' in Popper's conception of scientific truth, i.e., falsifiable by appropriate experimental procedures, but not falsified as of now).

> The second level, intermixed here and there, is a 'scientifically and politically correct', though not exhaustive, description of how our nervous system and brain are structurally and functionally organized, and of the main mechanisms of information processing and recording, with notes on the mechanisms of emotional life, motivational control, learning.
> It is dispensable if one is only interested in getting a general picture.

The third level is intermezzo. Images, free thoughts, metaphors, suggestions, not necessarily needed to follow the line of reasoning, but helping to set the appropriate mood and mental climate to appreciate the argument.

dedicated to those who will not
give up growing, discovering, wondering,
and even more to those who did give up,
but might change their mind

I
Infinity, just to begin

'To infinity, and beyond!'

Easy, for the imaginative cartoonists of *Toy story*, to put this challenging cry in the mouth of an improbable, awkward and foolish toy-astronaut, paranoically unconscious of its being a toy, and indeed positively and tragicomically identified in its role of interplanetary envoy in defense of the universe, against the forces of evil...

Yes, easy, because this way, thanks to sympathy and smiling, nobody rejects the shocking force of the extraordinary insight – not at all comical – that underlies this apparently innocent motto. If one stops smiling and suspends the benign sympathy that this novel don Quixote for children (for children?!?) evokes, because he is so serious and naive, and proud and firm, and plump and nonsensical..., then one realizes that the paradox and the explosive contradiction are not at all unacceptable. It may be difficult for the most logical part of ourselves to accept the idea of 'beyond infinity', but the most open, receptive, intuitive regions of our spirit are perfectly at ease with the idea that infinity can be inhabited, and nothing is more precisely natural to our spirit than trespassing in it, and indeed progressing further, well beyond!

Infinity frightens us because we cannot embrace it all (comprehend it). But even more upsetting is that, were we ever able to do it, we should stop on its border and admit the vacuum, the *nothing*, farther on. It is unacceptable that infinity, wide as you wish, may enclose everything.

Even more unacceptable, indeed, is that one could not move beyond. So: beyond infinity, but not into the vacuum. Rather, towards an even wider infinity, outside of which higher and wider infinities are waiting for us. Honestly, one feels much better if infinity, infinite as it may be, does not claim it can encompass everything, and leaves us some more to explore.

An infinity larger than the physical one...

$$* * *$$

Mathematicians, who can always find some tricks and algorithms to abstractly reproduce the music of spirit, have long solved the problem, elegantly as they usually do it. You write '∞' to say infinity, square it, and there it is: ∞^2, and go on with ∞^3, ∞^{10}, ∞^n, ∞^∞, and all higher order infinities. Elegant, and veeeeery mathematical, as you don't understand it, unless you decide a priori that you *WANT* to understand it.

What does it mean? it means that it is not even enough to say that there is always something bigger. It is not a matter of being bigger (be rich as you wish, if I give you a dollar you become richer...): here the question is about being *definitely* bigger, quite a huge lot bigger, intrinsically, foolishly, *infinitely* bigger, QUALITATIVELY bigger. Infinity is something else, with respect to any magnitude. Still, an infinity to the second power is conceivable, and it is definitely something more than any simple infinity...

It seems like spewing hot air. Instead, it is an obvious perception, deep in the soul, even for a child, though one may not be able to tell it.

Take a line. Take it long, but really, really long. Okay, take it *infinitely* long: will it ever manage to cover just the surface of a toasted bread slice? Take a surface as big as you wish, extending to infinity this side and the other, will you ever be able to play ball with it, if it does not have at least the thickness of a rag, which is no longer a surface, but a tri-dimensional object?

No surprise, we know it well: infinity, large as it may be, cannot do it, it is not enough, does not reach there. There is always something farther. Always. Anyway.

And after all the dimensions that multiply infinities?

Maybe some god, or God, the spirit of the world, maybe the soul...? Where does this commotion of endlessness come from, where does the visceral certainty of the *'beyond'* ?

A long-preferred hypothesis is spirit-god, who imposes to intellect, and calls us. This was in the myth of the cavern: we can perceive a limited 'reality' of the conceivable, livable experience, but we feel that a truth must exist, and a reality, of a different and more solid, *true* nature. We find this in every form of religion and mysticism. It seems that humans have always needed this: a reality that be immense, higher, something to surrender to, and let the spirit wander, relax, dream.

It is interesting that this way the infinity of the universe is diminished, enclosed in a box in the hands of God...

An alternative explanation is that – God or not God – we need something 'beyond' as a defense: it is necessary, it helps; perceiving something that is greater than, and beyond, infinity is the easiest and most effective way of negating the *infiniteness* of infinity, and the commotion-confusion that follows.

As is always the case, there is a third way (is it always the case? in Italy, decades back, many were convinced there was a third way! now, it has remained few of us...). But the third way is always the most demanding one, and according to many it does not exist at all, and anyway cannot be found, cannot be followed.

The third way to look at it is that infinity is admissible, it is real and conceivable, but is irrelevant, it is just the first step. Because no infinity can exclude the possibility of a further dimension, in which all infinities considered hereto just project as a small dot, while the space of the 'real' infinitely expands as each new dimension is added. It is not simply a problem of lines that cannot enclose a surface, of infinite surfaces that can wrap an object but cannot fill and pervade it. The question is that no infinite space can encompass more than an instant or include movement.

The question is that no physical reality in space or time can embrace an emotion, an idea, an interpretation, a desire, a passion, a dream.

* * *

Warning!

Avoid reading the following section, and in general all sections written with this character. This is material containing mostly data and information – pretty rigorous but dispensable, by the way – at difference with the rest of the text, that is made up of accurate combinations of words, aimed at evoking the fleeting and misleading sensation of understanding, and illumination, with subsequent disappointment, uncertainty, confusion and regret – 'for a moment everything seemed so clear !' – from which pleasant languor follows, and admiration for the author, and tender remembrance, which is our not-least, unconfessed and badly concealed aim.

We apologize, but it has been necessary to include these 'technical' sections, to comply with the regulations of the Ministry of Education, in case this were to become – as it should in our most optimistic expectations – the official textbook of neurophysiology (or metaphysiology), as soon as this topic breaks in into the study programs of high schools and elementary schools, and possibly in experimental nursery schools.

INFINITE OR NOT?

'Only two things are infinite, the universe and human stupidity, and I'm not sure about the former.' (Albert Einstein) Indeed, scientists do not love infinity: you don't know how to place it, how to fix it to the bench to do an experiment on it, how to be sure that it does not run away as you try to harness it into a theory. Scientists like 'brain' more than they like 'soul', because 'soul' directly evokes infinity, and perhaps 'mind' plays a similar trick, while 'brain' is less dangerous.

A grayish and little poetic jelly, much easier to trap into physical schemes: cause-effect, action-reaction, stimulus-response.

We shall discuss later what a biological system is, how it is characterized, but we can already anticipate some hints. Briefly, it is a system that presents some structural, ordering and functional features that maintain a certain degree of persistence and stability although they continually change and evolve. This is made possible by a complex system of mechanisms that enact physical and chemical responses to any possible stimulus or influence that the external world exerts on the biological system. This way, the system can maintain most of its characteristics unaltered, while it partially modifies some others, thereby changing no more than what is necessary to survive.

In complex systems, such as multi-cellular organisms, responses cannot be performed by the same sub-system that records external influences (for example the skin is stimulated by the heat of the iron, but the muscles must react, and pull the skin away from the contact, to avoid getting burned). Therefore, there must be mechanisms and systems to grant communication among the parts of the organism. The principal such mechanisms are the hormonal and nervous systems.

Hormones are substances that a group of cells produce and release in response to a stimulus. Through blood circulation, hormones reach all cells in the organism, so that they evoke the appropriate responses by those cells that are supposed to produce them. Conversely, the nervous system is a network of cells – neurons. Each neuron can generate an electrical response, if it is appropriately stimulated; it will then propagate such electrical signal along the membrane of its processes, to several millimeters or even meters away, and transmit the impulse to other neurons, or a muscle or gland cell. The first role played by neurons is therefore to 'transfer' a signal from one point to another in the organism.

In many simple animals several groups of neurons are organized to generate variably complex responses to external signals, but there is no single control center that organizes and 'interprets' all this activity. Typically, in invertebrates, groups of neurons constitute 'ganglions' in distinct portions of the body that coordinate specific local responses.

In vertebrates most of the neurons and their connections are organized into a central axis (*neuraxis*) that, in addition to producing local responses, also performs a general coordination of all neural activity. This gives rise to a *central nervous system* (CNS).

As one ascends the zoological scale, the mass and complexity of the coordinating and supervising structures grow, until a *brain* can definitely be recognized, and its complexity tremendously grows, from the few grams of a frog to more than three pounds in human brain.

* * *

Classical science does not depart from this vision. – No infinities there.

The nervous tissue is an evolutional conquest that makes it possible to build multi-cellular organisms capable of complex and coordinated functions and responses. Its meaning, goal and fate are to make it possible to generate the appropriate responses to any external (or internal) stimulus.

Stimulus, response.

In between, the nervous system.

We study how it perceives and records phenomena, stimuli and conditions from within and outside the organism (sensory systems) and how it produces the appropriate vegetative (autonomic nervous system) or behavioral responses (motor systems).

Classical science does not depart from this view.

Nice and simple way of looking at things. Then, little surprise if none of us is willing to identify themselves, their mind, their own experience, identity and consciousness with this purely reactive apparatus, made up of sensory, autonomic and motor systems, but where there are no interpretative or creative entities, capable of passion, fantasy, desire, dreams and ideals.

Hundreds of billions of neurons are not enough to suggest infinity, if they are indeed organized into a device that is only built to produce responses.

But really there is nothing more than that in the nervous system?

No infinity at all?

II
LET'S START AGAIN: LIFE

Uncertain, rough, jagged and confusing is the border between *life* and *soul*. Still, the different matter they are made of is evident. It may even be easier to deny a machine a 'life' – a feature that even the most stupid worm or thread of grass possess – than the possibility of a soul. Robots and spaceships in science fiction do not *live*, but some have been capable of suffering, desiring, dreaming, loving.

To preserve a minimum of scientific dignity some definitions must be crystallized, some scaffolds erected to try and look farther. So, let's put down some definitions, let's draw some clear limits.

Let's forget, for a moment, *our* life, the *life* of humans, *life* as history, *life* as memory. And let us talk of 'life' – *bios*, the life of biologists, theologists, cosmologists: where there is life, and where there isn't, what makes the difference between a living entity and an inanimate one, how life begins and ends. Pretty light and easy questions...

In this world it is possible to persist, or survive, or to live.

Structures and objects, up to a certain degree of complexity – wonderful crystals of purple quartz – reach stable equilibrium, each molecule resting as comfortably as possible, nobody nervous, no energy to give away. Cold. Dead. In the absence of external perturbations and forces they do not change; they exist and persist for ever. They may grow, sometimes, by engulfing in their – senseless and wonderful – dead organization new molecules, that they subtract to the external world, where life quivers. Sometimes they disaggregate, they get lost.

More dynamical and complex structures are sustained by unstable balances, that are not 'equilibrium'. Static appearances with no peace, they survive thanks to forces that corrode and nick and change them, but they can change so skillfully that they dissipate the forces that undermine them; they even exploit the energy that comes from this dissipation to repair, regenerate and perpetuate – as long as it is possible – the features that define their fundamental nature, and to reproduce their own equilibriums and to reproduce themselves by generating living 'copies' of themselves. This is the main feature of biological systems: they are dynamical systems that maintain their integrity and evolve during their life by means of complex processes of regulation of their internal parameters, and of a continuous interaction with the external environment. This is what we can rigorously call 'life'.

An aspect may help better than others in clarifying the difference. Left alone, a crystal does not change and persists. Conversely, with no interactions with the exterior, with no forces that try and change it, with no exchanges to gain energy, a living being nevertheless does change, but does not persist, does not survive, it degenerates and dies. A fragile and demanding balance. Like music that seems to develop and persist in an admirable equilibrium of vibrations, but wanes into echoes if one stops singing, and dies in still air.

* * *

"Ninetta bella, morire di maggio / ci vuole tanto, troppo coraggio"
My lovely Ninetta, one must be really brave to die in May, too brave"

This was Fabrizio De André in one of his songs. Precisely.

Who would not agree?

As usual, poetry is the one that does the magic. Because, strictly speaking, it does not make sense. Bravery... One dies even without having any. And if one has to be brave, why more in May than in November?

But yes. War, sickness, pain, death, at night, while it is raining, no moon, the earth grey and forsaken, the branches dead and dried... maybe death, loss, suffering, pain are more tolerable, they seem inevitable.

How can you accept them when the sun shines and colors to the fields, the breeze whispers among green and tender leaves, the whole nature promises new life and awakens every hope to grow and blossom, to be reborn?

How can you talk about being reborn and blossom just now, in December, among hurricanes and floods, never-ending wars, public debt, unemployment, hopeless crises, youngsters who can't see a future?

Nature, life, enact a continuous show around us, which restarts again every day after the curtain has fallen; it has always been like this, everything dies and is reborn, new and ever different.

So, it is not strange than man cannot accept death as a final event, with no return: eternal souls, lives in other dimensions, metempsychosis...

Because one cannot imagine consciousness that switches off, the soul that stops looking around, understanding, enjoying and suffering, waking up every morning to dream, to love...

Life is a strange trick, an ingenious wonderful game. Fake unstable balance that sustains and reproduces itself in its apparent stability while slowly changing.

But the laws of Physics are inexorable: as long as a system is stable, ok, but if you crack it, let it move toward disorder, it will inevitably march that way.

What, then, sustains life?

What force pushes the living organism to continually fight to survive and repair the damages of time and rebuild, moment by moment, arduous balances, and reproduce itself, and proliferate?

* * *

Physical chemistry, in principle, is not complex.

It is like running a nursery school. Many hyperactive children: they run, jump, scream, they chase one another, flounder and turn around. If you organize them in such a way that they have room, distractions, amusements, and the possibility of settling down in all imaginable ways, of saying and doing what they want, then it is more likely that they will not run away or destroy everything. Also, it is less likely that they build something, or efficiently perform some work...

The question is energy. The more they waste in running and playing (hell, this always ruins us, post-catholic thinkers: who says that this is *wasted* energy, who says that only the energy that is used to work is good, well spent?), the more energy they *devote* to move around and play, the less they will have to build or destroy, in or outside the school.

Atoms and molecules are admirable equilibriums of ridiculously small matter particles and huge energies. They get closer, match, combine and move apart. The more the electrons are at ease in a molecule, wide paths for them to run around, some beloved protons at reach, other electrons out of the way, the more they can shake and play without disturbing the general balance, the less they are likely to perform a work, by running away, or moving or changing other molecules.

The same is true for big molecules, such as proteins. They are at ease when their regions can turn around and resettle, graciously combining among one-another, electrical charges well organized, water molecules trapped where they fit well, hydrophobic regions in reciprocal contact... Portions of the molecule that wish to rearrange and explore other positions can do it without compromising the general structure, and the protein is well and stable.

But if the possibilities of rearranging and changing position are limited, as when one sleeps on a chair, or a hard and narrow couch, sooner or later the equilibrium breaks down, the protein changes its form and interacts with other substances. Possibly performing work.

Physicists and mathematicians can tell it precisely, as usual.

The more numerous the ways a system can rearrange itself (states or conformations), the more energy is trapped in this babbling: it is energy that 'faces inward', *entropy* – yes, let's say it, entropy, although it is an arcane word, that repels most people who encountered it, and who hope nobody will ever ask them about it. The more energy faces inward, the less can be given away to perform external work: the 'free energy', the fraction that can perform work, is less.

The equation is precise and is one of the most general equations in physics. The probability that a system rests in a certain conformation is proportional to the number of states that this conformation admits – like playing the roulette: only one good number, 36 losing numbers; either the wheel is deceitful or most of the times a losing number will come out.

Probability. Entropy is proportional to the logarithm of probability. Mathematics tells us the probability that a system rests in a particular state, and such probability tells us what part of the energy associated to the system is entropy and cannot be used.

Entropy reflects probability, disorder: did it ever happen that something reordered itself (a single ordered conformation versus innumerable disordered ones) on its own? Entropy reflects the ease for electrons, molecules, forces and relations to fool around without doing damage.

Maybe happiness itself is a metaphor, or even a form, of entropy.

The possibility of discharging energy, pursuing desires, expressing wishes and not needing to change modes and situations.

A consequence of this is that if one is too happy, one gets drowsy and dull and may lose the drive to do, build, fight, even to merely preserve happiness (and happy marriages break apart...).

'Happiness' is a heavy word. One should be more cautious: well-being, maybe. Happiness is something more. But how much more, why more? to be, not to be, to die, to sleep, perchance to dream...

But it is not time for this, yet.

* * *

Entropy and TIME.

Time is abstract. As such, it has its meter. It is absolute distance, and relative. Past and future are far away and equally remote.

But the time of things has a direction.
The time of things erodes, smooths, corrodes, disintegrates.

It does not create. It cannot. It does not move backwards.
And it plays the role of an inexorable force of nature and matter.

But not even time is omnipotent. Time only erodes and disintegrates what allows it to do it.

A force is needed, possibly the slightest gust of wind, to upset even the weakest and most unstable balance. Be it ready to ruinously break down, it will persist as long as it is left alone. The time of things is powerful, but it cannot start its own job by itself. It is blocked, it just watches and waits, until the balance gets compromised; then, time breaks in, efficient, rapid or quiet, but inexorable. It dismantles. Until a new balance is reached, be it necessary or fortuitous, be it greatly or only slightly more stable. Then, time gets back to its patiently waiting for another cracked balance that it might destroy. Think of a card tower. It could rest there for eternity. A slight shake, and it breaks down. You can make it more accurate, solid, ingenious. It may still break down, but it will take a stronger shake.

Here is the law of time. And of physics and chemistry. Often, improbable orders and equilibriums would wish to break apart, but they cannot. This is *potential energy*, ready to be set free, as in a match or a bomb. On the other side, there stand brakes, limits and restraints that someone must crack to let order disperse and vanish. This is *activation energy*, that must hit the house of cards for it to crash down or trigger the bomb to detonate it.

Everything whirls and vibrates in the world of matter. Temperature is but a measure of molecular frenzy. Give it some heat, the temperature rises, every molecule vibrates more, each atom twirls to snake out of the molecule that traps it, each electron, proton, neutron bites more strongly the brake straps that binds it to its atom. For each intensity of a shake, only some card towers are possible. For each value of temperature only certain molecules and atoms are possible: only those in which attractions and restraints are stronger than frenzy. And time is there. It peers in, ready to break in and destroy improbable and cracked castles.

Just after the Big Bang, while the universe was cooling down, in the first moments of its billions of years, inert matter clotted on each possible combination, more numerous and complex as the temperature was decreasing, and allowed more precarious arrangements to stabilize. Matter piled up on each single possible shelf of the chemical vocabulary, like snow on the branches of the trees. Like snow, ready to fall at the first blow of the storm or at the fist bump of an unskilled skier.

Sunrays arrive to the earth. Everything could warm up slowly, and matter could experience new instabilities and balances. Just like the snow, thrown up again in the air by the storm.

Thereafter, some million years later, the sun old and weakened, everything would cool down again, the storm would gradually wane. The same snow would not be on the same branches, but some snow would still be on the branches, just like before. And everything slowly getting colder, quiet, coagulated, still and immutable.

Poor time! With all its impatience and care and tricks, it cannot make sure that each snowflake finds its way to the ground, while the wind is blowing. But afterwards, when the wind has calmed down, it is too late, the snowflakes have settled down again and nothing cracks their unstable balance, at the border of the branch, to let them free to finally lie on the ground.

Time cannot make sure that while the universe cools down each atom, each electron escapes soon enough from fatal attractions, that it finds its best environment, so that it will eventually be happy, once the frenzy has cooled down, when it no longer has the energy to disengage from unlucky, fortuitous and gloomy restraints.

Tasteless history of matter. Senseless and wonderful in the evocative games of stalactites and stalagmites, in admirable quartz crystals, in the astonishing ambiance of the Grand Canyon, in the charm of a crystalline water spring...

* * *

Here they are, chemistry and physics...

A world of constrained order. Ready to fall apart if only someone helps. Someone clever enough, maybe, to use that same energy, the energy released by a blocked order when it breaks down, to crack other balances, other orders that may also fall apart. It is like a line of dominoes, that stand up and wish they could lie down, if only someone gave them the kick that is needed: the slight, gentle touch that unbalances just one of them. In losing its balance it will release the energy that is hidden in its standing up, smash down the second domino; this will do the same to the next, and so on for all the others.

A world of constrained order. And possibly someone so clever to guide the production of disorder, the release of hidden potential energy, maybe even so clever – alive! - not only to do that, but to use that same energy that is released to build, and maintain, and strengthen and reproduce *its own* order, that could not exist and persist without care and maintenance and repairs, without energy, its own *life*.

Among the possible equilibriums experimented by matter, there is a class of intriguing molecules: RNA, a type of nucleic acids. RNA is a well-designed balance of smaller molecules – assemblies of a sugar, a base, two phosphates – linked in long twirled chains. A revolutionary equilibrium, because it favors the association of other similar assemblies, which orderly align on its blueprint and produce a perfect replica, a new identical chain (more properly, a complementary, mirroring chain, but that makes little difference). The molecules that constitute RNA can stay perfectly well on their own, but if they approach an RNA chain already formed they are strained and attracted, their small card tower may crack while they settle down into a more complex and stable house of cards: a new chain of RNA, complementary to the first one and mirroring it. Certainly, this is not life, yet. But it recalls a crucial aspect of life itself, the capacity and tendency to reproduce itself. And, even more important, the capacity to exploit the energy hidden in relatively stable, restless molecules and calm them down into more complex structures, into higher orders.

* * *

ROS: Reactive Oxygen Species. Free energy (too free?...) that sustains life.

Oxygen is life. Because it is eager for electrons. He who is truly alive is equally eager and greedy for emotions and ideas. Without oxygen each molecule in an organism would rest quietly in a deadly inertia, like me when I boil the same usual thoughts, again and again.

But the puzzle of life, with its chaotic, unexpected and complicated matches, is never complete. It is renewed and reborn at all times, by continuously rediscovering previously experimented combinations and inventing new, improbable arrangements. Because there is no rest. Because oxygen chases and requires electrons, it asks for answers, and questions, agitates doubts and proposals, novel readings, possible metaphors and audacious flights.

The cell breaths by stealing electrons and protons from sugar – which is thus dismantled until it vaporizes into sterile carbon dioxide – the same way we steal images and sensations and emotions from the world.

The cell cautiously handles these electrons, one by one, to the greedy oxygen, while protons are spun and shuffled around until they can get married, in the end, to the oxygen so charged, to yield placid, stable water molecules. So, the cell lives by accumulating the energy that shaky, reactive compounds release in calming down into solid unions.

Energy and tension that fosters the continuous remodeling of the cell, tension that forces us to incessantly reread and revisit, and to try and continually rewrite, reality and life.

Alas, precisely because of its sacred and compulsory avidity and vitality oxygen sometimes runs away with an extra electron, unpaired and explosive. It runs away alone, or together with the atoms it stripped it from, or with others that enjoy sharing the daring instability of the single and turbulent electron, of the unfulfilled emotion, of the barely imagined thought, incomplete, unfinished and infinite.

They call them ROS, reactive oxygen species, they call them radicals — free, vagabond, reactive, boisterous, out of control.

Indispensable, to attack snobbish and apparently incorruptible molecules, that must anyway be dragged, them too, in the continuous merry-go-round of biochemical dances, a process that moment by moment rearranges and rebuilds immutable, ever new and ever-changing equilibriums.

Indispensable, but they may spoil and harm. They may crack and demolish antique, delicate balances. And other electrons are needed, other stimuli, and emotions and affects and ideas, to calm them down, so that unpredictably balanced, new combinations of forces and masses may happen, and transform, dance, live, rather than collapsing, disaggregating, leaving the game and dying.

A thousand substances, continuously renewed and gathered from outside, protect the cells, by donating their electrons to radicals that have gone mad. They are called antioxidants. A thousand policemen and teachers and mercenaries and clowns and poets offer you rules and lashes and scoldings and smiles and emotions to calm you down when the soul breaks apart and energy does not find a way out.

Often, a harmed soul can soothe another one, often ROS can pacify each other by sharing their injured electrons.

Neurons, brave cells, noble and selfless, hyperactive in taking note of the history they see and live, by translating it into ever-new reorganizations of their own biochemical and functional balances; neurons, that because of this are unpredictable cells, more difficult to protect, sometimes can't face the tension of a life that is made of continuous asking, retrying, and going back over, full of storms and raids of molecules gone wild. So, neurons get old. Mechanisms of admirable efficiency and precision may get oxidized and misfire. Thus, any tiny defect is amplified.

Serious, efficient, reliable proteins miss their duties, are secluded and start to die: aggregates appear that reveal neuronal suffering to the pathologist, as the unequivocal signs of diseases with terrible names, Parkinson, Alzheimer, ALS...

But there is no Evil. And Good. — There is only Life.
It is a challenging bet, hard, demanding. It turns out winning an incredible number of times, and is promptly renewed, continuously, always on the edge of a shaky balance, lost and regained. ROS, wild thoughts and wounds of the soul are not demons, they are sublime forces that move the world. They can hurt because they don't know how to sit aside and just watch.

Free radicals damage the skin, antioxidants protect it... But radicals are but moments of life, and our vegetables, drugs and vitamins, are not capable of shutting them up to protect the skin that needs most their uncontrolled vitality, and protection from their excesses: neurons, the skin of the soul. And if the whirls of the soul damage the quiet management of society, without them there is no life. Let them anti-oxidize us as they wish! as long as in the world there is injustice, and hunger, war and pain, there will be sympathy, surprise, desire and love, and there will be curious souls, wounded, tense, lighted. There will be life.

* * *

But that's enough with games. What is life, in the end?

Life is a principle, abstract as you wish, that differentiates the systems that persist quiet, as long as external forces don't put their balance at risk, from those systems that instead can only survive by means of interactions with the outside, and are sufficiently complex to be able to exploit external sources of energy to reproduce moment by moment their own structure and organization, their shaky and mutable balance; systems that are capable of reproducing themselves by regenerating that same order, that same organization, in new exemplars.

Life is a well-conceived mechanism that sustains and reproduces itself using the energy it gathers in guiding the degradation of energy rich compounds, thus helping time, who could not by itself attack them, to crack and dismantle them, and helping the sun to build – rather than merely and stupidly heating the Earth – ever new unstable balances. Life is a one-way road that lets the second principle of thermodynamics come true: it allows entropy to grow under conditions where it would not find its way by itself, it allows the time of things to flow more free and powerful.

Indeed, life is not an abundance of resources and room to throw away garbage, but rather the admirable capability of transforming resources into garbage, of producing disorder, while pursuing a project. Maybe, more simply, it is the project itself.

We survive by protecting ourselves, but we live by changing in the *tourbillon de la vie*. Life itself is nothing but a WAY. Life is real, but its reality consists in the WAY the living being is. You need a name for this – life, precisely – and an ontological value: anybody would clearly perceive the absolute reality of life, thus defined.

But the question is exactly this: per se, life has no reality whatsoever, if by REALITY we mean palpable matter. Life is only an abstract concept. But life is real, ontologically real, as an immanent property, unavoidably inborn to the organism that possesses and expresses it.

Life is a physical mechanism, an organization criterion, an abstract principle. It is form, that is not less real than matter, inherent in living matter, a form that is physical but also outside of Physics. Internal and going beyond. Metaphysical, indeed, exactly and precisely.

And if the cleverest ones already got where we are heading – and what all this has to do with the soul – then they are kindly asked not to unveil the end to more peaceful and eager readers.

* * *

WHAT DO WE KNOW, IN THE END? – Animal Neurophysiology

Some neurophysiology, at last! here I feel at ease....

Among those that are attracted – by intellectual curiosity or by their study plans and duties – to neurophysiology, a large majority comfortably sits back in the perspective that is widely supported by the lazy and little creative dominant mechanicism: the nervous system is a complex device, very complex, hypercomplex, god! how it is extremely complex!, but with a clear design principle: it is structured and organized to produce the right behavioral response to the stimuli that are present at any moment and in any situation.

Nice and clear, but then no surprise if one steps back, wrinkles their nose and says to themselves 'sure, but the soul is something else'. Sure, the soul is something else. But the brain too, the human brain at least, is something else!

Let us proceed with some order.

The nervous system

The nervous system is constituted by hundreds of billions of nervous cells (neurons), most of which exhibit a rich branching of processes (dendrites), where thousands of terminals from other neurons make contact. Each contact (synapse) generates a small electrical signal, when it is activated, and all signals in the neuron get summed in space and time to generate a fluctuating electrical signal in the cell body of the neuron. Each time this signal trespasses some 'threshold' value, a rapid potential spike is generated (a wave about 1/10 of a Volt high) where the principal process of the neuron (axon) leaves the cell body. When a neuron generates a spike, this is propagated by means of a regenerative process: it is identically reproduced in the nearby portion of the membrane and gradually invades all the axon, that can be a few millimeters long, but in some cases may reach tens of centimeters in length. The axon may branch close to its target and ends in small varicosities (nerve terminals) that contact other neurons (or muscle or gland cells) making synapses – structures where the membranes of the two cells are very close: when the spike invades the terminal, small quantities of chemical substances (neurotransmitters) are released and generate the abovementioned small electrical signals on the target cell.

Central Nervous System (CNS)

The great majority of neurons are in the central nervous system, constituted by the spinal cord and the encephalon (the part located in the head). In the CNS there are groups of neuronal cellular bodies, dendritic trees, synaptic buttons and short local axons (the gray matter), and bundles of axons that connect the gray regions; these longer axons are generally sheathed by an isolating material (myelin), that facilitates and accelerates the conduction of the spike, and are collected in bundles that are visible to the naked eye (white matter).

Spinal cord

All sensory information coming from a segment of the body – from the skin, the joints, the muscles and the internal organs – enters the spinal cord at the corresponding level, by means of axon bundles (nerves) collected in the dorsal nerve root. The neuronal circuits contained in the spine elaborate simple reflex responses (such as the patellar reflex that the neurologist tests by hitting your leg with a small hammer, just below the knee); they simultaneously send all information upwards and receive control signals from higher structures. The anterior gray portion of the spine contains neurons that are regulated by this complex integration of local signals and controls from above and send their impulses toward the muscles and the glands, through axon bundles that exit through the ventral nervous roots of the spinal cord.

Brainstem

The structure of the spinal cord continues within the skull (brainstem), where it executes the same functions for the skin, the muscles and the glands of the face and the head, but also integrates specific sensory information – that coming from the vestibule, the organ of equilibrium, from the ears, the tongue, the eyes.

However, in the brainstem the burden of elaborating and coordinating what is going on at lower levels of the medulla becomes more and more massive and complex. In the nervous axis we therefore observe an input-output polarization, dorso-ventral – from posterior (input) to anterior (output) – and a hierarchical organization, climbing from the tail (missing in humans...) to the head, the hierarchy being particularly relevant in the intra-cranial portion.

The impressive amount of information that passes through the inferior regions of the brainstem (medulla and pons) is partly dispatched to the cerebellum, that executes complex control elaborations and returns part of its results to the brainstem itself. Motor behaviors is largely performed and coordinated at this level, with no need for serious involvement of higher structures (cerebral cortex); this is true in particular for instinctive motor schemes and learnt schemes that have become automatic (a fundamental role of the cerebellum is precisely to learn and conduct automatic movements).

The rich information and local elaboration in the brainstem give rise to intense activity, that diffusely project to various higher regions, and is indispensable to maintain the cerebral cortex active, and sustains alertness, attention and active behavior. If this input to the brain is missing (or is attenuated due to lesions, inflammation, pressure from internal bleeding or other causes), a coma ensues.

The highest (and most anterior) region of the brainstem – midbrain – is the last tract that receives sensory information (important sensory processing occurs here in the 'colliculi', the roof of the midbrain). And the connections with the two cerebral hemispheres are inserted here. At this level, the coordination of all motor behaviors is complete: higher structures are not needed to perform complex tasks, such as breathing and swallowing, maintaining the upright position and executing the refined and coordinated sequence of movements needed to walk, at least on plane ground and in the absence of obstacles.

In addition, in the midbrain some important groups of neurons (nuclei) are located, that project to higher structures. One such nucleus, the substantia nigra, performs an essential activity of modulation of movements, and dysfunction of this structure results in Parkinson's disease.

Another system of nuclei, in the ventral tegmental area (VTA), modulates in a coordinated way two distinct regions of the brain: one of these, the so-called limbic system, guides the elaboration of emotional experiences (part of this projection constitutes the so-called 'reward pathway', we shall talk about this later); the other target region, that is constituted by the most anterior portions of the frontal cortex, is in charge of motivational control, thought and behavioral programming. The incorrect balance between these two control systems, originating from the VTA in the midbrain, results in schizophrenia

III
Everything and more – the limit

The child proceeds, resolute but careful, he places his foot with studied measure. Two long steps, a short one, two more small steps, a longer one. He made it!, he crossed the whole paved ground without stepping on any junctions between two tiles, without betraying any one of the abstract and inviolable limits that marked his way.

Oh, not easy at all to escape this, even when you grow up. As it is not so easy to connect the nine dots below with four straight lines, without lifting the pen from the paper (see end of chapter if you can't solve it):

● ● ●
● ● ●
● ● ●

The trouble is that the limit strikes us, it attracts us, hypnotizes us. And limits us.

The reality of objects has taught us to examine their profile and border, to recognize where the limit separates the ground from the sky.

Uncertain borders thrill us like dangerous transgressions. They fascinate us, but they elicit an intense desire for *terra firma*, of solid and reliable ground onto which to set our foot. So, we end up searching for clear limits and borders, even when there is no reason for them to be there, simply not to get confused, to be able to discern and orientate.

But to subsist, life relies on changing, remodeling, and overcoming at any moment its border with the world, with external reality; so, in front of life even our sublime capacity of imposing names, and borders and limits and differences, turns out inadequate. We feel the inescapable need to reconcile two approaches, two perspectives: matter and its laws, on one side, and something else, other, that requires a gaze that can capture vague and vanishing aspects, that can sense multiplicity.

Yes. Life puts us in trouble. In what precise moment the caterpillar, hidden in its cocoon, is no longer a caterpillar and has become a butterfly? Not to mention the question of abortion, embryos, and vegetative life, and postponed deaths, and when does the soul arrive and when does it leave?...

Accustomed to the obvious limit that encloses a body, separates two types of matter, gives reality to objects, we feel as if we had to separate and dissect in the same way events, processes and developments that gradually, quickly or imperceptibly, flow through different phases.

It might be indispensable; it might be useless. Certainly, it is difficult: few things are so clearly different from each-other as life and death are, but still, it is not easy to grasp where the precise border is.

This happens precisely because what has no life only persists when it is so strong, or protected, that it cannot be attacked and modified, but life can only sustain itself by continuously changing, by eroding the limit; life confirms itself by negating in any moment what it has been up to a moment earlier, by overcoming the border between how it is now – what it is in this moment – and how and what it is going to be.

* * *

Life persists by eroding its limit. So, it might be appropriate to try and change our perspective on LIMITS in general, and consider them as lines of passage, of interaction. Does this mean that we can extend the approach that works so well in simple domains of our knowledge to any other, more complex domain? Does this mean that physics can explain, in addition to forces and processes in the inanimate world, also our life, maybe even our thought, as if we were simply built using inter-changeable circuits, the same for all of us?

Certainly not. Nobody would dare to state that our neural circuits are interchangeable. My own circuits are not even the same they used to be yesterday. We shall discuss this later. And we are certainly not *reducible* to circuits, formulas, waves, equations.
We are not *reducible!*

But is it possible that we need to change our view, not on ourselves, but rather on Physics?

The fundamental problem of reductionism may not be that it is wrong to try and reduce the soul to equations, but rather that it is wrong to try and reduce *Physics itself* to equations, overlooking indeterminacy, un-knowableness, charm, wonder and poetry that are in the things, in the world, in Physics itself.

To this purpose, a new outlook is really necessary.

Physics is clear and reassuring. Objects, energy and measurable forces. Precise and finite things, limits, causal relations. The relations may be complex, and where relations are complex and ordered there appears to be a project. But it is not so; as regards physics, phenomena are but the inevitable result of the factors and the forces involved.

Our everyday experience, instead, is marked by man. Events guided by motivations and aims, hidden or explicit, valid or not. More obscure, mediated, sometimes inaccessible are the causes.

Where causes and mechanisms are masked and difficult to perceive it is easier to imagine motivations, aims, or some form of will whatsoever, arcane and arbitrary as it might be. Arbitrary, because arbitrariness is the domain of life in general, and the quintessence of human life: will, apparent freedom from material causes, because material causes should arise from ineluctable, necessary mechanisms, hidden as you wish but coherent and predictable (at least if you know enough).

This is an easy, malleable, powerful and satisfactory interpretative paradigm. An effective and tranquilizing perspective: what is not inevitably produced by evident physical causes is produced by choice and will (sensible or absurd). Human choices and will; or, where no humans appear to be involved, divine will.

It is the perspective of the child, who only grasps a few causal relations, and in all the rest sees the omnipotence of the adult at work. It is the perspective of myth: when you run out of physical explanations, entrust yourself to the omnipotence of the gods.

It is not stupid credulousness. In some respects, this is also Aristotle's perspective, cautious and creative, systematic and sharp: to build a house you need bricks (material cause), a mason (efficient cause), the project (formal cause) and the need of a roof to cover you (final cause).

There must be an aim and a design, a project. Wherever Man is involved.

But this is false! Aims and projects are not there in all things.

One needs to be able to stop, to draw a line and recognize where formal and final causes are not necessary, and they are there only to fulfill our ancestral need of attributing the design of an order to a superior mind. Especially when the order appears too accurate to be self-generated, so accurate that it can persist indefinitely solely due to causal rules that do not imply any choice or will, any skipper with a destination, any master with a target, any god (unless a miracle is to occur by infringing and humiliating the rules).

All that we know today lets us understand storms and eclipses, planetary orbits and earthquakes, holes in the ozone... and even the extinction of dinosaurs, the architecture of anthills, the language of bees, and Sybille's epileptic convulsions too, without bothering any higher wills, formal causes, finalisms, demons or providences.

Human history is a story of ever-new readings: each new discovery displaces the border between physics and metaphysics. Between known and mystery. Between a theory of causes and a theory of aims.

Physics and metaphysics. Maybe the border is there, where causes no longer suffice and choice, motivation, aim are needed. Human will, or the design of fate, the arbitrariness of a god.

As long as a frog only croaks, and runs away from noise, and jumps to catch flies, as long as it always and only does what you expect it to do, it is difficult to concede it a soul, notwithstanding all the complexity and finesse of the mechanisms and processes that have brought it there from being a tadpole, with all the wonder of life that pushes it and guides it and pervades it.

Conversely, it is hard to see mechanistic rules down deep in our heart, in that mayhem where we pick our sensations and judgments, so clear-cut and definitive that they seem to have been profoundly engraved there by somebody else, before, since the beginning...

There one can find the signs of the soul. It is where a choice is possible, where there is more than one reading of the world, where acts are not only instinctive, where selfless behaviors are possible. And they are not possible because of a species instinct, but because they are guided by social, ethical, ideal values, by forces that are not causes arising from the world of things, but rather motivations, aims, aspirations, dreams, passions, that come from somewhere else, from what we have always liked to call the world of ideas.

So, this may be the border. But not a limit, rather a border that science must dare trespass, invading the domain of CHOICE and WILL. Because many aspects of the neuronal mechanisms of choice, of motivation, of behavior finalization have by now been clarified.

* * *

Here comes again the problem of limit, separation, diversity, 'other'.

Is the soul 'other', then? Is the world of ideas 'other', something else, and material reality is only a deceptive simulacrum of such 'something else', that one can agnostically disregard, captured by the frantic fibrillation of the real world...

Physics, guided by causes and laws, on one side; and metaphysics, guided by choices and aim, on the other; science on one side, poetry on the other. Or, perhaps, this is precisely the way to trespass the border: a science that does not give up poetry.

A science that does not fear the limit, that is able to look at life as a process and to venture to study the soul, at least as far as it can be reasonably explored, investigated, known, understood.

To gain this new perspective one needs to exercise in looking at each aspect of reality, and knowledge process, from both inside and outside, one must appreciate the limitations of each single approach and each logic, but not repudiate it in looking beyond.

Perhaps the LIMIT is not the only problem. But the most difficult problems are indeed those that require trespassing a limit, evading a frame, a scheme that nobody has imposed on us, but we ourselves have imagined to be there to stop us, insurmountable.

In order to explore scientifically what has been traditionally precluded from science, to find the roots of consciousness and will in the brain, it is necessary to avoid getting stopped by LIMIT, to be capable of *meta*, to be able to perceive the relationship among worlds that seem different, 'other'. One must overcome the sensation that 'ok, the brain as far as you wish, but the soul begins where the brain ends'.

If one assumes a fracture between the physical perspective, guided by causes and laws, and metaphysics guided by choices and aims, the relation between mechanisms and active deeds becomes uncertain, the field of research, exploration and empirical investigation abruptly and unduly collapses, the gap between scientific approach and humanistic culture gets widened, and the logic and culture of *limit* is strengthened.

Instead, this should be the time of great unification!

It should be about time to understand that one and the same place, calm and welcoming, can host meditation and prayer of believers of any religions. Time to understand that different perspectives add light and depth, and do not fragment but rather expand comprehension and knowledge, that different logics do not discourage and divide but rather help understanding reality and life in their splendid complexity.

It should be about time, because the healthy part of culture has overcome the need of contemplating inexistent monotonous universal harmonies and totalizing coherences, whether revealed or not. Exact sciences have denuded themselves and negated dogmas by showing unexpected impotencies. Gödel has sublimated mathematics and logics by showing that no logical system can be coherent unless it admits a limited field of application, and cannot be complete unless it accepts some incoherencies: it is not merely word-games, the phrase 'this sentence is false' does not admit any judgment of truth and is an example of a clearly demonstrated property of any formal system: its rules can be clear and coherent only if they apply to a limited domain and do not demand to be apply outside its borders. The logic of true and false does not apply to discussions about the truth.

Euclidean geometry does not apply to a universe where nothing is flat. Galilean physics does not apply when speeds approach the velocity of light. And the laws of Physics do not apply to the soul. But one can build logics that deal with criteria of truth though they can't tell whether specific statements are true; one can build geometries in which parallel lines do not make sense, but that can describe curved universes; one can state and demonstrate theories of Relativity that analyze physics in the neighborhood of light speed and redraw space and time and matter and energy, and the infiniteness itself of the universe. All this can be done with coherence and rigor, putting these systems side by side, although each of them, inside itself, obeys inviolable rules that do not apply in the other systems, and negates applicability of fundamental principles of the other systems within its own domain.

One can construct perspectives capable of exploring the soul, using instruments that have no use in physics and putting aside physical laws that cannot say anything about the soul. On can do this without imposing physical causality outside its limits, but nonetheless without subtracting from physics all that changes and lives; without searching for mechanistic interpretations of dreams and love, but nonetheless without confining aspirations, passions, forces and flights of the soul in a cave of the ideas, in a limbo of revealed truths, in a mystical ether that reason could never reach.

* * *

Why the block imposed by the concepts itself of *limit* is so difficult to overcome? First, framing a problem, fitting a scheme is convenient, the limit simplifies, overlooks difficulties, reduces distress; in addition, and this is an elusive factor, but not less relevant, the limit negates evolution, crystallizes, underscores the antithesis between preserving (protect, defend) and changing, between coherence and development; it generates and sustains the horror for new and 'different'.

When I was young and Marxist (I can't be proud of being young any longer and, alas!, it appears that one can no longer be proud of being a Marxist either) I wanted to write a book (yes, sooner or later it was bound to happen) about *the limit*. About giving names to things to trap them, separate them, disarm them.

Like any organism, the social organization persists by evolving and changing its relations within itself and with the outside.

The health of an organism relies on the coherence between the dynamics of the subsystems that constitute it and its own dynamics.

Life is based on the simultaneous presence of forces and mechanisms that tend to consolidate and reproduce the prevailing organization, and forces and processes that push to interact with the outside, suffer changes, and evolve by guiding such changes. So, the conflict between components of the society that act to maintain the current social, political and economic status unchanged (generally because of their conditions of privilege) and components that push to change (generally moved by their disadvantageous conditions) is not a sign of social suffering, per se, but rather of vitality. Indeed, this might be a scientific flaw and ideological limit of historical materialism, of Marx's analysis and the idea itself of a society with no classes, non-antagonistic.

However, the dominant classes and lobbies, that are 'automatically' inclined to preserve the momentary sociopolitical status, greatly profit (indeed, the Nation itself may profit) of a diffuse fear and aversion versus any change, because change is perceived as limit, negation, destruction. Thus, the dominant culture tends to be strongly founded on the concept of limit, separation, diversity, as a bulwark in defense of the existing (entities, rules, relationships, perspectives).

The solidity and stability of a social system is based on and measured by the force with which the limit, the fear of diversity and exclusion, the aspiration to homologation, are imposed and profoundly rooted in common thinking. And this is particularly true in antagonistic, not equalitarian, systems. This is reminiscent of what was discussed about molecules and energy and entropy: a society can be quite stable, even if it is strongly conflictual (like a high free energy compound), provided that the barriers to changing it are solid enough: a culture of the limit, of difference, a strong enough fear of change (like the activation energy in a chemical reaction, the heat needed to ignite a match).

But the inability to see the limit as a line of encounter-passage-communication, rather than separation, to see change as evolution, rather than diversity and negation, precludes any serious analysis of life as a process. Even more – let's finally say it – it precludes any serious analysis of the 'soul', at least of what in it can be somehow explored, known, analyzed, understood.

* * *

Thalamus and hypothalamus
Anterior to the midbrain we find two fundamental structures: the hypothalamus, the highest center of coordination of visceral and vegetative information, and the thalamus, the last stage for all input signals to the cerebral cortex.

The *hypothalamus* operates by maintaining constant values for all vital parameters (*homeostasis*). Blood pressure, body temperature, blood levels of sugar, oxygen and carbon dioxide, water/electrolyte ratio, etc., are maintained and controlled by coordinating all visceral and vegetative responses.

The hypothalamus supervises cardiac activity, renal function, vasoconstriction and dilatation in various districts, digestive activity, sweating, and sexual organ functions. It does so through three systems.

The first system of vegetative control is the autonomic nervous system (*orthosympathetic* and *parasympathetic*), that innervates the heart, blood vessels, visceral muscles and glands.

The second control mechanism for vital and vegetative functions is the production of *hormones*, some of them by the hypothalamus itself, others by the *hypophysis* (the small, *pituitary* gland located above the roof of the pharynx, just below the hypothalamus) under its strict control.

The third control mechanism is the generation of neuronal signals that are distributed to various nervous structures of the brainstem and higher centers, to ask for the performance of active behaviors: in higher organisms, in fact, it is not possible to maintain homeostatic equilibrium, and therefore not even a mere vegetative survival, without performing oriented motor activities, such as searching for food and water, protecting oneself from heat and cold, sexual and reproductive behaviors.

One must realize the importance of these aspects: without voluntary activity humans cannot survive, even though they may breathe and possess healthy heart, liver and kidneys, unless one attaches them to machines that nourish and hydrate them and protect them from extreme temperatures.

Above the hypothalamus, a big structure with the shape of two collated globes, the *thalamus* (this is the ancient word for nuptial bed, presumably there were no king-size mattresses at that time), constitutes the last stage of organization and control for the information that must reach the cerebral cortex.

The thalamus performs an essential function of elaboration and filtering on the passing information. If the thalamus prevents the sensory information from reaching the cortex, the latter works in a completely different way, by elaborating according to its own rhythms in a state of altered consciousness, independent of sensory information (sleep).

Thalamic centers may work in any intermediate situations, between stopping the flow of information and having specific portions of the cortex elaborating it in a discriminative way, so that selective attention can be focused, in each moment, on a specific sensory input or an internal elaboration.

Cerebral cortex

The cerebral cortex constitutes most of the encephalic mass in humans. Cortex development is what mostly differentiates human encephalon from that of other animals, even primates. In less brilliant animals, the cortex constitutes a small portion of the brain, almost an optional accessory, which suggests that it must not be strictly indispensable to permit the animal to correctly react to stimuli and behave in the most appropriate way. This is why the doubt arises that looking at a man's brain – and possibly a woman's one, in particular – as a mere instrument to optimize behavior, in a stimulus-response logic, might be quite minimizing and will prevent us from grasping and appreciating its potentialities, its essence itself.

The cortex is comprised of two hemispheres, characterized by a rough and complicated surface, like the kernel of a nut, rich of ridges (cortical gyri) separated by troughs. In lower animals it is much less bumpy and jagged. Cortex organization is symmetrical in the two hemispheres, even though several higher functions in humans are performed asymmetrically by the right or left hemisphere.

Information reaches the cortex mostly through the thalamus; in general information coming from the left part of the body reaches the right thalamus and hemisphere, and vice versa. The various cortical areas are intensely interconnected by massive bundles of axonal fibers (white matter) that run partly on the surface and partly in the depth of the brain. The two hemispheres are strictly connected by an antero-posterior arch of white matter (callous body) that is constituted by a massive ribbon of transversal axon fibers. The hemispheres enclose a large mass of nervous tissue, located in the deep central region: a region where white connection areas alternate with gray regions of neuronal bodies with their intricate local connections (*basal ganglia or nuclei*). A major fraction of cortical elaboration is relayed to the cerebellum and basal ganglia. Both structures return their own elaboration to the cortex, through the thalamus, although the cerebellum also has direct output connections towards the brainstem. The function of these reciprocal connections of the cortex with the cerebellum and basal ganglia is very important and will be discussed later.

Learning

Most functions in cells are performed by proteins, large molecules that can change their shape (more properly *conformation*). When they change their shape some proteins (referred to as 'enzymes') may bind chemical substances and bring them together in such a way to favor a specific chemical reaction;

other proteins may move molecules or cellular organelles along filaments, or slide different filaments on one another to produce movement (muscle contraction, for example); other proteins may be inserted in the cellular membrane and cross it: by changing their shape they can transport small molecules or electrolytes, or let them through in a regulated way, from one side to the other of the membrane; proteins can recognize specific molecules, change conformation upon binding them, and this way initiate specific reactions in the cell; thus they are called 'receptors': if they are proteins that cross the cellular membrane they will be able to produce an effect inside the cell by binding a signal molecule outside the cell.

Briefly, by changing their shape proteins control and regulate all the chemical activity of the cell, produce movement, define the composition of the internal fluid in the cell and its organelles, and produce electrical activities by actively transporting ions (electrically charged) across the membranes or letting them through. In turn, the proteins are regulated and modulated in various ways by the momentary – rapidly reversible – binding of ions or small molecules, or by the electric field, or following chemical modifications, such as the addition, removal or modification of pieces of the molecule (e.g., a phosphate group), in turn produced by other enzyme-proteins. Finally, the presence itself of each protein, and thus the function it performs, can be regulated by controlling its synthesis, starting from the gene that codes for the protein, or its degradation.

As mentioned, nervous cells can produce electric signals and use them to elaborate and transfer information, and communicate through synapses. The elaboration of the electric signal, the secretion of transmitter molecules, and the response to the neurotransmitter can be regulated in thousands of ways by influencing the activity of the proteins involved. The functional organization and the number of synapses can also be modified by changing the activity of proteins.

The crucial point, in nerve cells, is that one of the most efficient and flexible means to modify the activity of their proteins is electrical activity itself. Therefore, neurons modify many of their properties in time, and may strengthen or weaken synapses, or even destroy them or make new ones, and all this *as a function of their own activity*, or in other words as a function of the information they are elaborating.

Thus, the functionality and organization of neural circuits, and the way they process information, change as a function of the information itself they are elaborating. This constitutes the cellular basis of the capacity of neural circuits – of the brain – to learn, and the cellular basis of memory.

Typically, a synapse can be strengthened if it is stimulated in an intense and repetitive way. However, the fundamental feature of learning processes in the central nervous system is associativity: a synapse strengthens, or in some systems weakens, when it is activated several times in synchrony with a nearby synapse, or just after it, with the result that the neuron learns to respond to one of the two signals as if both signals were present: thanks to this associative learning it is sufficient to recognize some elements to have the brain work as if it had recognized the whole, it is enough to recognize a few tracts of a face to revive the pleasure that we have experienced in the past with that person...

<u>The 'paleo-cortex' and the limbic system</u>

The most 'ancient' portions of the cerebral cortex, the ones we find first in ascending the evolutionary scale, extract signals, from sensory and visceral information, that are relevant for survival and wellbeing, and generate the signals to coordinate the appropriate response. They are regions in which the most rudimentary aspects of 'emotional' life are elaborated (pain, pleasure, well-being, distress), together with the resulting 'motivational drives', capable of producing active behaviors, i.e., not only reflexes but endogenously generated reactions. In lower animals, the schemes to execute these behaviors – such as fetching food, building a lair, courting, sexual activity – are already pre-wired to a major extent in the sub-cortical neural network, and constitute instinctive behavior.

Therefore, the role of the cortex is almost exclusively that of evaluating the opportunity of initiating instinctive behavior, possibly choosing the appropriate response among several different possibilities, and triggering such behaviors in the appropriate situation and moment. The structures that constitute this portion of the cortex are in strict connection with the hypothalamus and with two nervous structures that have a rather precise function and a marked learning capability: *amygdala* and ventral striatum (aka *nucleus accumbens*).

The *amygdala* is an almond-shaped nervous nucleus, whose neurons have the job of discharging impulses when signals that have vital relevance (that indicate danger in particular) reach the nervous system. The *amygdala* not only responds to signals instinctively relevant but learns to recognize other signals important for survival and well-being, based on experience. Activation of the *amygdala* at increasing levels triggers the visceral, mimic and behavioral reactions typically associated to anxiety, fear and terror.

The *nucleus accumbens* is a low ventral portion of the basal ganglia, that receives information from many regions of the central nervous system and has the role of signaling the possibility of satisfying a physiological need or obtaining a gratification, and of confirming success in attaining it.

An important pathway that reaches the *nucleus accumbens* comes from regions of the midbrain (*VTA*, ventral tegmental area) that are activated when a positive event occurs, a need is being fulfilled, a distress is overcome, or a situation of well-being has been reached. This neuronal connection is called 'reward pathway' and produces two distinct and equally important effects in the *nucleus accumbens*: first, it activates the *accumbens* to signal success by producing pleasure and gratification; second, it trains specific neurons in the *accumbens* to fire in the future when a situation occurs that may lead to this same gratification. So, when the possibility of well-being shows itself, the *accumbens* starts firing, thereby acting as a powerful source of motivational drive (*anticipation*) to enact behaviors that are adequate to obtain the desired result.

The capacity of directly or indirectly activating the 'reward pathway' is shared by many drugs acting on the nervous system, such as nicotine, cannabinoids, amphetamines, cocaine, heroin, and constitutes the fundamental mechanism by which these drugs establish a condition of psychological dependence.

Amygdala and *accumbens*, together with some other communication pathways and the most ancient portions of the cerebral cortex (in the innermost portion of the cortex, where the two hemispheres face each other) constitute the system that performs the general elaboration of emotions and motivational drives, the so-called *limbic system*. The name itself is evocative, as if it were to indicate the region where deep urges, physiological needs, pain and pleasure approach, through emotional elaboration, the threshold of conscious perception: a 'limbus' (margin) between the storms generated by conflicts between vital urges and the ethereal lands of conscious cognitive elaboration.

* * *

Between emotion and logics – imagining the future

I was born when you could still smell the post-war atmosphere, the spirit of reconstructing, getting back life and happiness. It seemed that it was important to heal people, build houses and bridges and roads, extinguish fires, win analphabetism, write bold articles of denounce, get committed in politics to change everything for the better, go to the Moon…

In the Seventies we were pervaded by the sensation that we would change the world, because everything was changing. There was enthusiasm in our recounting our own future, there were infinite possibilities. It seemed that the world was full of room, and jobs: a large possibility of choice to give a meaning to life, and getting family, wellbeing, serenity and security in return: a future, many futures among which to choose.

We played with our imagination, no way was banned, we could become whatever we wished, we simply had to choose and prefigure.
We were in love with the future. With our future. With that of society, with the future of the world.

It seems to me this is no longer exactly the same…
Dreams still exist, and youngsters still think of their future. But too often the imagination stumbles on problems, difficulties, bottlenecks, lack of perspectives and security. One does not dare let imagination free to fly and prefigure what probably will never be true.

One does not dare get in love with their future.
I live in an environment full of young people, I would say of young people with high hopes: I teach in a School of Medicine. They start with an initial advantage, they do have a perspective of a future, hard, but fascinating.

Still, I often see them disoriented: they attend a ward, and it seems to them that is their future, they are all cardiologists; then they attend another ward and do not know what to choose anymore. Now they may prefer anesthesiology, or neurosurgery, they meet me in the corridor and ask for advice. My advice is simple: do not get deceived by the appearance, try and imagine the job: imagine how the day goes, what you do in the working hours, how much and how and with whom you interact, what is expected of you, where your rewards come from – having solved a problem, or saved a life, or received a sign of gratitude – what targets you can set for yourself, how tired and how satisfied you will be at night, and with which expectations you will wake up in the morning…

In a sense, it is just a suggestion to grow. Not to be a child, who cannot tell their own story yet, cannot get in love yet, and – if you ask them about their future – imagine themselves in a picture that they cannot draw correctly in its various aspects: the chores, the problems, the targets, the delays and the satisfactions, big and small. They simply dress up as firemen and see themselves fleeting on the fire engine with their yellow caps or climbing up a tree to save a frightened kitten; or they see themselves as astronauts floating in their capsule, or as aircraft pilots.

We live in a society of appearance, and this does not help to grow.
The dominating weak thought is made of short and axiomatic sentences, which exclude any discrepancy or disagreement: "America to Americans", "we follow the will of the people", "with this law we put 40 billion dollars in the pockets of the citizens" (but, pardon me, where do you get them from?)… And we are flooded by "icons".

Nothing strange that the term has been so inflated: static images, with no thickness, no motion, no life. It seems that in order to be happy – or to succeed in life – the problem is to conquer an image, to have something: fame, or at least a god number of followers on Facebook or Instagram, a nice house, being rich or powerful.

Imagination stops there: as if everything could be solved by putting on a new dress, by throwing oneself into a future photograph, like children do. And if nobody can tell me what the path is to get there, where to find the dress, the image freezes, loses its attraction and wanes away.

Luckily many youngsters can escape this verdict: they can still dream, they know what makes them feel well and what they must look for, they have learned that happiness comes from what you ARE and what you DO, from what you can give the others and get back from them. So, rather than imagining oneself in an improbable, petty future photo, somewhat vaguely rich and famous, they can imagine a live future, in which they can be peaceful and satisfied because they ARE and they DO what can give a meaning to life, what lets them realize themselves and make them happy.

Luckily, many youngsters can still fly around imagining a future, a tridimensional and dynamic future, in which they can be alive, have a place in the world, a commitment, a meaning.
They can still fall in love with their future.
And the future, their own, ours as well, is in their hands.

* * *

Cerebral cortex specializations

Each cerebral hemisphere is crossed by a transverse furrow (*central fissure*), approximately at the center of the skull, that separates the anterior part (*frontal lobe*) from the middle-posterior part (*parietal, temporal, occipital lobes*).

In vague analogy with the organization of the medulla, the posterior part of the cerebral cortex is involved in elaborating sensory information ('input' to the brain), whereas the anterior part is involved in the elaboration and programming of behavior ('output'). In particular, the posterior part of the cortex (*occipital lobe*) elaborates visual information. Auditory information is elaborated in the *temporal lobe*. Taste information is elaborated in the internal region of the *temporal lobe* and olfactory information more anteriorly.

Just behind the central fissure, a stripe of cortex of the parietal lobe elaborates *somatosensory information* – tactile and skin sensory information, and *proprioceptive* information from joints and muscles that make it possible to know the position of each body segment at any moment.

This cortex stripe is topologically organized: information coming from the foot reaches the central region (toward the top and center of the head), while information from higher levels is distributed to more lateral and lower regions, thereby drawing a species of small monstrous man, upside down on the surface of the cortex, a warped troll with short and tiny legs and chest, huge hands, wide face and an enormous tongue, as the quantity of cortex dedicated to each region of the body depends on the quantity and importance of the information coming from that particular region. The 'homunculus' on the right parietal cortex reproduces the left part of the body, and vice versa.

Anterior to the central fissure, facing the sensory homunculus, a motor homunculus can be drawn on the surface of the frontal cortex, deformed in about the same way: this stripe of the frontal cortex constitutes the *primary motor area*, which is responsible for the voluntary control of muscles in the contra-lateral part of the body.

In the motor area many neurons (*pyramidal neurons*) send their signals directly to the neurons of the anterior gray matter of the medulla – *motor neurons* – which directly activate skeletal muscles, and to interneurons that modulate the local spinal circuits involved in motor control.

In addition to these regions with sensory and motor functions, the cortex comprises the above-mentioned limbic areas, more 'ancient', that elaborate information with emotional relevance.

Associative cortex

The regions of the cortex described up to here – limbic cortex, primary visual area, other primary sensory areas and primary motor area – comprise most of the cortex of a mouse, but they only account for a minor fraction of human cortex. Each primary region is encircled by 'associative' cortices, that elaborate in a thousand different ways the information coming from the corresponding primary areas. In humans, other areas are even more developed, broad and important: they are the regions in between these associative areas, that compare and relate information collected from distinct sensory modalities (*multimodal associative areas*).

Thus, in humans most of the cortex is taken by associative areas, and in particular multimodal areas. This is particularly true for the frontal lobe, which is tremendously developed in humans with respect to any other animal, because its function is not only to program the most refined movements, but also to elaborate a complex behavioral strategy, that is based on different time scales, aims and projects, and involves canceling, deferring, rescheduling the various purposes, conciliation and compromise.

The role of multimodal associative areas is no less important in parietal, occipital and temporal regions, where they sustain most cognitive, mnemonic, logic and linguistic activities.

More generally, as we shall see, the degree of vigilance and *consciousness* is a function, in man, of the intensity of neuronal activity in multimodal associative areas.

Here is the solution of the stupid quiz:

IV

MAYBE BOTH – Beyond the limit – meta

Natura non facit saltus.

Still, an important objection to Darwin's views has been that evolution does not appear to proceed so smoothly and quietly...

Indeed, the world itself does not proceed calmly. Nature does proceed through jumps. Or better, the jumps are not there, we just see them. We realize that properties and features suddenly appear, that were not there before and that require new interpretative approaches and new readings; thus, we decide that new and different orders have been achieved, and limits have been trespassed.

Life itself is the hugest of these jumps. Nucleic acids, for example. Molecules that can guide the surrounding potential energy of chemistry towards their own reproduction, then towards the synthesis of even more versatile molecules – proteins – and through these towards the organization of complex systems: ordered systems, such as cells, and organisms, which in turn can collect energy and use it to keep going, maintain themselves and change, evolve and reproduce themselves.

A jump, certainly a powerful and frightening jump towards infinite possibilities. But a jump that has no starting, or turning, or arrival points. What was holding back everything before – energy, potentials, entropy – still constrains everything, afterwards. But this possibility of reproducing a *form* by ordering external matter could not be detected in anything that existed before.

And the jump is twofold, with life: reproducing the form by ordering matter, sure; but the cell, the organism, can also *keep the form alive* in a never-ending exchange of matter with the outside, and can guide an individual entity through time, so that it remains recognizable in spite of its continuous changing, until, after decades, you will still recognize it though not a single molecule will still be there, out of what used to constitute it at the beginning.

Further, impressive jumps follow. The synthesis of molecules capable of capturing sun rays and using their energy to destroy stable, inert molecules such as water and carbon dioxide, to combine them into sugar, vigorous and energetic, ready to give out its energy for any possible use by the cell, or to donate itself as food for other organisms that are incapable to exploit sun's energy but are happy to permit sugar to disaggregate, and ready to use its euphoria to build themselves, repair their own cells and tissues, move around, and change the world.

It's the plants and then the animals.

It is the possibility of using not only the potential energy that has remained trapped in Earth's cooling down after the Big Bang (the snow trapped on the branches), but also the energy that comes from the sun, to make life.

The rules that used to be in force before each jump still are. The new system, with life in it, just adds new, additional rules that are needed to understand the new processes, mechanisms, and possibilities that life has brought about.

Another big jump: the development of cells that can signal at one site of the organism changes that have occurred at another site. The neural cells, neurons. And networks of neurons, more and more complex, that make it possible to simultaneously respond to different stimuli, to compare, to integrate and modulate complex responses, to organize coordinated behaviors of the whole organism.

More. The development of a central nervous system, where the bunch of information that pullulates among the neurons and their intricate connections begins to constitute a complete representation of all the complex relations that constitute the organism, the external reality, and their interactions. Or, better, a model, which makes it possible to develop a behavior based on predicting how interactions with the external reality may satisfy vegetative needs, and less easily describable motivational drives.

A meta-biology is born, that physics and life are not sufficient to interpret and understand, that has its own rules, forces and dynamics; a meta-biology that invades the field of immaterial, of knowledge, of cybernetics (the science of control systems, κυβερνήτης is the Greek word for pilot), characterized by anticipation and finalized action.

Finally, in humans, the cerebral cortex undergoes an impressive growth and becomes capable of escaping the function of merely producing a response to each stimulus: innumerable circuits in the cortex elaborate available information according to specific modalities, perspectives and contexts, and generate a cohort of different readings of the reality, which pullulate and evolve in the cortex, each of them complex in itself and in many ways autonomous, but integrated with the others. Each reading is an image of a specific aspect of oneself or of the world; it arises, grows and evolves like a meta-organism, endowed with its own life, although confined in the immateriality of a formal, abstract representation.

But there is no contradiction. The rules developed so far are still in force, the energies, forces, mechanisms, processes.

The fundamental rule also holds, unchanged: each event has its own cause, energies that would push but are restrained and mechanisms that make them be released to produce one or the other effect. Mechanisms are often so complex that it becomes difficult to understand, or even describe them.

But mechanisms are there, however, reasonably clear and well defined, even though they begin to hide behind processes that seem no longer guided by physical forces, but by aspirations and aims.

There is no contradiction, but at each step and jump a new dimension appears, that must be noted to appreciate what we are facing.

At each new jump a novel formal description is more appropriate, because the rules that have guided simpler systems, though they continue to operate in depth, are no longer relevant to describe and understand the general dynamics of the new system, which is governed by certain specific relations and requisites that in simpler systems could not even be thought of.

Finally, the ultimate step (up to now, at least). From representation of objects, events, simple and complex relations, to conceptual and symbolic manipulation.

The innumerable readings that waggle in the brain carve the concepts, build a multiple, complex and variegated vision of reality and of oneself, made of metaphors, capable of symbols and of abstract manipulation. Specific regions of the cortex evaluate visible aspects, sounds, smell, taste of each element of experience, and its spatial and temporal relationships with other elements, its order, affective valence and value for satisfying vital needs. In associative areas nervous circuits collect all the readings of an object, present in the various regions of the brain, compare and correlate them; as these associative areas greatly develop, the possibility arises of an abstract representation of the object in all its aspects, of a concept, the unifying principle of a coherent multiplicity. The possibility of a concept not only for an object, for an event, but also for a set of objects, for a sequence of events, the concept itself for relation among objects, and among events, for a relation among relations...

Here, in the systems that interconnect the thousands of readings, consciousness sprouts: a gaze that is conscious of itself and of the world. Once more it is a synthesis and unification of multiplicity. The regulation of behavior becomes more careful and delicate, considering the variegated interaction among vegetative, hedonic and socio-cultural drives, and ideal aims; a clear and real possibility of choice appears: finalized behavior, strictly speaking.

Here biology and cybernetics are no longer sufficient, the fields of epistemology, of ethics, of freedom are invaded. We are trespassing into the territories of the soul.

It is the concomitance of metaphors, consciousness and free will.

All this, empowered by language. The quintessence, and admirable tool and toy, for symbolic representation and manipulation. Language is a useful paradigm to understand the brain and the powerful jump that humans constitute in evolution.

'Ipse' (Aristotle for friends) had many defects; he was authoritative and systematic, he might have been so careless (as Galileo accused him) not to realize that three dimensions are enough to define space because of a simple reason, i.e. that no more than three perpendicular lines can be drawn through a single point: there was no need to involve idealities for this, there was no need to claim that 'the dimension of a body MUST be three and no more than three', no need at all of using sophistic and mystical arguments about the perfection of number 3... He had his limitations, all right, but about *logos*, about the language, *Ipse* was not careless at all: he understood it well, he had a clear vision.

The sounds that animals produce have a meaning, and the human voice, with its modulations, can naturally express many meanings and nuances. But language is something else. In his *De Anima* Ipse unveils the trick: it has been necessary to strip the sounds the voice can produce of their natural meaning; to extract and crystallize phonemes, vocal sounds, without any meaning; and finally to give them new meanings by combining them, partly in an arbitrary way, partly by similitude, assonance and association, according to many criteria and rules, ending up with a full system of symbols. A system that exists as a set of signals that take on a precise meaning only within that same system. The same phonemes have different meanings in a different language, the same meanings in a different language require different phonemes. But why did he put all this in a book that he called *De Anima*? Because one perceives straight away that manipulating symbols has nothing to do with the material reality, it is beyond physics, it's metaphysics (μετὰ τὰ φυσικά), we are abandoning the perceivable reality, we are taking off towards the spirit, that portion of our intellect that no longer has anything left that looks mechanical or predictable.

Then, let us recount each other that bees talk, that they perform symbolic flights to explain the others how to find food, that our cat understands us and meows in a way it seems it's talking...

There is a difference, and not a small one.

All animal sounds and communication modes simulate, represent, describe according to natural or instinctual associations; they are mimical languages. A symbol is something else: nothing in it links it to its meaning, it could mean something completely different in another symbolic system, in another *language*. They teach us in school that there exist words that remind and represent their meaning by natural association, we learn to call them onomatopoeic. They are but rare exceptions; nothing strange in this. Because they are useless, except in a few cases, to evoke in a direct and precise way – in an instinctive way – objects, actions and images, or the emotions that we spontaneously associate to those objects, actions, images.

The capacity of symbolic manipulation is a new dimension of life that is born with *Homo*. Curiously, there is no need for formal models to inject language in the brain: the way neural circuits elaborate information precisely draws the limits, the modalities and the rules with which we generate symbols and combine them into a symbolic system.

So, many formal, fundamental features are common to all natural languages in the world: they essentially reflect the modes in which the cerebral cortex recognizes and classifies the objects, the spatial, temporal, causal relations that appear to link them, and the events and possible interactions, with them and among them...

But we are running too fast. Let's wait until we have described, at least roughly, how the brain works. As of now, we shall be contented of having described this hopping-jumping by nature, in creating more and more complex systems, that transcend the rules and the mechanisms of the preceding ones, and invade ever wider and higher domains of order, form, immateriality.

Up to language. Up to thought. And complexity grows, and multiplicity.

* * *

Everybody knows how Natural Selection works: the more fit will prevail.

To be precise, nobody prevails, as nobody survives. Try and explain how nice it is to the poor mate of the black widow, who gets poisoned to death during sex, but may thus favor genetic diversity, and survival of the species, by allowing its spouse to mate with other males… The matter is about whether your species will prevail, because it has some reproductive advantages.

The paradox is exasperated in unicellular organisms: bacteria have quite dynamic genetic material, they may be infected by phages, they may exchange pieces of DNA, they display high mutation rates.

All this may in most cases impair their survival as individuals, but simultaneously favor the appearance of novel features that may make the progeny more apt to survive. We all know about antibiotic abuse and antibiotic resistance.

With this trick of hypervariability to favor adaptation, Evolution has anticipated our geniuses of finance, who invented hedge funds. You cannot always win, so split your money, invest in different sectors, bet hedge: you will certainly lose on some tables, but you may win overall. A perfect strategy for Evolution, as it does not care much if some of its experiments fail; those that succeed carry on life in its innumerable versions on Earth.

An even more fascinating trick has been discovered in some bacterial species: true genetic bet hedging. Mechanisms to regulate genes in a random way, so that in front of changing environments some individuals will lose their bet, fail to adapt and die, but others will guess the winning genetic make-up and prosper. Expose a bacterial population to stressing conditions that should kill most of them ("bottleneck" conditions), do it repetitively, and if some of the bacteria develop such capability – the capability of epigenetic bet hedging – they will be selected and keep proliferating, because some of them will be able to overcome each one of the repeated challenges.

Again, most will die.

The story is not about individuals, but about the species. Bet-hedging bacteria will keep dying, all the ones that bet on the wrong genetic make-up; but for every new bottleneck some will win their bet and overcome, while bourgeois, conformist bacteria, who stick to a fixed genetic regulation, will be decimated by every new challenge.

Bet-hedging bacteria will much more likely be resistant to antibiotics, even many of them: some bacteria will survive every attack and proliferate, but they will keep betting, and remain a heterogenous population.

Sometimes we see even more threatening strategies: bacteria that turn off error-proofing mechanisms in gene replication, which implies enormously amplifying mutation rates: in most cases this will be sure death. But it might, by pure chance, yield an unexpected way of surviving.

Hypermutable bacteria and viruses escape the attempts of the immune system at eliminating them: for every antibody we make, some of them will be able to survive... Think of flu: every year a new strand comes about that is insensitive to the antibodies we made last year...

Crazy, gruesome and cruel games of Evolution.

We feel more comfortable with the alternate strategy Evolution has chosen for us: stop playing with numbers – innumerable individuals just to have some surviving – and produce an organism so complex that it can adapt to every climate and situation, from the equator to the poles, from the seaside to the Pamir, facing hurricanes, pests, famines and diseases, thanks to the many survival strategies that we can adopt when the environment attacks us, and to the capability of modifying the environment itself when we cannot adapt.

We feel more comfortable, but Evolution keeps playing its "game of life", within our own bodies: some cells happen to suffer some random mutation, and this way evade the mechanisms that control proliferation and growth in the organism. Tumors may develop.

It happens much more frequently than we realize. In most cases, the modified cells die, our immune system manages to spot and kill them. But sometimes they undergo further mutations, or even turn off error proofing mechanisms, like those evil and invincible bacteria, and one ends up with no defense: they keep mutating, and become more and more defective, and weak and unstable; in every new generation, though, there will be some cells that not only manage to survive, but will now be able to escape the attacks of our immune system, and will be insensitive to the antitumor drugs that seemed to be so effective yesterday...

It is like in the movie, "Jurassic Park": you cannot win against life.

Life will find its way around any obstacle you may build on its way.

* * *

Maybe evolution does have a meaning, a dominant direction. It proceeds blindly, true, any path is good to produce and multiply life, life that keeps discovering ever new ways to consume blocked energy.

Surely evolution does not abandon any alternative path, it simply shuts them down when they can no longer compete, but as far as possible it keeps every tactic open.

The direction is multiplicity, 'biodiversity', the thousand different solutions for any problem. But in this search Nature sometimes encounters 'qualitative jumps', new solutions that are substantially more complex, that offer higher flexibility and multiplicity of strategies by one and the same organism. In this direction, complexity accompanies multiplicity: evolution does not abandon simple solutions, but in addition to multiplying simple solutions it can find more and more complex solutions, that escape the domain of mere survival and begin to modify the world, instead of only adapting to it, and then begin to represent it, to model and interpret it, and understand it, and end up looking at themselves and interpret and understand themselves.

In this direction – complexity and multiplicity, solutions that depart from practically facing the problem and explore instead implications, and colors and atmospheres, and higher harmonies – it is evident that man is not the endpoint. Evolution has already made at least another step: woman...

* * *

The created creator, or: Evolution and History, but whose history? ([1])

Usually, one thinks that Homo lives its history and marks its stages in stones and papyruses, in traditions, in knowledge, in products, in myths and religious creeds, in political structures and social organization. Curious idea...

Geneticists and molecular biologists play puzzles –which they like defining scientific studies and camouflage with intense conceptuality – through which one generates schemes that resemble genealogical trees, where yeasts, worms, humans, rabbits and bacteria are located on branches, close or far apart, depending on the differences between the respective sequences in the gene of interest.

Here is the puzzle: in ordering all the differences and deducing where each of them has arisen, to reconstruct the evolutionary path of the gene...
Not much of an enigmatic challenge, however, or of mental gymnastics, as the computer takes care of it. Looking at these schemes usually bores you, sometimes it upsets you – especially when the ghost of an exam impinges...

But if we exploit all the resources that our brain can offer us, in offering similitudes and getaways from boredom, we may be caught by the fantasy of looking for a meaning, a story, some kind of a poetry. Then, the clear, fascinating and intriguing image appears of a colored tiny snake, an infinite winding little staircase of nucleic acid that, by coiling and curling in the millennia has been able to reproduce itself, thanks to the sexual

---

[1] This piece comes from an idea encountered some time ago on the network, that presumably drew a lot from Dawkins' idea of the 'selfish gene'. I cannot find out who the author was. I thought that by the 2nd edition the author would certainly have emerged. I am still waiting, but I hereby declare that I will not recognize paternity of the idea to more than 10 philosophers.

appetites of stupid animate beings that believe that air is there for them to breath, water for them to drink and the whole world to be eaten and destroyed...

The colored tiny staircase may be the only thing that has really survived, and evolved, during all this time. Strictly speaking, not even the small snake has survived across prehistory and history and the black Monday and the new-year day of the prophesized 'a thousand and no more thousand' (1.1.2000 or 1.1.2001?); not the snake, indeed, THE SEQUENCE.

Now think of written stuff, the 'text'. Doesn't it evolve as well? knowledge, ideas, interpretations, images, written histories have their own pathway, their own growth and evolution, every written thing feeds on what has been written before, after having been digested in a solitary meal by the abstruse erudite writer or mixed up, contaminated, crushed, thrown up and recomposed by a crowd bath, read, taught, discussed, refused, and revisited...

THE SEQUENCE, *in order to live and reproduce itself, has been able to create life and, after recombining everything in every way, has ended up relying on living beings that are capable of drawing and representing the reality that surrounds them. Then, why should not* THE TEXT, *that was embryonically born in scratches in the rocks on the walls of a cave, profit of this situation, to organize, grow up and live its own history, using the brains and sometimes the viscera and emotions of humans to coagulate in ever new and ever more complex combinations, and to embrace ever wider horizons?*

And what can we say about ART? *What has it got to do with us? It is like feeling proud, ants in a queue, for the magnificence of the anthill, for the sublime and superior equilibriums that not us, but some strange emerging properties of the coordinated ensemble of billions of us, have created!*
*'*ART*', the pictorial, volumetric, linguistic expression of some persistent moods in nature and humans, of relations unexpectedly discovered in many different domains, of unimagined, improbable harmonies, of the* QUINTESSENCE *of things…*

*'*ART*' has developed in history like a fantastic drawing in continuous evolution, a process of which we are only unaware creators and spectators, like the ten thousand participants to that old Coca-Cola advertisement: a Christmas tree that transformed them, small candles in their hand, into the molecules of Global Market's poetical aspect.*

So Homo has been used. By the TEXT *and by the* QUINTESSENCE. *And by many others.* ECONOMY *and* MARKET *used Homo to grow and proliferate, and change and adapt, and crawl in their uncertain and doubtful evolution; so has social* ORGANIZATION, *that transforms into* HISTORY *through our working, using humans as picture cards for a millenary role-playing game.*

Finally, support, opium and superstition.

Myth, and spiritual, mystical interpretation of good and evil.

Of evil, especially, that is more difficult to bear, and death itself, that is more difficult to cope with.

From the simplest natural puck to the sophisticated One and Triune God, mysterious and incomprehensible, revealed in His Divine Humanity to elude reason and keep alive the devoted, faithful, unaware and humble acceptance and submission; uppermost justification of the value of life in a world that kills for money, of the value of love in a world that only loves what it can possess; sublime justification needed to grant the desire of copulating and proliferating even in the face of misery, famine and war, disease and pain, thereby keeping RELIGION *itself alive in the millennia. And keeping* GOD *alive, but this way* THE TEXT *as well, and the* QUINTESSENCE, *and* THE SEQUENCE, *mother of any things that live...*

Maybe, then, not a GOD *who creates Man who will recognize His creation and appraise Him/Her/It and honor Him/Her/It, but the* SEQUENCE *that creates* LIFE *to merely survive, and through life manages to create Homo, and through it the* TEXT, *to be described, the* QUINTESSENCE, *to perceive and love itself, the* ORGANIZATION, *to consolidate these conquests, and finally* GOD *himself, to give a meaning to its own stupid and insensate life.*

But was it really necessary that all of us were here, and Giacomo Leopardi and William Shakespeare and Michelangelo and Tom Waits and Einstein, and Countries and Flags and Churches, and God, and War... merely to justify the stability of four molecules in a line...?

* * *

Now, let alone the reference to religion, that may taste too much Marxism and people's opium, and certainly has offended somebody; but from the point of view of RNA, and of life in general, and of animal kingdom, and maybe of the human species in particular, histories and fascinating developments such as art and music, philosophy and literature, are nothing but incidents, collateral effects. Life itself, indeed, for the history of the SEQUENCE that all governs, is but a collateral effect.

Here is the question: a complex system that interacts, persists and reproduces itself asks for a new perspective, *another* reading frame, that recognizes its own specific evolution rules. It generates a meta-system.

The development of complex systems tells about new agents, organisms and meta-realities that are born, grow up and seem to live their own life outside the system that has generated them, in another domain of what is conceivable, of reality. It is a curious, exciting interplay of collateral effects. Unforeseen collateral effects, unpredictable based on the system that has generated them, on the relations that define it, on the rules that govern it, on its most complete and organic formal description.

They are unpredictable products because they blossom in unexpected domains, that are ruled by other criteria, forces and fates: complex systems, for which students and lovers have created the term 'emergent property', to indicate the appearance of those unexpected collateral effects, because such features only appear – emerge – when a complex system is considered as a whole, *from the outside*, in its relations with higher systems, examining its behavior in spheres that are not contemplated and predicted by its internal relations and rules.

Well, from the impressive development of cognitive, cybernetic and behavioral power of the human brain, a collateral effect was born: an unexpected and fascinating mixture of interpretative power, emotions and motivations, memory and desire, pleasure and pain, and conscious understanding and feeling, and blue and happiness, love, passion and will, curiosity and fear, wonder and shame, fervor and commitment.

A mixture that is a new level of life, interior and superior, not secluded and excluded, but rather capable of etching reality and carving the world, and of doing so in a new and different way, following plans and aims, desires and ideals.

Even more, from this mixture of gazes, wishes and fantasies, a new unexpected dimension of life blossoms, the need for *other*, infinite in time and space, the need for transcending the self to wander in eternity and infinity...

It is a curious collateral effect, something for which it is difficult to find out a name that be nicer and more appropriate than 'soul'.

* * *

All this is 'meta'.
The logic that governs the *system* is useless to understand, explain, interpret the *reading*, the meta-system. Still, the latter, and its logic and its life, are based on the logic and life of the underlying system.

This is meta. This is Gödel.

We live in a world full of complex systems, that because of their complexity are something different from the sum of their components and invade domains that their elements do not know of. Emergent properties cannot be predicted by analyzing the elements which constitute a system – and their reciprocal interactions.

But then one must forget that objects and systems end where they end, and perceive and understand the *border* that *connects* them to (rather than a *limit* that separates them from) the surrounding reality: the apple is green only because the light hits it and somebody observes it; it is not a property of its own, and in any case it does not depend on (and is not relevant to understand) its structure, its organization, its equilibrium.

Still, from outside it *is green*, and we do not know the apple if we do not know it under this respect as well, if we do not know it in aspects that arise and remain outside it but contribute to defining it in reality.

That's baloney, isn't it? sure! until it only concerns apples.

But it becomes a little alarming and worrying if all this also messes up logic, and mathematics, because these matters are what appears to most closely approach perfection, to many of us.

Gödel has bewildered and upset modern thought by demonstrating a theorem that stated more or less as follows: 'there cannot exist a logic and/or mathematical system that simultaneously be coherent and complete'.

In other words: if a logic system wants to be coherent it must accept to be applicable to a limited domain only, and if it wants to be complete it will certainly contain some incoherencies.

A trivial example: in a logic system that permits deciding with absolute certainty and coherence whether a sentence (statement) is true or false, what happens to a statement such as 'this same sentence is false', i.e. to a sentence that states its own falsity? It is acceptable and correct, grammatically, syntactically and even (abstractly speaking) logically. Still, it is not possible to define its truth/falsity. Then, a logical system that attributes a value of truth/falsity to statements must admit that there exist at least one class of statements that it cannot deal with (to be coherent it must be incomplete), because it cannot classify such statements as either true or false: it cannot deal with those statements that talk about the truth of statements (*meta-statements*), for which a different and complementary logic is needed (a *meta-logic*).

Somebody will disagree and claim that the logical system can easily apply to meta-statements. Here is a good one: 'the statement 'the snow is white' is true'. A logical statement, correct, true, and talks about the truth of other statements. Then let us try: 'the statement 'this same sentence is false' cannot be defined as true or false because it is true if it is false and is false if it is true, ergo it is absolutely possible that it be both false *and* true'. Perfect. Now we have a logic statement, grammatically correct, syntactically correct and true, that talks about truth and applies to other statements. We did it. Now our logic is complete.

Just a small problem: our logic now admits as a true statement one that states the incapacity of the logic itself to judge the truth/falsity of a statement that belongs to the logic itself. Our logic is now complete, but incoherent, by its own claim. Was the previous incomplete logic better than this?

Word games? No. It is not the place to recall the rigorous demonstration of Gödel's theorem, but it is not word games. The question is not the precise claim of the theorem, but its philosophical relevance. Not only mathematics, and logics, and reason itself that is based on the two of them, are not perfect (*ouch!*), but the most coherent, rigorous and sophisticated logic that can be applied to the analysis of a system cannot be applied 'as is' to the interactions of the system itself with the exterior. The correct analysis of the components and the internal dynamics of a system is not an adequate approach to evaluate the system in its wholeness, its interactions with other systems, or the way it will emerge in a different cognitive or ontological dimension.

One must surrender, then?

No. But an approach must be developed, a meta-analysis approach, that be capable of looking at the system from outside; without exiting the system; using new canons and criteria that will say nothing about the internal logics of the system and ignore irrelevant details that cannot be interpreted in the new perspective, but correctly describe and interpret and understand the modes, times, roles and behaviors of the system, in the higher reality it belongs to, in the new dimensions it has invaded.

* * *

Back to infinity, then. Because '*all*' encloses, and one cannot go further, maniac for coherence, while '*infinity*' does not stop, and finds new rules where the old ones no longer hold. Back to the power of multiple perspectives, that surrenders the certainty of universal coherence but can offer multifaceted readings that see different views and perspectives instead of seeing limits, that do not amputate the soul of its freedom.

It is difficult, anyway. It is difficult to give up the protection of four walls that limit, surround and warrant a *whole*, a small one perhaps, but an entire one. It is difficult not to dream of freedom as a wider space, wider but anyway protected, please, a castle maybe with its flourished garden. But there is another freedom, that of American Indians, who died if they were trapped among four walls, because the eye must fly far away, the skin must feel the wind, the spirit must travel, free.

The desire of infinity is meta, is consciousness of the soul, is going beyond, out of oneself, it is living and feeling oneself living. It is trespassing the limit between self and non self, expanding and transcending oneself. It is flying and enjoying the flight while remaining ourselves: it is the naturalness of flight in our dreams, the pleasant discovery that we can fly, that unexpectedly does not disagree with our own being and our idea of ourselves. It is transcending ourselves in space and time, but in an intensely dialectic way: it is not Peter Pan, it is not flying away, it is living, here and now, and still being able to fly and see ourselves from outside, and see the world. It is not being outside. It is beyond, it is *meta*. It is being *also* outside.

The contradiction is apparent, but so is also the absolute reality, and equally apparent is the reconcilability of the contradiction. This is the magic of dialectics, that does not demand ontology to be static, and by permitting a contradictory ontology gives (gives back) life to reality.

Luigi Pirandello once said 'life, either you live it, or you write about it'... It may be true, strictly speaking, but the soul precisely consists in reconciling the two things: *maybe both*, feel and read and write life, while you live it.

* * *

If you try playing the scientist, today, you must be able to alternate two opposed approaches. The biological processes that occur in any organism are so evidently useful and appropriate for the survival of the subject, or the species, that one is led to stop and describe their admirable organization and interactions in making possible the incredible equilibriums, the intricate processes of life.

One is led to look for the AIM that appears to be driving every process, forgetting that a '*scientific*' explanation must instead clarify what forces and energies feed it and make it possible and accomplish it (the CAUSES).

For the neuroscientist everything is even more difficult, because forces and mechanisms are multiple, intertwined and hidden by the anatomical and functional complexity of the brain, whereas the usefulness of any aspect of neuronal elaboration for a specific aim is more easily discernible and traceable. It is comfortable to reason that each response that is produced by the nervous system be triggered and guided by the stimuli that reach it, and the circuits and modes of elaboration be selected so to give the most appropriate and suitable response to each stimulus.

Following this reasoning, one must follow the stimulus-response pathway to understand something, paying attention not to get lost. Thus, one ends up reasoning backwards, from the observation of human behavior to the causes that determine and guide it, as if the brain were a black box whose functioning could be understood by studying the responses it gives to the stimuli it receives. This is totally misleading. Because it does not work this way. Or, better, it does, in one sense, but otherwise it does not. From the mechanistic point of view, this idea is somehow correct: for each signal that moves around in the brain it is possible to track back a signal, near or far away in space and time, that has determined it, either directly or through variably complex mediations (it seems that determinism governs on Nature).

But if one looks at human behavior, the sum of stimuli and causes is clearly not sufficient to predict it, neither is it possible to track the paths and the mechanisms that have generated it. To understand human behavior, one must accept that *something*, in the brain or elsewhere, has elaborated and accumulated and drudged information, and clearly has not done this by considering and weighting each piece of information solely in terms of their relevance to (momentary) behavioral and practical aims. Humans extract from this 'something', at each moment, the forces that generate autonomous acts and modify the responses that would be expected, based only on the stimuli that are present or have occurred in the near past. This 'something', in the brain or elsewhere, generates autonomous, endogenous motivational drives, capable of initiative, choice, creativity.

We must restart from the right perspective.

Forwards, not backwards. From the information that arrives to the brain and the use it makes of such information. Along this path one encounters bifurcations, wanderings and collateral effects that strongly characterize the functioning of the brain and generate emergent properties and processes.

These processes definitely depart from the stimulus-response path, complex as it might be. They are collateral effects that may appear little relevant in terms of response to the stimuli, but must be considered to understand human behavior, the drives that guide humans, and their endogenous and creative aspects.

Collateral effects that do constitute human peculiarity and profoundly permeate human life, opening infinite, yet unexplored, spaces, in the cognitive, ethical, esthetic domains.

Here is the 'meta' of the brain. In its playing and spending most of its time re-elaborating, re-drawing, re-interpreting and re-modeling the world, freely following its multiple and varied tastes, with no practical aims, generating sketches, impressions, readings and metaphors of reality. So, when a thousand metaphors live and push and compete in the brain and drive ACTS that are no longer mere choices among possible RESPONSES, then something is born that can no longer be studied by the same approach one would use to study a cause-effect chain. Direct causes are no longer sufficient, elementary mechanisms do not explain much. A new perspective, a new gaze is necessary to understand, ideas are needed, and aims, objectives, possibly dreams and desires and imagination, to explain acts that are no longer responses, but rather autonomous initiatives.

* * *

The other way around: from the stimulus up.

If you are smart (but not too young, or smart enough not to care – indeed, one lives pretty well disregarding the problem) you have probably looked closely at the screen of an old television set, at least once, and noticed that each point of the image was actually divided into three sectors, a blue one, a green one and a red one, more or less luminous and more or less intense (please do not look at led or plasma screens..). All the colors arise from this. Sure, it is obvious that all colors arise from this, because this is exactly the way our eye builds them: a sensory cell recognizes the red light, another one the green, a third type the blue light, and a task for other nervous cells is to combine these sources of information to decide what is the color of each point of the visual field.

Then, once the color of each point has been recognized, the image is projected (upside-down! this we all know well) on the posterior part of the cerebral cortex, isn't it? Didn't they explain the story this way, in high-school textbooks? – there is no single textbook that does not print the candle, or the pine tree, upside down, at the back of the head...

No. No images stroll around in our brain. And certainly, there is no 'intellect' in our brain that looks at such images, interprets them, records them in 'memory' and recalls them when it needs it. Each cell that is there to recognize a stimulus (*receptor*) generates an electric signal. As an isolated electrical blip, the signal remains there – in the skin, in the retina, in the olfactory epithelium in the nose: it is not reproduced identically in any other part of the brain.

Before leaving the eye toward the central nervous system, visual information (the ensemble of the blips generated by millions of photoreceptors) is decomposed into distinct aspects – general luminance, light conditions, local contrast, color ratios – and is not simply bounced around the brain, but re-elaborated according to specific criteria, reading canons; it is not transmitted and reproduced but translated, narrated.

This is true for any external stimulus: a photon that hits a cell in the retina, a sound vibration that excites a cell in the cochlea, a molecule of perfume captured by an olfactory cell in the nasal mucosa, the terminal of a pain neuron stretched by an air bubble in the intestine.

The receptor generates a signal that directly reaches numerous neurons in the nervous system, and at each of these it is related, compared, summed and integrated with many other signals coming from other similar sensory cells and from many other neurons. Only the results of these elaborations proceed towards further neuronal stages.

In the retina, for example, several layers of neurons are present in addition to sensory cells, and most of them do not respond to the intensity and color of the light that hits a single point of the retina, but to the difference in light and/or color between this point and the surrounding ones... It is not strange that even the most trained painter cannot select, on their palette, the exact color they want to put in a precise point of the painting, among the other neighboring colors, because we cannot 'see' a color independently from the context.

One may wonder... It is natural to ask why it should be this way, what is the advantage of all this. Well, it is not difficult to support the claim that it is much more useful to see color differences and relations, rather than absolute values. This lets us recognize a ripe fruit from an unrip, or rotten one, both in the white sunlight at noon and in the red light of sunset... And if the light dims while we are reading a book, it is absolutely no use to note that all points have become darker in the image we have in front; it is much better to simply perceive that there is less light (overall, by combining signals that come from many points) but realize that the image composition is essentially the same, as the differences among neighboring points have not changed much.

Nothing strange, therefore, if mother nature selected sensory mechanisms capable of performing such elaboration.

Let's neglect for a moment the practical usefulness of these manipulations of sensory data by our nervous system and turn our attention to the underlying mechanisms. Intriguing and fascinating consequences will arise.

In fact, we cannot watch, listen, perceive elements that occur together, without noticing and elaborating their reciprocal relations. No colored points exist for us but shapes, no vibrations but sounds, not even sounds but possible melodies or words, not words but sentences, talks, stories, poetry. Then, let's forget for a moment what is more or less useful, and try to understand how all this works, why (what is the cause, not the aim) our brain does not let in reality, but rather elaborations of sensory data: reality does pop in, but is chewed and ground at once, because these processes do not apply a posteriori to recorded and saved information, they are not 'cognitive' elaborations; they occur in real time, are the result of an automatic computation that is 'pre-wired' in the network of neuronal connections in the brain, an absolutely unconscious computation that starts taking place even before the sensory data reach the cerebral cortex.

These are computations that occur exactly in the same way, no offense, in the head of a mouse.

Each one of the myriads of sensory signals that reach the brain at any instant contacts numerous neurons; and at each neuron it is combined with other similar signals, some of them with similar meaning and some with a different one, because they come from other neuronal systems. In each neuron, the signal will enter a different and specific computation.

Imagine having to explore a wood, with a hundred boy scouts: would you assign one hundredth of the woods to each of them, asking them to record whatever they see?

Much better would be to divide them in teams, assign a larger portion of the woods to each team, but asking each member of each team to record a specific aspect: the structure of the ground, the paths, the presence of water, and which plants, animals, mushrooms, fruits... The gathered information will be much easier to elaborate and interpret – they will actually be already interpreted to a large extent. And after repeating the exploration, the scouts who look for mushrooms may have learned to recognize the poisonous from the good ones, and those observing the plants to recognize the different species.

If many scouts look at *the same things*, but each of them focuses on different aspects and features, the myriad of meaningless data becomes an interpretation (or a number of simultaneous interpretations) of reality.

This way of dealing with signals characterizes all elaborations by the nervous system. Typically, each nervous cell can receive tens of thousands of synaptic contacts, through which other neurons transmit signals to it. Each neuron collects an impressive amount of information in a precisely ordered way on its dendrites, so that activation of each neuron has a 'meaning', indicates that a certain pattern, a feature, a relation, an organizational principle, a sequence is present and detectable in the collection of stimuli that reach the brain.

Going back to eyesight, in the cortex there are neurons that receive information from a certain number of receptors that are positioned with a precise spatial organization in the retina, so that their coordinated activation indicates that a profile between two colors or gray levels occurs in a specific area of the visual field; other neurons recognize, by the same principle, a horizontal line, or a vertical, or an oblique one. By combining the information elaborated by these neurons, other cells detect the presence of geometrical figures (squares, triangles, circles) or even more complex figures such as stars, targets... By refining more and more this game of feature and relation detection, one reaches neurons that are located in the temporal lobe, more lateral and anterior, at a distance from the primary visual areas of the occipital cortex; these neurons perform even more 'abstract' or general tasks, and are capable of detecting objects and complex figures in the visual image, or even any possible combination of elements in which a human face or expression can be perceived: :o) :-(:-p ^__^ are smile, sadness, bleah!, another smile.

Children in their first months, as soon as they begin to see well, are happy – are quieter and smile – if we position a face sketch, ☺, in front of them. And when we raise our gaze to the sky and look at the clouds, whenever it is possible we see faces, profiles, smiles. It is not just chance.

Each nerve cell in the brain produces its own synthesis and reading of the small piece of reality it is in contact with – according to the signals it receives and the way it is designed to elaborate them, – and sends this result to hundreds of other neurons, which in turn perform the same operations on similar information coming from thousands of other neurons.

The raw sensory data (sound, image, smell...) is digested and decomposed in a myriad of different ways by many distinct brain circuits: no longer an image, but lines, colors, masses, volumes, light and tone contrasts, geometrical figures, faces...). The raw sensory datum produces a specific pattern of activity in millions of specific neurons and connections. A set of activity patterns occurring in specific sets of neurons reports a specific sensory experience. Each pattern represents a specific trait, a feature, a way of looking at the sensory datum: the brain has invented 'parallel architecture' – in which information is distributed, and elaborated, in a thousand pathways, in parallel – well before information scientists.

Parallel processing lets distinct circuits extract different features and characteristics simultaneously.

In our brain there are no 'photographs' of our experiences but records of the aspects and elements that comprise them, and of the relations among such elements, and of the relations among such relations. Reality is redrawn and interpreted in innumerable ways, from many points of view, with many perspectives and different gazes, simultaneously. The brain incessantly elaborates information, and at each step information is messed up, decomposed and re-unified. Each element and detail is only preserved in its relations with other elements and its relevance.

But information simultaneously gains thickness and new dimensions. Each neural system can be considered as an *organ* that operates as a transcendental system, in that it receives information and rearranges it by extracting the specific features it is 'interested' in. And in each neuronal system it invades, information becomes a concert of colors and melodies typical of that particular system.

* * *

This capability of transforming sensory data into a representation of elements and relations has an obvious usefulness, because it makes the recognition of objects and situations possible, and effective, so that the appropriate behavioral response can be evoked. It is an elaboration modality that characterizes the brain of all animals that possess one.

The main difference, in humans, is not only the mass, and the number of neurons and circuits, of the regions of the cortex that take care of these combined and 'interpreted' readings of a piece of sensory information; even more important than that is the enormous development, with respect to any other animal, of the associative *multimodal* areas of the cortex.

These are the regions where complex evaluations are performed by combining and putting into reciprocal relation the information that comes from different sensory modalities (and not only sensory) and bears variable relevance and meaning: sound information, and visual, and visceral, motor, emotional...

We shall discuss these aspects further on. But an unusual perspective already emerges here.

A very complex neuronal machinery designed for appropriate behavioral responses produces a representation, or better a multifaceted series of representations of reality as a collateral effect, as a precious byproduct. Relations among objects and events are represented by patterns of neuronal activation, that can be recognized when they occur again, perceived by analogy in other situations, and generalized to drive a predictive reading of reality. Each pattern of neuronal activation can therefore be profitably used to optimize behavior; but in the meantime it is related to others to build a MODEL of the world and its dynamics, to generate a new dimension of life, a meta-biology of the representation, modeling and interpretation of reality, more and more complex as the dimension and organization of the cortex expands and becomes more sophisticated, in ascending the evolutionary scale. The idea that the stimulus-response scheme is not sufficient in discussing the development of brain cortex already arises in examining animal behavior. The stimulus-response paradigm may not even be the most appropriate paradigm to understand what is going on. Sure, there are reflex responses; there are, in the brain, connections and circuitries that produce predictable reactions; but input information does not control responses, it coalesces into a multifaceted, ever-changing, simmering representation of reality, a MODEL of how reality is and changes.

This informational turmoil generates its own impulses, that are capable of evoking behaviors that none of the present or past stimuli could justify per se. If one wants to stick to the idea that the nervous system serves to produce adequate responses and behaviors, well, let them stand there. But one cannot deny that in complicating the circuitries ever more, Mother Nature has found itself facing something novel: a neural *inner experience*, built by re-elaborating sensory experiences, that is capable of flanking external stimuli and substituting for them in guiding and determining animal behavior.

* * *

Life is sustained by a cosmic force, the potential energy enclosed in molecules, that urges to get dispersed into the disorder of entropy. Life effectively helps it to overcome barriers and constraints, to escape immutable and ordered ballets: a molecule of glucose will never release the free energy it contains, to turn into dead water and carbon dioxide, if there is not an animal, or at least a bacterium or a yeast, that burns it down to use the energy that such digestion releases.

But life, in helping *the force*, also sustains and reproduces itself. So, why should it not exploit this?

Life can perpetuate and find ever new ways and paths; it is sustained by its own capability of perpetuating and reproducing itself by granting an efficient production of entropy.

Thus, any new idea that strengthens survival capacity, the ability to cope with environments that are difficult, mutable, insidious, will have the tendency to get fixed evolutionarily.

The combination of sophisticated control mechanisms and processes – the *cybernetic* power – of the living organism, and the jump represented by the brain, in terms of complexity and versatility of such control, offer even greater help in releasing *the force*. But through this last jump life overcomes the limits of cybernetics and invades the immaterial territories of information, representation, inner experience of the world; the possibility arises of predictive, and unpredictable, behavior...

Welcome, then, to this runaway from biology toward knowledge, raw and rudimentary as it may be.

The *force* itself gets an advantage from this. So, the same way it sustains life and biology, *the force* will be happy to sustain meta-biology, knowledge and wisdom.

What do we know, then? – Cognitive neurophysiology

Doctor Franz Joseph Gall, at the beginning of the nineteenth century, had already understood it all: here is the area of comparison, there is music, time, color, order, weight, dimension...

Here is calculus, if this area is more developed one will be cleverer in computing and the skull will have a bump here: the *'bump of mathematics'*.

He had already explained everything to us. And please do not say that these are only cognitive capacities, nothing to do with the soul, because there we also have the bumps of seriousness, hope, ideality, spirituality; here we have love, parental love, even conjugal faithfulness (if one does not have the bump...).

Soul, uncertain word. One of those words like life, intelligence, memory (love?), that change their meaning and color depending on the moments and the context, that have a different meaning – a thousand different meanings – for each of us. Difficult to grasp. Looking at the brain, it appears equally rich in processes, modes, representations, approaches and interpretations. It is capable of innumerable multiplicities, simultaneous and contrasting, and a thousand levels of analysis and synthesis, meta-analysis and re-synthesis, and re-discussion.

A science that dares study such a complex, intricate and multifarious system cannot recoil in front of the commotion of complexity and infinity. Brain's mission is precisely this, facing complexity ad infinity: it transforms each information that comes in, and reads it in a thousand different ways, simultaneously. It decomposes and reunifies elements and relationships, thereby building not only representations but criteria and interpretations: a MODEL.

May we define the capacity of transforming sensory data into a representation of elements and relations as a process of 'abstraction'? Immanuel Kant would possibly recognize in it an unexpected materiality of his beloved process of transcendental knowledge: the application of a 'filter' to sensory experience.

But then he would have to admit that at least some of the 'categories', that constituted his transcendental scheme and would mediate between the sensory perception and the intellectual conceptualization of a phenomenon, are interposed well before reaching consciousness: categories (more or less rigorous) such as Unity, Plurality, Negation, Limitation, Cause, Community, Necessity, Analogies, are immanent to the neuronal schemes themselves that pre-elaborate sensory signals.

It might be more precise, then, to talk of *translation.*

If there is an *intellect* that interprets sensory data, these have already been *translated* before they arrive there, according to a series of re-elaboration schemes not at all elementary. These same re-elaboration schemes are real and material (they can be recognized in neuronal circuitries) and as such they are the object of scientific investigation. An investigation that has undergone an impressive acceleration in the last twenty years.

* * *

As we already mentioned, the main difference between humans and the other animals consists of in the extraordinary development of multimodal associative areas, regions in the cerebral cortex that take care of combining readings performed by other areas and 'interpreting' them, by integrating information that comes from distinct sensory modalities and have different relevance: visual, auditory, visceral, motor, emotional information...

The regions where pieces of information of different nature converge extract properties that are not present or detectable in the single sources and modalities of information: it is a novel reinterpretation, multiple and multifaceted; most relevantly, it differs in each of the 'multimodal' regions of the cerebral cortex: the multiple readings thus generated add emphasis, thickness and depth to raw and flat information, as the standpoints and complexity levels multiply.

The fundamental result of this process is that each sensory datum – object, phenomenon, situation – is translated into the activation of a certain number of neurons in the cortex; on the one hand, this scheme of neuron activation constitutes the cerebral equivalent of that sensory datum; on the other hand each neuron – or group or neurons – that participates to such scheme represents a feature of the datum itself, and will also be activated by other sensory data that present that same feature – and will also participate to the activation schemes that correspond to such other data.

In a sense, it is like translating a drawing into its description: there, a rounded pinky shape, with two blotches of shade surmounted by black dashes, a central prominence, an extended horizontal reddish mark that moves, changes its shape and sometimes lets through a number of small whitish blocks or a central darker region, and the whole surrounded by a scrawl of an uncertain dark color, and slightly to the right... Those who play with the computer know that it is possible to draw on the screen by using, in place of a virtual brush, instruments that generate squares, triangles, circles, polygonal or curled shapes, filled or empty, colored as one wishes, possibly with shades. It is a way of drawing that saves room on the computer disk, in comparison to creating a file where an image is represented by a value of red, green and blue intensity for each of its points (pixels). It is a way of drawing ('vectorial') that lets you modify elements and relations with great facility, without erasing and redrawing, simply by changing the geometrical features, the color, the visibility properties of the graphic objects that constitute the drawing.

The most relevant aspect of this translation of each experience into a scheme of neuronal activity possibly lies in the fact that the activity of certain neurons or groups of neurons represents the presence of specific relations in the sensory experience.

An example: all somato-sensory information (tactile and skin sensibility, and 'proprioception' that informs on the position of muscles and joints) arrives to the anterior gyrus of the parietal cortex, topologically ordered, so that a virtual map of the whole body is drawn on this strip of cerebral cortex; visual information arrives posteriorly and is mostly interpreted in terms of spatial relations, as it proceeds forward, moving away from the primary visual area toward the parietal lobe; the central region of the parietal lobe, interposed between these two regions, simultaneously elaborates and compares information about one's own body and about the external space. Several groups of neurons in this region are therefore in charge of detecting relations of proximity, distance, repetitiveness, order: each group will be activated every time one of this kind of relationships is detected in space, and its activation will precisely represent the occurrence of the relationship, the experience of the relationship, the relationship itself (the concept?).

As the complexity of elaboration grows, other specific neurons will elaborate, rather than simple spatial relationships, the reciprocal relations among such relationships, until the objects and events of experience are framed in a complicated network of spatial relationships that essentially constitutes the idea itself of 'space'.

Yes, the consciousness of spatial relationships precisely arises from the activity of these groups of neurons: a subject that suffers a lesion in this area of the cortex, on one side of the brain, loses any conscious interest for spatial relations in the opposite half of the space (information that arrives from the left half of the body are processed by the right half of the brain, and vice versa); if the lesion is on the right the consciousness of the left half of the world is fully lost: they hit obstacles and furniture that are located on the left, and if asked to reproduce the drawing of a flower they will reproduce the right part of the flower only; still they can see, well, because if you ask to draw two flowers they do reproduce both flowers, but only the right part of each one...

* * *

A scheme of neuronal activity for each object, a scheme for each relationship; in a way, a specific scheme – those neurons activated in that way – for each *concept*. Disappointing as it may be, this is precisely the right word. In regions close to the ones that elaborate spatial relationships, groups of neurons recognize spatial sequences, any forms of order and ordered series: one element close to the next, each one greater than the next, or smaller, darker, nearer...

It might astonish, but these neurons and circuitries also elaborate information that comes from other areas of the cortex and has nothing to do with spatial relationships and sensory information: their activity is indispensable to count, enumerate, recognize hierarchies (of position, dimension or luminosity, but also of age, importance, even emotional relevance): every time a mental operation involves some form of counting or ordering, enumeration or sophisticated mathematical computation, the neurons of that region are the ones that show intense activity.

In general, the modalities of information processing are essentially similar, although rougher, in less developed animals: the sophistication, depth, versatility and precision of most processes of feature / relation recognition may be more rudimentary. The crucial difference, however, does not lie in that, but rather in the intensity and richness of multimodal elaborations, in the capacity of relating different kinds of information – visual, auditory, tactile, kinetic, visceral, proprioceptive, emotional – in a thousand ways, to create schemes of neuronal activation that correspond to that specific set of sensory and relational (*cognitive*, in a word) aspects, which synthetically characterizes a *concept*, that abstract entity that lets us classify dogs as different from cats although all have four legs, hair and a tail (and a Chihuahua is more similar to a cat than to a firedog or a Neapolitan Mastiff);

that abstract entity that lets us classify a photograph as different from a painting, or a dream as different from a desire.

The impressive development of associative multimodal regions in human brain cortex creates the possibility of an almost infinite multiplication of concepts, that can be represented in their complexity, in their finest differences and their most subtle, intricate and delicate relationships. This massive expansion is accompanied by another big evolutionary jump, the enormous progress in the capacity of modulating sounds, thanks to a vocal apparatus that is much more sophisticated than in any other animal, and to the huge enlargement of the portions of cortex that process the emission and the perception (and elaboration) of sounds. It is not easy to tell which of these two developments has preceded and possibly favored the other one: presumably, each of the two has made the other one possible, the richness of the sensory and cognitive material to be elaborated and the complexity of circuits and modes of elaboration have grown in parallel, and not suddenly.

But it should be clear that we are talking of *elaboration* of sound perception, because this is what is much more sophisticated in man, not the *possibility* of *perceiving* sounds: a monkey, or even a mouse, hears like we do, it similarly distinguishes two different sounds, but it elaborates such perception in a much less complex and refined way.

The extraordinary capacity of relational and interpreted classification, together with the availability of an infinite repertory of sounds (phonemes) that can be combined into precise sequences, creates the possibility of associating a sequence of phonemes (a word) to each pattern of neuronal activation – to each sensory concept – and to each relationship between such concepts; these combination of phonemes can be reciprocally linked by interactions – phonetic, morphological, grammatical and syntactical bonds between and among words – that can reproduce any possible relationship among objects, events and relations themselves: each possible, observed or merely imagined relations, or even absurd or impossible ones.

The production of such a set of abstract relations among elements, that are arbitrarily associated to objects, relations, acts and events, makes up a *symbolic* system. This is the fundamental feature of neuronal elaboration in humans, that is made possible by the motor and phonetic versatility and by the substantial development of the multimodal cortex: symbolic manipulation of reality becomes possible. And modeling reality (and possible realities) becomes much more sophisticated...

One region plays a fundamental role in the production of the most versatile and powerful symbolic system that is generated by the human brain, *language*. Who diligently studied the 'neurophysiology in pills', above, will have no doubts on where this area must be located: in the lateral portion of the cortex, somehow in between the areas of visual, auditory, somesthetic elaboration, close to the limbic system as well, and possibly sufficiently anterior to be able to consider information about motor schemes as well. This way, it is possible to collect here the information about shape, color, texture, sound, possible practical use, emotional and affective value of an object, and to associate to it a set of sounds – a word – that represents it; a word, both as we hear it with our ear and how we pronounce it by means of a complex modulation of movements of the larynx and tongue, but also how we see it written.

This area is called Wernicke's area, and it is fundamental for language, not so much for phonation (emission of sounds and words), but rather for connecting meanings to words, and therefore for the capacity to correctly choose words and combining them to express a concept. A lesion in this area does not impair the capacity of repeating a sentence but that of forming original sentences without confounding sounds in forming words and making errors in choosing the appropriate words.

Intriguingly, small lesions in the nearby temporal areas (the supero-lateral portion) interfere with the ability of fetching and using specific groups of words, such as those that refer to working instruments, or geographical names or people's names. This is most disheartening for those who refuse a 'neuronal' view of cognitive functions, because it undoubtedly confirms how the organized and classified memory is based on saving learnt responses into precise neuronal schemes, well localized in a certain region of the nervous mass of the brain.

Presumably, phonetic versatility is what makes the symbolic leap possible, because it brings about an extremely efficient – precisely, symbolic – translation. This conquest in turn pushes and sustains the further development of cortical areas that are capable of symbolic elaboration, from the first prototypes of *Homo* to *Homo sapiens sapiens* (who knows, might the next be, perhaps, *Homo modestus*...?).
Still, without speech it is perfectly possible to develop symbolic capacity: the human brain is so rich in such possibilities that it can use any modality of symbolic coding – from mimic and skeletal-motor gestures to drawing and writing – to that aim. However, without verbal coding, and this mutual enhancement between symbolic capability and speech-related motor-sensory proficiency, the development of human cortex would not have been so impressive and revolutionary.

* * *

The generation of the capability of symbolic representation through the precise working modalities of specific neuronal systems is not only fascinating – at least for those who suffer from that deformation of intellectual curiosity that makes them sensitive to the appeal of *understanding* how and why; it also evokes a subtle form of wonder, and the clear feeling that something big is going on here. Something that asks us to stop reasoning in terms of connections, functional relations, neuronal networks and strictly mechanistic processes.

When a system like the brain learns to manipulate symbols and not only information, the possibility arises of interpreting reality rather than merely representing it, of imagining it different, of finding answers to questions such as 'and what if now...?', of inventing, this way, the instruments and the strategies to change it.

A new dimension is born this way, in human brain; the world of ideas, that Plato imagined as the site of true reality, invisible to man – prisoner in a cavern – but through the shadows of the perceptible appearances of the material world. An intriguing overturning, this one. Reality out there and the world of ideas hidden in the brain... Or possibly nothing new: the noumenon, from Plato to Kant...

Between our senses and the world of ideas there are indeed complex and relevant mediations, but such mediations appear to be in our own brain: they have biological and physiological bases and explanations and can be studied and clarified in ever greater detail. True, we cannot reach any certainty about reality out there, our senses may deceive us. The world of ideas, in which our intellect rambles, would then be a construction of our own brain that does not reflect at all the deepest and most precise essence of external reality, as Plato used to like believing. Sure, it is possible. A margin is there of unknowable, nobody could deny this, a philosophical domain, or better a mystical domain, where the flight can only be blind, and perhaps because of this even more exciting: the world and life can be imagined, different from how we see and live them. If one wants, one has the full right to play this way. One has the right to fly away, let's hope they find their window open when they decide to fly back, and will not end up commuting forever, like Peter Pan, to and from Neverland...

* * *

In the complex schemes of neuronal activity that represent aspects of the external reality (objects and relationships) various types of sub-schemes can be identified.

A specific pattern of activation of certain neurons will represent persistent aspects of the object (or relationship), *essential* aspects: similar objects (relationships) will also display such aspects, which can be generalized and permit to classify and recognize as 'similar' any objects (relationships) that also display such traits, even though they have never been encountered before, just because they are capable of producing these same patterns of neuronal activation. It is like saying they are the *same thing* (please, pick a *name* to indicate them all). On the other hand, there will be sub-schemes that represent features of the objects (relationships) that may or may not be present, *qualifying* sub-schemes; these aspects may also be shared by other objects or relationships, though they are not *essentially* similar. They are accidental features (*attributes*) that may or may not be there and apply to the object. A further kind of sub-schemes, finally, will represent *relations* with the context or with other objects/relations: spatial or temporal relations, similitude/difference, analog behavior, association, sequence in past experience, and therefore possible causality...

This semantic classification of neuronal sub-schemes that constitute our experience may remain implicit, unnoticed, unreported. It may not be verbalized. It still works perfectly as a tool for an implicit reading and interpretation of reality, through a rapid adaptation to new experiences, by recognizing previously acquired scheme, and manipulating them to adapt them to the new situation, and through anticipatory behavior based on the predictions offered by the application of known schemes to the new situation. An implicit intelligence arises from this, a non-verbal intelligence, that permits solving operational problems, even complex ones. It is a capability of modeling, and thus understanding, though not necessarily explicitly, and therefore not necessarily being able to explain.

The animal halts here. Conversely, if symbolic manipulation flanks associative mechanisms, comparison and generalization, then the situation drastically changes. The coordinated, systematic association of a sign to each scheme or sub-scheme of neuronal activity implies the automatic generation of an intricate and sophisticated system of *relations among the signs themselves*, of a structure that reproduces the formal features of the system of relations that exists among neuronal activation schemes. A true symbolic system, in which each sign becomes a symbol, i.e. is given *not only a meaning but also a reticule of precise and inevitable relations* with the other symbols.

Two general consequences derive from this, on the symbolic system as a whole: a morphological one and a structural one.

The morphological consequence: inevitably, entire families of symbols will be generated by variations on the theme, by applying standard transformation rules to each symbol. In language this translates into the possibility of adding prefixes and endings, repetitions and accents to indicate variations in number (singular/plural), gender (masculine/feminine, in many languages), temporal location or modes of an event or action (mode and tense of a verb).

A simple principle of economy will inevitably lead to this kind of evolution of the symbolic system, since each datum of experience can present itself with variable characteristics and will therefore generate a scheme of neuronal activation that can exhibit multiple alternative sub-schemes: these variable characteristics are easily translated into morphological modifications of one and the same symbol; the same variable characteristic, recognized in other data of experience, is easily translated by applying to the corresponding symbols the same (or similar) morphological modifications...

Full families of new symbols can be generated this way by analogy.

The structural aspect is perhaps even more inevitable and substantial. In the structure of the symbolic system, the symbols that have a distinct semantic value – and represent *essences*, or *characteristics*, or *modalities*, or *relations* – cannot be interchangeable: their relations can only follow a certain number of schemes.

Symbolic representation of any aspect of reality requires that there be:
- at least one symbol that represents the *essence* of an object or relationship (a symbol with the function of a *noun*);
- *qualifying* symbols may only be associated to other symbols, which may also have a qualifying function but in the end must more or less directly refer to a *noun*;
- symbols that represent *relations* (verbal forms) constitute the most relevant semantic aspect of symbolic representation: since most relations are asymmetric they must be located with respect to other symbols (or modified in their form, conjugation and suffixes) according to precise rules that let you identify in an unambiguous way the direction of the relationship (who is the subject and who the object of an action, for example);
- symbols that represent modalities (like the adverbial forms in any language) are typically dispensable – they only *add* information – but specific rules will determine which other symbols they have to be put in relation to.

All this brings us to an observation that is initially intriguing: given that the symbol system is generated by a neuron network with the properties of the human brain, whatever symbolic instrument will be employed to represent and interpret reality – and possibly to analyze it abstractly or reproduce it, or to communicate one's own reading – will necessarily share some features of the morphological variation and the syntactical-grammatical structure with any other symbolic system that has been generated by a similar neuronal network. In other words, all human natural languages must share some structural features and traits of morphological variability.

This must be true because of how incoming information is decomposed and analyzed, translated into neuronal activation schemes that reproduce the specific and general aspects detected in the sensory experience: elements, characteristics, relations, and modalities.

As usual, though intriguing, this observation is hardly original. Nothing new here. The analysis of human natural languages, rigorously undertaken by Noam Chomsky, has already given us this reading frame, extraordinarily powerful, capable of unifying traditionally scientific themes with fundamental philosophical questions.

Apart from the critiques that any new idea is exposed to – and the more revolutionary the idea is the more numerous will the objections be, and less relevant to the substance of the argument – nobody can deny that Chomsky's discoveries have framed with extreme clarity and on new bases any modern attempt at facing the topic of natural languages. His fundamental intuition, solidly supported by evidence, is that natural languages, although they show spectacular phonetic and terminological differences, are linked by strong analogies in terms of structure and by common fundamental grammatical characteristics, that indicate that a major fraction of the structure of any natural language must be based on biological, genetic, neurological properties of the human being.

* * *

So, information enters the brain, branches, disintegrates into myriads of readings and this way triggers an abstract ballet that justifies abstract logic and even language. But we must come back to ground, sooner or later, if we want to discuss what rules our behavioral response.

However, it is still too soon. We have not talked about emotions yet. We have not even named consciousness.

Later! We shall discuss the way one acts. But let's think, before acting!

VI
WHO ARE WE, THEN ? – Memory

Memory can be defined in various ways, or better many kinds of memory can be defined. It can be decomposed into many simple or complex functions, some of them already present in worms, others only in humans, and each one can be considered as one aspect of memory.

The response to a stimulus that is applied repetitively decreases: if you wish, this already is some kind of memory, isn't it? But the response can be restored by associating other stimuli; this happens even in very dull marine mollusks, which this way seem to 'remember' what has happened. And who is unaware of Pavlov's experiments, who made his dog's mouth water by ringing a bell? Riding a bike (a bear can do it) or playing the saxophone (a brighter subject appears to be needed here) also require that memories (motor schemes) be 'fixed' somewhere in the brain and that it be possible to recall them. And one could go on with much more complex examples...

Usually, we think of memory as a more specific function: the capacity of fixing memory traces that persist for a long time, rather than their momentary registration. Our interest therefore focuses on the process of memory consolidation: a term that suggests that the question is, after having carved a trace in the clay, to let it dry and cook it so that it does not get spoiled.

This is precisely the way one generally thinks about memory traces: sensations, sounds, images, captured and etched in some hidden spot in the brain – in some protein? in DNA? – and preserved for the moment one will want to fetch them back. Computer culture reinforces this vision of memory as an 'archive'.

But memory – as it takes place in our brain – is instead an active process that does not even come close to the ideal of accurate and reliable preservation of documents: it is a mutable game of notes and drafts and sketches, that tells a lot about the owner, maybe even more on the owner than on the matter that was supposed to be archived there.

Along this line of thought, one may end up supposing that the owner is precisely what is archived there, in the end... Memory as personality and identity, *my* story as *I* have lived it. This is not so extravagant, because each activity of the nervous system leaves a mark, be it labile or permanent, that is not only a trace of what has happened: in the meanwhile, it constitutes a modification, slight and imperceptible as it may be, of the way the system will react to other signals in the future.

* * *

Memory is not a repository, no.
Memory IS YOU.
Memory is not even what you are made of, that is not enough, it IS YOU.

Memory grows and changes, memories are not closed boxes, they change with you. Reality, sensations, emotions create reticules of activity and relationships among the hundreds of billions of neurons you are made of.

Yes, you are made of neurons, of neurons your mind is made.

Sure, you are not your neurons. But each unimaginably complex net of activities and relationships, each moment of the activity of your brain, that changes at every moment, is an instant of your life, of you: and this IS YOU.

It is like music: it is not the piano, it is not the strings that vibrate, strictly speaking it is a vibration of air. It talks to us, it moves us, it appears as an energy and an incorporeal magic, but its essence is nothing but air and its capacity to vibrate.

* * *

But what do we remember? Memory does not tell our past; it tells the signs the past has left in our soul...

'Anyway, when we recount our past each of our breaths is a lie'. Why? What emotional, metaphysical, supernatural force makes us do this?

Oh, we do not necessarily 'do it'. If a car appears to proceed in a strange way, this does not necessarily imply the driver is drunk; sometimes it is the car itself – sometimes a fault or a defect – or it may even be precisely built to work like this. Many people are surprised by the imprecision of memory and the re-elaboration of reminiscences, as if they mourned the precision of a computer in recording data.

There are regions, in the brain, dedicated to fixing information, in an associative way: an object as an association of sensory features, names for objects, people and relationships, a word as a sequence of characters, a limerick as a sequence of words, or even better as a sequence of movements implied in repeating it. They are specific regions in the brain and cerebellum. And they do work well.

But a great part of memory has nothing to do with this secretarial work, a job for meticulous archivists. It is something much more complex, evanescent in many respects, but also much more fascinating.

Those who complain about malfunctioning and defects in how memory works – as if they envied the inflexible and inarguable precision of electronic memories – seem to forget that they would deny the slightest possibility of a hint of soul to the computer; and not so much because the Council of Trento only conceded it to women, but simply because the computer cannot invent its own reality, or live it: it just records it.

What makes the difference is the path that memory follows, between the one who records it and the one who reads it.

We do not recall with our eyes, our hands, our heart. Before anything arrives where something can be recorded, in the brain, a long way must be travelled, a lot of elaboration, interpretation.

We remember interpretations, and we reinterpret them by recalling them.

Is this a defect?

I do not think so, because there is where the soul is born.

* * *

The sensory data (a sound, an image, a perfume...) reaches the cerebral cortex and is re-elaborated at every passage, dematerializing into a collection of relationships and schemes. The raw data are digested and decomposed in a thousand different ways by many different cerebral structures (no longer images but lines, colors, masses, volumes, contrasts of lights and tones, geometrical shapes and faces, unknown or possibly well known...), and what is recorded is many activity schemes of specific groups of neurons. Each activity scheme represents a trait, a characteristic, a way of looking at the sensory data.

Each coherent activity pattern of neuronal cells tends to be fixed if it repeats (or if it occurs in a moment of intense attention or emotion): if a network of neurons is activated in a synchronous way several times, the connections among these neurons are strengthened. The pattern of neuronal activity that corresponds to an element of experience becomes fixed: our experience is thus recorded within us. Actually, not so much *within*. It becomes *part of* ourselves. In the end, this is what we (our identities) are made of. This is the way we grow, the way we change...

We can go back to these past moments: the brain 'recalls to memory' ...

The networks of neuronal activity evoked by reality, by sensations, by emotions, which are fixed when there is emotion or repetition, tend to come back and reactivate when the involved network of neurons is activated, even only in part; this occurs whenever we live a sensory, cognitive or emotional experience that is at least partially coincident.

Thus, the brain easily recognizes the features from schemes that have been already acquired, and the new memory is built employing such schemes, already present, and completes and enriches them.

In the last fifty years we have made great progress in understanding memory processes; but if you do not look at it the right way it is easy to overlook the relevance of what we have understood. We now know the cellular mechanisms by which the efficiency of a synapse (contact between neurons) changes as a function of previous activity: it can be strengthened or weakened, and the effect persists for minutes, or days; it may even trigger permanent modifications of the neuronal 'network'.

Changing synapse efficacy may not seem a great deal: memories, language, thought, are something else! But these processes of synaptic plasticity are progressive and associative: synapses that are activated together are stabilized and strengthened (in some cases weakened). Schemes of coordinated activity of neurons, even very complex ones, are thus consolidated, thereby 'fixing' sensations, mental states, memories.

This is what continually happens in 'working' or 'momentary parking' memory regions, where modifications only persist for a short time: this lets us repeat a telephone number or recall a name for a few minutes. This is a limited room, that must be continually reused: if a trace is not refreshed it fades and gets lost. But if a scheme is repeated again and again it will be reproduced and 'fixed' in less dynamic cerebral regions, where plastic alterations are more persistent, and will constitute a permanent memory item. Students know well that if we re-read what we have studied today, tomorrow and again in a few days or weeks, we shall not forget it (it has gone to the cortex!), while in a month we won't remember anything that we studied in a hurry just before the exam.

The repeated schemes of coherent activity by neuronal cells tend to be fixed. The connections among the involved neurons are strengthened, and the activity scheme tends to reappear every time at least part of this reticule of neurons is activated by a similar sensory, cognitive or emotional experience. Thus, what reappears, or persists, or comes back in your sensations, in your thoughts, in your emotions, is fixed and will be recalled every time a somewhat similar experience occurs, i.e. when 'something reminds you' of it: you will recognize it as part of a personal patrimony, as yourself; and when you meet it again you will recognize both the experience and your own reaction as parts of yourself.

Also, what is not recognized, what is new, becomes fixed, provided you are attentive. It also becomes integrated with what you are, it also becomes yourself, *the changing you.*

Just observe postures and expressions: each expression and gesture of ours reproduces a scheme of activity of neurons, from various parts of the brain, that predispose and perform movements. There are few things that you feel as your own more than your expressions, your typical gestures; you continually reproduce them. But if you reproduce several times new ones, in order to study them, or by unconscious imitation – this happens a lot to children, but also to us, with the people we love – then those become yours as well...

What is new gets fixed if you are attentive, and you are so if you are alert, tense. It gets even more fixed if you are upset, or troubled by emotion. We shall discuss this later, but emotion, and particularly fear, arises from the unconscious recognition of situations of great relevance for the survival or the well-being of the organism: deep regions of the nervous system are activated, they alert the whole brain but also fix all present perceptions and record them as possible hints of an emotionally relevant situation, important details that might in the future warn in time about a danger, or a possible emotional gratification.

What is new gets fixed. Or better, the schemes that represent new experiences get fixed. Because each scheme that is generated, that gets fixed, is indeed a response to reality. It is not *reality* in itself: it is *your way* of receiving it, *your* response, a complex framework, rich in cognitive aspects, but also emotional, and affective, esthetic, volitional, visceral ones. And they are *yours*.

It is *your* response; it is *you* in front of reality. It is you, but in the meanwhile you change. You change because now that instant of your life has also become part of *you*. From now on, the coordinated neuronal activity scheme that represents it will tend to turn on every time you activate a part of it and will recall this same instant; the more intensely you have lived it, the more inexorably the neuronal scheme will reappear. Each *similar* experience will propose this moment again to you. If you pay attention, you will realize that you are not living that same moment, you will notice the differences. This may be crucial to react properly. But noticing a difference in the scheme makes you fix a new scheme, similar to the old one, that will confound the memory, enriching it with new shades that were not there before. If you do not pay attention, you will feel as if you simply relived something you already knew, you simply WERE something you had already been. But in the meantime, the subtle game of neurons – strengthening interactions with whomever is in tune – can gradually erode the etching of your memory trace and make it more and more similar to what you are living now, to *how* you are living it now.

Each new frame of activity that is generated in the brain is a way of assimilating the world and the experience (making it as similar as possible to what we already possess, and to what we already are). But as we assimilate, we also change. And the more we care, we are affected, hit, troubled, upset, emotional and passionate, the more we change.

Try and say the most original and sharp and extravagant thing that you can think of: there will always be somebody who honestly and sincerely reacts as if you told him something they already knew, already saw, already thought of. Sure, already seen everything: it is sufficient not to pay attention, not to care, not to detect differences, what is new, not to get involved... Still, etchings get eroded (less so, perhaps, if one sticks to the idea that nothing is there to be learnt, if they can only see what they already know), and everybody changes, at least a little. In every moment you are no longer the same; even those who *already saw*, those who knew everything, are no longer the same. You are no longer the same, materially: if you love yourself exactly the way you are, you may not like it, but new connections are established, strengthened or weakened among your innumerable neurons, and you will no longer even be able to precisely reproduce (recall) how you used to be.

In every moment you try to assimilate but meanwhile you do change – another metaphor of the general rule of life, changing in trying to persist – you change because in every instant each reticule, each scheme of activity that you would recognize as yours, as *yourself* who already lived it, has actually become richer, and different.

New and different like a word, used many times: one day you find it in a poem, charged with a color, an emotion, an atmosphere that it had never possessed before. That word will never be the same in your vocabulary, and all your language will not be the same, because now it has a new instrument, renewed and refined, capable of rendering novel shades and perspectives.

Yes, memories like words; our memory – each of us, after all – is like a language, like the language of a child, who may one day become a poet.

Each word enters our language having a meaning, a semantic value, an esthetic value, an emotional value, an affective value, a color and a rhythm. Each time its sound occurs, its sequence of written letters, the concepts and emotions linked to it will appear. But they may reappear associated to different, possibly unexpected and surprising, objects, concepts, emotions, tones, colors, rhythms. So, the word itself changes, gets enriched, its light and color change, its tonality, its agreeability, its evocative power, its music, its commitment.

The language changes, and the child does become a poet, or maybe a lawyer. Or an engineer, or a stylist... But language, this way, is personal, individual. To each of us, each word has a different sound, emotion and color. Is it surprising that we often don't understand each other?

* * *

Sometimes it is easier to remember stupid things, the text of baby songs, the names of the characters of TV serials, or even the absurd ones of videogames, and people may experience great difficulty to learn by heart things they consider important, while unwanted, irrelevant rigmaroles keep rolling in their mind. Maybe this is a way of sitting back, under the pressure of changes and novelty, turning to familiar sounds and words, perhaps unimportant, but reassuring. Because memory is also this, feeling home with what one is acquainted with. Like life in general, memory is thorn by the eternal conflict between avoiding novelty and change, to affirm and recognize oneself, and curiosity, the need to interact, to change and be changed, to live.

The brain preserves a multifaceted representation of each experience of ours, based on numerous schemes of coordinated activity of nervous cells. It will easily detect, for each new sensory data, features that correspond to already acquired schemes. The new memory trace can thus be built using the schemes already present, and in turn it completes and enriches them. Memory is not a photographic film, that captures the image projected on it; it is an active process of assimilation of incoming data with the ensemble of information previously acquired: thus, it faithfully reproduces not reality, but subjective perception, mostly determined by previously recorded information. In these terms – a dynamic process in building as well as in saving, updating and recalling remembrances – memory is not at all reminiscent of a dusty archive, but it rather reminds of language, language that evolves and grows: a set of objects-words that live in the relationships that link them reciprocally, and in generating and sketching new objects and relationships, in attaining new meanings and richness.

The same way as words sometimes seem to detach from the objects they represent, and assume new meanings and colors, as if they were animated and alive, thus our memories, conceived and kept alive, grow and transform with us, like words employed each time in a different context; when we recall an old memory we rebuild the scheme of neuronal activity that corresponded to it at that time, but we do that in a brain that has changed in the meanwhile, in which new meanings may have been associated to the activity of each group of neurons.

The memory turns up different, it is an experience that the momentary ego rebuilds, not the experience that was 'fixed' long ago by a long-gone ego. Though some aspects of the memory, especially emotional ones, may be perceived as, and may actually be, genuinely identical.

Memory is then an imprecise recording device, flawed by prejudice and remodeled. An imperfect machine? Well, it may be so, if you wish to say so; but were it not so, how could it enable us to give a 'meaning' to an image, to a sound, to life itself? It is an instrument that interprets while it records. Imprecise, distorted? So, what? This is only a further reason to exchange impressions and opinions with other similarly imprecise observers of reality!

* * *

As one learns to speak, the same way one learns to remember.

For one who possesses few words it is hard work to acquire a new word, to perceive its richness and complexity, to learn to use it in all its expressive power. It is not strange that it is harder to fix and retain complex memories for the very young child, although they have great potentiality of synaptic plasticity, few fixed memories and 'lots of room' to accumulate new ones; their memories may even be more intense but are less precise, detailed, rich. That is because there are not myriads of other memory traces with which to build the new one in all its facets and relationships, in all its complexity.

The poet, who deeply knows the word and its origin, who can eviscerate its semantic implications and metric, musical, evocative properties, who knows many ways to tell the same thought, will not be put to silence by simply stealing some words from their vocabulary.

Similarly, an active memory, oriented to capturing relations in reality, rather that fixing static images, a memory based on a continuous re-elaboration of one's own knowledge, by putting it in relation with ever new data and information, will display a much greater resistance to deterioration by time and age: notions are forgotten and lost, but the mesh of conceptual references that entraps them – one's *culture* – remains.

We have learnt to take care of our body: hygiene, attention to what and how much we eat.

Even greater attention we should dedicate to our mind. Emigrants, who come back after many years during which they have not spoken their mother tongue, seem to have not only forgotten many words, but also lost their proficiency in using the native language to express themselves.

Language is enriched by speaking, it parches in not using it.

So does memory, the crucial instrument for any higher cerebral function: it rusts with age if no stimuli keep it exercised.

The deterioration of mental abilities in many elderly people is caused not only by disease, but also by dereliction, social neglect, loss of affective relations, lack of physical and especially mental exercise.

* * *

The concept of memory that emerges from this varied picture is multifaceted, in certain respects contradictory and elusive: one thing and a thousand different other things. Seeing memory as a process of fixation and reproduction of schemes of neuronal activity, in fact, leads us to extend the concept of memory and perceive its multiplicity.

Neuronal plasticity is present and active – though to a variable extent – in most structures of the nervous system, especially in cortical areas. Each region, with its own way of elaborating and 'interpreting' specific information, will exhibit its own form of memory: in the field of cognitive sciences the term 'memory' is almost never used alone, as a vague category of cognitive activity. Today the study of memory is based on precise classifications.

Memory, divided in short-term and long-term, is classified as *declarative* (explicit, reportable in words and conscious) on the one hand, and *non-declarative* (implicit, nonverbal, unconscious) on the other hand: procedural memory (skills, ability, habits, motor schemes), priming and basic non-associative learning (habituation and sensitization), associative learning (conditioning). Memory subsystems are considered and described: episodic memory (remember that), semantic memory (know that) and procedural memory (know how).

* * *

The processes involved in various aspects of memory:

<u>Priming</u>
Sensory areas can fix schemes that correspond to sensory experiences, ready to be activated to *recognize* aspects of experience previously encountered.

Is it memory if we recognize something seen before? This is exactly the technical meaning of *priming*, as opposed to naiveté, something in between preparation, predisposition and loss of virginity. It is not a sensation of familiarity, clear or elusive but anyway conscious, something like the so-called *déjà-vu*.

It is something more elementary, an accelerated (or attenuated) response to a stimulus that has been presented before as compared to a novel stimulus;

it is a rearrangement of neuronal circuitry, that generates the perception that something has been recognized, but such perception will be elaborated by other areas of the brain, areas that are in charge of meta-analysis, semantic evaluation, interpretation, alerting and focusing attention.

Here are the cellular bases of something we already mentioned: in experience, responses of the brain to what is known and what is new are different. Priming is a fundamental process in memory, and relevant at least as much as surprise: both call for attention, one because it suggests familiarity, responses already tested and customary, support and safety; the other because it demands hesitation, doubts and change, and the slight vertigo of curiosity and discovery. But these latter aspects do not concern *memory*, this is reading and meta-reading of what happens in regions of sensory elaboration, following changes that are linked to memory, by systems of 'higher' elaboration and interpretation.

If this process of recognition is strictly related to sensory activities, a very similar process also occurs in areas of complex elaboration and correlation among sensory modalities: in those areas, where various sensory modalities converge, compound schemes are fixed and enable to recognize objects, relationships, features, to learn conceptual readings and interpretations.

Priming phenomena may also be present in circuits involved in even more complex elaborations, to help handling more and more abstract logical aspects, and elaborations of symbolic systems, which can be detected and fixed to sustain learning and rational elaboration.

<u>Classical conditioning</u>
The place in the central nervous system where associative mechanisms dominate is the cerebellum, which contains more than a half of the total number of neurons in the human brain. It coordinates entire groups of muscles, operating with perfect timing and control of intensity in coordinating the distinct muscles that cooperate to produce complex movements; it compares the motor orders output by the brain and brainstem with their results, and it intervenes to correct and modulate when needed. It similarly participates to the activities in various regions of the encephalon and cortex, behaving as an extremely powerful and rapid servocontrol, that permits attaining maximal accuracy of motor and behavioral responses and their rapid and dynamic tuning.

Lesions to the cerebellum impair rapidity, calibration, accuracy, fluidity and automatism of movements: if the cerebellum is injured, an aimed movement (for example bringing a finger to one's nose) becomes uncertain and oscillating, it departs from the optimal pathway, is overcorrected, goes beyond the target and must regress.

The cerebellum is an enormously powerful system, organized in a repetitive, modular and systematic way. It receives two kinds of inputs: one carries information from specific senses, vestibule, muscles and joints and descending pathways that control movements; it is directed to the deep cerebellar nuclei, which may intervene to refine movements based on the complex sensory-motor picture; the second input comes from the inferior olivary nucleus, which compares descending commands with the actual situation and sends error signals to the cerebellum, if something does not fit, to correct the output from the deep nuclei. Both kinds of input also reach the cortex of the cerebellum, a structure comprised of more than half of the neurons of the whole nervous system. Here, the main neurons – Purkinje cells – send an inhibitory signal down to the deep nuclei, so that every activation is rapidly switched off and remains strictly confined in time; also, the response of the deep nuclei is corrected, if needed. The synapses in the cortex are modified every time an error signal is received from the inferior olive, so that next time the movement will be corrected with no need for the intervention of the olivary nucleus.

This great plasticity of the cerebellum, guided by the comparison of input signals, makes it so that if a particular stimulus or situation comes about in the moment in which a certain response is being performed, the cerebellum 'associates' the stimulus to the response, i.e., it learns to generate this same response each time that same stimulus or situation (which would have nothing to do with the reaction, in principle) occur again.

This is the basic mechanism of classical conditioning: a puff on the eye each time a bell rings, and I shall blink every time it rings in the future. An interesting consequence comes from this capability: since a lot of information reaches the brain, concerning the position and the movement of muscles and joints, performing a specific movement generates a sensory picture, a 'situation', and if this movement is accompanied or directly followed by another movement, twice, three, fifty times, the sequence will become automatic. Then, it will be finely and rapidly controlled by the cerebellum, with no need for attention and consciousness, and will be performed more rapidly and precisely, automatically, indeed. After a sequence of three keys pressed on the piano, the fourth one will come by itself: better not to think about that, or you will make mistakes, or anyhow interfere with the fluidity of the sequence of movements. Yes, it comes by itself, like 'Klaus' after 'Santa'. This servo-control circuitry for reproducing sequences is too useful and efficient, as concerns any automatic aspect of elaboration, for it not to be used by cognitive elaboration areas as well: it is not necessary to compute how much is three times four, because you studied this in primary school and your cerebellum automatically suggests the answer 'twelve' much more rapidly than you can compute it.

The cerebellum helps to repeat poetries and prayers learnt by heart, without interfering with our thinking of something else; it even appears there are at least three levels: automatic repetition in the background, a me who thinks of something else, and another me who clearly realizes – observes from *above*, proud – those other two thinking machines in my own head. By the same token, the cerebellum controls word morphology, grammatical and syntactical concordances, *consecutio temporum*, and the order of the words in the sentence, leaving the brain available to us to think of WHAT we want to say and HOW we want to say it.

Pretty useful, this little machine that works there behind the curtain, in the back of our head, to simplify our lives. At least in those situations where it is good to simplify, in the name of efficiency, as in TV quizzes, where you must have the answer, possibly the right one, but above all rapid, because stopping to think about it is like getting it wrong... (not so useful, alas!, when we face a novel situation or a hard question that calls for reasoning).

Many sub-cortical circuits operate to react to dangerous situations; many signals (odors, images, events) that are indifferent to one animal species are danger indicators for another and can determine instinctive reaction of 'fight or flight'. In addition to instinctive reactions, animals (and humans) need to learn to recognize and fear what constitutes a danger, even where instinct does not help. This is an important aspect of memory; possibly not as exciting as other aspects, from the philosophical point of view, but certainly it is not less relevant for survival. The learning capacity of the *amygdala* (a deep nucleus in the temporal region) sustains these processes: simple associative mechanisms account for how the *amygdala* can fix relations between elements – simple or complex – of experience and danger situations, thereby learning to generate alarm, avoidance and defense reactions when a stimulus is associated several times to an unpleasant, dangerous or painful signal or stimulus (this is called *aversive conditioning*). Learning by the amygdala may in volve plastic changes occurring also in structures external to it, such as the cerebellum.

Similar neuronal mechanisms may sustain other forms of learning, such as *operating conditioning:* the repeated association between a behavior (e.g. pressing a knob) and a reward (e.g. receiving food) can guide the acquisition of a new behavior.

<u>Implicit and explicit memory</u>
The most thoroughly studied structure in the nervous system, to understand learning and memory, is the *hippocampus*. It is an important structure, buried deep in the temporal lobe, with some regions of the temporal cortex specifically associated with it. In lower animals it constitutes a major fraction of the brain.

Many circuits in the brain are extremely plastic during development, and this accounts both for the maturation of sensory and cognitive capacities in the embryo and in the infant, and for the impressive learning capacity of the child. Once adulthood has been reached, plasticity phenomena become more limited in many areas, but they remain very active in the hippocampus and some other specific structures (such as *amygdala*, cerebellum and many cortical regions). Its extraordinary plasticity allows the hippocampus to continuously remodel its connections and circuits, to fix associations and sequences; to fix them the deeper and longer, the more frequently these relations re-appear.

Hippocampal plasticity is associative: inputs that reach the same neuron together, or arrive on it in rapid and reproducible sequence, are reinforced, for minutes, hours, days; this writes and consolidates networks of relations, into the circuitry of the hippocampus, that can assemble a *context* for any sensory or cognitive information.

It is important to realize **what** the hippocampus memorizes: information about recognized objects is relayed to the perirhinal cortex and their localization, and general information on space, reach the para-hippocampal cortex. Both streams of data converge on the entorhinal cortex, which also receives information about the emotional state and relays all this to the hippocampus.

The hippocampus operates a contextualization of this information, in space, in time, and in the emotional domain; this way the stream of raw data is transformed into a multifaceted, consistent, emotionally colored experience. No sensory data, but such experience is bounced back to the cortex to generate the conscious perception of the moment, the situation, the event. And this – not any raw sensory data – is memorized: not the reality or the event, but the way it has been experienced.

In lower animals all this contextualization mainly reduces to sustaining *spatial* memory (for example learning the way out of mazes); in humans it helps contextualizing new pieces of information into the complex network of experimental and symbolic relations that constitutes our knowledge.

The memory trace is complex, in the hippocampus, intricate and rich of relationships; it is an 'explicit' description of experience, easily mapped on a symbolic and linguistic system: it can be verbalized, at least in the human brain, precisely capable of symbolic elaboration and language. This is opposed to the other associative memory aspects discussed hereto, that were mostly aimed at creating connections between stimuli and responses, or within logical or behavioral sequences, that are fixed and operate with no need – often with no possibility – of explicit reading and verbalization.

* * *

The modalities and the systems of memory

As mentioned, several subsystems can be recognized: episodic memory (*remember that*), semantic memory (*know facts*) and procedural memory (*know how*).

Episodic memory is declarative and refers to subjective experiences. Recalling the memory trace does not *reproduce* the episode, but *revives* it based on how the subject has lived it; the remembrance is manipulated with time, as the reference context of the subject evolves. This is an important aspect in attributing truth value to a memory: it has been clearly shown that the subjective remembrance of an episode one has assisted to can be substantially modified by simply talking about it repetitively and 'convincing' the subject that the episode was different from what he recalled. This is nicely argued and played with in the book 'Testimone inconsapevole' (Unaware witness) by Gianrico Carofiglio.

One portion of the temporal lobe is particularly involved in this kind of memory: actually, electrical stimulation in that region induces the sensation of déjà-vu, that elusive but strong impression of having already seen and lived this moment, so exactly and precisely...

Semantic memory (memory of facts) is also declarative and refers to meaning; it is intrinsically linked to association and generalization, to language, in general to 'interpretation' of experience.

It is a complex function that involves several distinct areas of the brain: hippocampus in memorization, and especially in contextualization; structures in the prefrontal cortex (those regions that we shall see implied in focusing attention) to search for and recall a memory.

Large areas of the cortex are involved in memory consolidation, depending on the kind of knowledge: principally the parietal lobe for spatial relationships, hierarchies, order, mathematical relations; mainly the temporal lobe for classification of objects, instruments, faces and names, and the associated lexicon; principally the frontal lobe for strategies, propositions and projects.

Procedural memory, finally, is for a large part implicit, mostly depending on basal nuclei and cerebellum, but it also involves the frontal lobe, and pre-motor areas in particular, for its explicit and 'reportable' aspects.

Two further systems implied in memory and learning have been clearly described.

The first one is a perceptual representation system, semi-automatic, principally linked to recognition/interpretation, mainly comprised of

- a visual subsystem for word/form recognition (visual cortex), that identifies with a great efficiency, for example, the word, and extracts it from the written context, rapidly proposing *plossibe redanigs, bsaed on the egeds, and mtosly on the frsit and lsat ltteer, mcuh bferoe an atnettive and dtaelied eaxm is prefrmoed*. Or not?
- an auditory subsystem for word/form recognition (auditory cortex), that continuously proposes, while you hear, hypotheses of subdivision of the flow of sounds into phonemes and words, and makes it possible to choose the most meaningful sequence to rebuild a sentence even from interrupted fragments; this way sometimes you think you heard wha... smb ..els h'nt sed: you really seem to have heard it, to the point of ending up discussing even heartedly, 'you said that!', 'no, maybe you interpreted that', 'no, I heard perfectly well that you did say that'...
- a structural subsystem for pre-semantic recognition of the structure of words, objects or anything else that can be characterized by a structure (here the temporal-occipital junction is important); this subsystem obviously has a central role in both recognition processes cited above.

The second important system is the 'working memory', that is a set of cerebral structures that retain for a few seconds sensory or cognitive information to perform cognitive elaboration on it.

The working memory system is operated by a "central executive" (a function played by the prefrontal cortex) that manipulates information, that may come from the sensory systems or be retrieved from long-term memory.

The central executive uses a limited number of (short time) memory banks to handle the retrieved information and two servo-systems: a phonological loop for testing and recycling small amounts of verbal information not to be saved in long term memory (it makes it possible to retain the phonemes recognized in the speech heard up to now, until interpretation of the word or sentence is completed, to rehearse it and to repeat meaningless sequences, such as a telephone number, without remembering them after a few seconds); and a visual-spatial sketchpad for the short term retention and logical, geometrical and mathematical manipulation of visual and spatial information. The working memory system involves several cortical areas and helps in detecting and analyzing relations, changes, movements and processes, also by means of a continuous comparison of current and recent past information.

* * *

In summary, memory with all its sophisticated complexity turns out to be a set of refined functions, partly connected, partly independent, and partly subordinate to other neuronal systems of elaboration. A set of functions, each of which has a specific, individual neuronal base and displays operative modalities that can be studied experimentally in detail and are today reasonably clear in their fundamental features.

However, those who are beginning to be bored now are right.

Up to here, we have discussed mechanisms of information processing, preservation and learning, that are obviously related to memory; but memory, what we normally mean by MEMORY, the thing that captivates us and we recognize as a part of us, as OURSELVES, is something else.

Correct, indeed.

It is also true that all the processes seen up to here operate, some of them identical, some others less sophisticated, in animals as well. On the other hand, we have mostly discussed sub-cortical structures – *amygdala*, hippocampus, cerebellum – or sensory areas of the cortex. Still, in humans it is the rest of the cortex that makes the difference, the associative multimodal areas that read, compare, combine and interpret the information that each brain system elaborates. The rest of the cortex is what sustains abstraction and symbolic elaboration processes. Thus, it is obvious that in humans there exists another kind, another level, another mode of memory: the possibility of building a model of reality and fixing, learning and remembering representations, analyses, interpretations, and intuitions, and of re-reading them as a complex and live matter, of writing an explicit and conscious story of reality and life, one's own history.

Here, once more we find ourselves trespassing limits, encountering again the META, a different dimension that poses new questions, asks for new eyes, and takes us elsewhere.

Once again, we face the elusive dimension of awareness and consciousness, a trait that occupies a good deal of the soul: its neural base flees, it bounces us once more to metaphysics, myths, spirituality and faiths.

One cannot stop here without dedicating some attention to this dimension of memory, memory as history, our own history. An entire world, rich in fascination and mystery.

Taken together, all the functions we mentioned make it possible to 'write' in the brain (in the connections among nerve cells) events, data and circumstances, information and knowledge, to record our history.

A history that is not told from the beginning to the end, but rather intermingled like a big box of old photos, knocked over and put together again by a curious child: you will find, close to one another, old photographs that are somewhat alike or have similar colors or shapes, or share a detail, and may possibly come from points incredibly distant in time and in space. Indeed, this is the way our history is written, closing a page every night, day after day, but continuously going back to old notes to add and delete, redraw, collect on one day memos that were written at the seaside and on another day the letters to mum, or the library tickets.

What history is that? something is missing! something that should be the axis of history: that something is *time*...

No time.

Neural circuits that analyze temporal sequences can order schemes of experiences, remember and recall events and actions, seen or performed. Areas and systems that control motor procedures help in such restorations. But indeed, each remembrance is a picture of neuronal activity, recalled and proposed again in the brain, abstracted and isolated from time: memory, as a capacity of recalling past sensory experiences, is fragmented, without time. A memory trace can refer to a process, a sequence of acts and words, but as a whole, as an isolated compound entity, with no temporal continuity with other traces.

It is often difficult to recall whether something in our life has happened before or after something else: we can associate a date, a job, a social or familiar condition, to spot the period, perhaps the exact date, but in our memory that event is not close to the events of the day before, there is no rewind or fast-forward button, there is no ordered sequence, there is no scanning. Rather, there are sets of places, people, events, emotions, ideas and projects that draw the background of the epochs of our life and let us locate our memories in a relative and absolute time.

There are times – those of each experience, action, event and sequence that we have fixed in our memory – but TIME is not there.

Because of this, memory is indeed what most fully and precisely resembles us, as we precisely are now: not what we have been, but what remains in us, of what we have been. Everything here, now, not in a line that fades away; everything – highlighted, pale or concealed – present in guiding our thoughts, our choices, our fantasies, desires and dreams.

Each of our thoughts is affected by what has passed through our body, our mind, our soul, in every moment of our life.

Memory reflects our history but does not tell it in an ordered sequence, TIME is not there. The same way as our culture is not what we know, but the sign left in our soul by what we have learnt, so we *are* our memory. We are not our history, but the way we have lived it, and we see it today. What our history has written in our soul.

* * *

'Tame me,' said the fox...

'What does that mean – 'tame'?'

'It is an act too often neglected,' said the fox. 'It means to establish ties.'

''To establish ties'?'

'Just that' said the fox. '...if you tame me, it will be as if the sun came to shine on my life. I shall know the sound of a step that will be different from all the others... And then look: you see the grain-fields down yonder? I do not eat bread. Wheat is of no use to me. The wheat fields have nothing to say to me. And that is sad. But you have hair that is the color of gold. Think how wonderful that will be when you have tamed me! The grain, which is also golden, will bring me back the thought of you... Please – tame me!' he said.

... So the little prince tamed the fox. And when the hour of his departure drew near

'Ah,' said the fox, 'I shall cry.'

'It is your own fault,' said the little prince. 'I never wished you any sort of harm; but you wanted me to tame you...'

'Yes, that is so,' said the fox.

'But now you are going to cry!' said the little prince.

'Yes, that is so,' said the fox.

'Then it has done you no good at all!'

'It has done me good,' said the fox, 'because of the color of the wheat fields.'

[THE LITTLE PRINCE – Antoine de Saint Exupéry]

* * *

Links. Connections. This is memory.

It is not what is there that make the space; it is the relationships.

Emotional relationships – and memory – keep you in the space of your history. Imagine traveling in an unknown territory, fog, possibly, no indications, no buildings, trees, rocks, cars that might remind you of somewhere else... The main sensation would be vacuum, unreality.

Precisely because of the lack of connections and links. Somewhat like the essence and angst of schizophrenia, characterized by a fracture between the emotional and cognitive spheres: incapable of establishing appropriate connections with the surrounding reality, the patient is disoriented in space and time and is heavily impaired in producing a coherent thought, and reasoning in a way appropriate to the situation.

Even more dreadful is the thought of being deprived of our memory...

This would isolate us from reality, and even more from OUR reality, from all that we love, from people we care, from all that has been and is important in our life. Because our history is our memory. Memory of the life we are living: not WHAT happens to us, but HOW we live it remains in us. It perhaps constitutes the crucial aspect of our identity, the way out from the dilemma 'am I simply what is written in my DNA' or 'am I simply the sum of what has happened to me':

I am the sum of HOW I HAVE LIVED what has happened to me, and *how I lived it* was written – at any moment – in *what I already was* in that moment. This is my history...

At any time, we are writing the memory of our future.
We do that as individuals, we do that as a society. But each one does it their own way. Each one lives reality their own way, giving attention to this or the other aspect, detail or emotion, link, memory or fantasy.

And what we live remains written there, in our memory: it is not an encyclopedia, or a telephone directory, it is a tale, to be read and reread playing with time and space, along unpredictable paths.

Memory as a tale. A tale which does not follow a single thread but can be told starting from any point and jumping here and there, following rational, emotional, musical, evocative links.

And each of us like a language, in which each word has a personal color, sound, emotion. Remembrances like words, memory like a language. But a live language, rich in complex and mutable relationships, in unexpected colors and ways of escape.

It is not the language of the encyclopedia, no. It is the language of poetry, rather. A language made of meanings, but also of images, emotions, evocations, capable of rhythm, music, emotion. And a memory that is easily carried away, like we are, by images and emotions, and runs away and comes back, or gets lost in evermore distant and unpredictable evocations.

Thought itself, on the other hand, looks like a tale.

A poetic tale that follows a thread, but at all times can evoke images and other paths in which to get lost.

> *APRIL is the cruelest month, breeding*
> *Lilacs out of the dead land, mixing*
> *Memory and desire, stirring*
> *Dull roots with spring rain.*   *[Thomas Stearns Eliot]*

* * *

Mixing, confounding memory and desire...

Indeed, what is really difficult is to keep them apart. Is there a signal – which one? – that distinguishes in our brain a representation that is a memory from another one that we would like it were a memory? If there is one, it is an uncertain and labile signal, as suggested by the facility with which our memories evolve, are deformed and deceive us.

Maybe it is only a qualification that is associated to them, perhaps the linkage with the word 'true', or 'real'.

Maybe because of this, humans have always been looking for a god, a principle, a harmony that taught them what is true and real, and what is not.

Maybe the whole history of philosophy is nothing but a search for criteria not to confuse fantasy and reality, not to mix memory and desire.

VII
EMOTIONS – *'Croce e delizia, delizia al cor'*

Now, enough with the brain. Let us talk a little about the heart.

Yes, about those feelings that arise down deep in the heart, propagate to the stomach, and may travel down to your belly if you try to retain them inside; but if you cannot control them then they climb up and block your throat...

Try to understand them, to control them and guide them, if you wish, but generally you will have to resign yourself to let them bud and grow and wobble and shake your soul. You may look at them, perhaps, and taste them, to feel alive. Or perhaps shut them down there and pretend you do not hear them calling and screaming, turn your head and look at something else, and keep playing with the things, the problems, the tasks, the projects of life.

Emotions. A physiologist should have no doubts: the heart is there solely to play its hydraulic role; it is just a pump; it is a matter of pipes. The place for emotions is the brain, in the middle of neurons. However, this is an example of the arrogance of scientists, who from the top of someone else's experiments (that they think they have correctly grasped) are ready to betray roots and centuries of history of the thought as if they were infantile myths. But history has its revenges.

In the Nineteen twenties, after the heart had been robbed of emotions, claimed to itself by the omnipotent and omniscient Nervous System, some slightly fizzier scientists, Lange for example, in a rebound of 'heart-ism', suggested a novel and provoking reading of the processes underlying emotions: *'we do not shiver because we are afraid, we do not cry because we are sad; rather, we are afraid because we shiver, we are sad because we cry'.* The body is the one who suffers emotions. We, the brain, simply feel and realize it.

It was not merely a joke. There is a profound insight into this statement. Deep motions move in hidden parts of our body, in addition to the soul, and guide reactions that we do not decide or control, sometimes we do not even understand.

Fear, angst. Oppressive sensations, almost physical. Surprising maybe, but nonetheless pervasive. At times you feel like laughing, reluctantly, you laugh and would like not to; sometimes one can hardly believe you are there laughing, while you would weep, fight, hate, or get lost.

The question is that pain, fear, discomfort and well-being, pleasure and stupor and joy evoke visceral and behavioral responses, well before one 'realizes'. Deep, direct emotional responses like those of animals, not decided, unwanted, maybe not even understood until, cognitively examined later, we can look at them and explain them to ourselves.

It is the 'unconscious' or 'subconscious' – Freud's wild ES that does not listen to any argument and has certainly fascinated all of us. But it is curious how our feelings on this remind us of the words of Cushing, in talking, in 1929, of a well precise and defined nervous structure, the hypothalamus, that controls all the vegetative functions:

'Here in this well concealed spot, almost to be covered by a thumb nail, lies the very mainspring of primitive existence – vegetative, emotional, reproductive – on which, with more or less success, man has come to superimpose a cortex of inhibitions'.

Actually, Cannon discovered how the hypothalamus, which is in charge of controlling and managing physiological, vegetative and visceral responses, and of evoking behaviors that are required for vegetative life (eating, drinking, sleeping...), has the capacity of triggering oriented and coordinated responses, such as the predisposition of the whole organism to fight or run away (fight/flight reaction), or the angry reaction to irritant stimuli; he showed that in the absence of inhibitory control by the brain, by the cortex, these reactions become exaggerated and uncontrolled ('sham rage').

* * *

As previously discussed, the hypothalamus is the fundamental control center of all physiological parameters, and its control function is exerted through the vegetative (autonomic) nervous system, through the endocrine system, and through the generation of motivational drives to initiate behaviors that are necessary to survive (fetching food and water, eating, drinking...).

In animals, the strength of these hypothalamic requests is almost unopposed: it is difficult to retain a mouse from eating if it is hungry; and if you put it in a cage together with a female in estrus it will not waste too much time in evaluating whether it is worth to try an approach or what may be the best approach... The possibilities of mediating, of retaining vegetative impulses from the hypothalamus and opposing other behavioral choices, grow with the development of the cortex in higher animals. Obviously, the picture becomes substantially different in humans (or at least it should, shouldn't it?). But not so much because *the cortex is there to inhibit*: rather, because much more numerous and varied motivational forces affect human behavior.

The responses directly generated by the hypothalamus give rise to modulation of cardiac activity, blood pressure, respiration, visceral activities – corporeal reactions aimed at reestablishing equilibrium and satisfying needs, which constitute the physical, visceral component of emotions. The hypothalamus does not justify or tell emotions by itself: there may be opposing needs, and their combination and the external situation will dictate choices and modes.

Neural circuits are capable of plasticity. In learning the most appropriate and effective modes and reactions, the capability of recognizing dangerous – or anyway relevant – situations is particularly important; a region in the nervous system has precisely the function of spotting signals and indicators of emotional relevance. Looking at photographs of a man who laughs, or smiles, or looks uncertain, worried, fearful or even frightened, the *amygdala* gets increasingly activated, deep in the temporal lobe, and triggers visceral, corporeal and mimic reactions that correspond to the intensity of the fear transmitted by the image.

Another deep region, also capable of learning, discharges in response to the resolution of a state of need, or when a prize, reward or gratification is obtained: it is the *nucleus accumbens*. Here, a subpopulation of cells discharge when the possibility appears of such a solution or prize; this system also learns, and these cells learn to recognize each signal that may suggest such a possibility. Finally, instinctual and learned strategies to adapt to social life and to be accepted control the system of serotonergic neurons in the *raphe* of the brainstem, to accordingly influence behavior.

The concerted action of hypothalamus, the 'vegetative control center for survival', *amygdala*, the 'alarm system', *nucleus accumbens*, the 'pleasure sensor', and median *raphe*, the 'be nice and get accepted' talking cricket, agitates a compound and mutable mood in the activity of deep regions of the nervous system. This translates into visceral responses – tachycardia, palpitation, breathlessness, digestive block, pallor, cold sweating – that prepare to react or suffer, and motor responses – muscular tremors, weeping, alterations of the voice, facial mimics and posture – that unambiguously communicate our emotions to those who see us. They communicate efficiently: the others not only perceive them, but have a hard time not to get influenced by them.

This set of vegetative adaptations and postural and mimic responses are accompanied, if a sufficiently complex nervous system is there, by changes in its mode of operation: cognitive elaboration becomes less discriminative (approximate but quick) and responsiveness immediate, more rapid; control of behavior becomes reflex, instinctive or heuristic, rather than strategical.

All this constitutes a merely biological and fully involuntary component of the reaction to affectively relevant events or situations, which Antonio Damasio proposed to call the 'somatic marker' of emotions, to distinguish it from the cognitive and affective elaboration of the emotions, which he proposed to refer to as 'feelings'.

* * *

Indeed, emotion wanders in parts of the nervous system over which we do not hold rational and conscious control, parts and circuits that we share with all animals that possess a sufficiently developed nervous system. These are systems capable of driving complex responses that prepare the organism for the appropriate reactions and simultaneously communicate to other members of the species what happens inside us. Yes: tremor, pallor, cold sweating, perception of a blocked stomach and intestine (digestion does block, indeed!), and palpitation, agitation, and all this up to the point of no longer being able to feel fatigue and fear and pain and limits, well, all this is not useless reactions of a baffled frightened soul who has lost its control on the body...

No, these are all reactions that have a physiological meaning and value: the heart pumps more strongly, the blood is displaced from where it is useless (the intestine and the skin, that becomes pallid and cold) to the muscles, to the liver that must share its reserves of sugar; the skin sweats to disperse the heat produced by muscles, activated to fight or run away; the regions of the brainstem that awaken the whole cortex, alerting it, are intensely activated, and the systems that might stop from action, by lamenting fatigue or pain, hunger, thirst, are silenced. It is almost discouraging, how simple all that is, how it is sufficient to inject adrenaline to identically elicit all these reactions, how easily the sensation of strength and invincibility, and immunity to fatigue, that are produced by cocaine and amphetamine, is explained by the mere potentiation of these neural circuits, that mainly employ noradrenaline and dopamine to transmit signals among their neurons.

Joy, and laughter, too, come from elsewhere, are not born in the regions where our conscious EGO looks and judges, but in low regions of the nervous system, in the basal forebrain and brainstem, where they finely modulate the activity of face muscles that communicate our emotions to the others, who in turn perceive them with no need for conscious reading and interpretation, the same way as animals understand arching of the spine, erected hair or lowered ears, or a cry or a sob.

Hard work, to try and reproduce a smile, a weeping, a sigh, to simulate an emotion! Oh, the face children make when you tell them to smile for the photograph... Still, a hemiplegic person, who cannot move half of the body and of the face, because of an ictus (a lesion of the cortex), smiles with almost perfect symmetry, because smile and weep are controlled down there.

Hard work for the actor, because body language is born from emotion and not from will. Often, to understand how to produce a credible smile or a weep one must try and live the emotion, rather than simulating it, and train and study oneself to learn to be credible. The face is harder to counterfeit than words; and if you are clever, you will trust faces more than words.

Again. Once more one realizes that in humans there is something more.

There is the way we tell, and narrate to ourselves, these underground movements. If you inject small doses of adrenaline, emotional reactions get enhanced: show shocking or moving images to subjects you have injected a bit of adrenaline and they will display more marked corporeal reactions (cardiac frequency, sweating...) and perceive much more intensely the emotional strength of the images. If you tell them in advance that adrenaline will amplify their visceral emotional responses, the corporeal reactions will still be enhanced, but notwithstanding the palpitations they will no longer attribute an excessive emotional value to the images.

The body, the nervous system, reacts, no control by consciousness or will, but the emotional experience – *feeling*, in neurophysiology language, distinct from the visceral-somatic expression of *emotion* – is generated by how we *tell* ourselves those submerged movements.

* * *

It may have happened to you to wake up early to enjoy the spectacle of the dawn – possibly on the sea: a succession and intersection of colors, faint, pale colors that gradually turn strong and bright, to finally melt in a glorious blue. Or possibly to let your gaze wander along the profile of the mountains, where the luminosity of snow plays with rebellious rocks that won't let the whiteness get a hold of them, red in the sun. Or again, in a clear night, to look at a full moon that looks like a hole, round, perfectly chiseled in the black dome of the sky, to let in the amazing light from another world out there; or a pale moon that, veiled by clouds, seems to slowly dissolve in the sky like an Alka-Seltzer.

Moving experiences.
But how much more intense, poignant, if you can say: "look!".

*If you can move your eyes for a moment,
encounter the gaze of the Other and exchange a smile.*

A smile that is involvement and complicity, sharing.

*Embracing and being embraced makes every pleasure more intense and
meaningful: no longer alone, the amazement of the sublime, the immense,
turns into the joy of moving free and safe in an infinite space and time.*

*It may be true that silence sometimes is worth a thousand words, but a
smile is certainly worth more. Because words are paths, sometimes long
and winding, to reach the Other's soul, but the smile is the highway.*

*The atmosphere changes around us: clouds mask the sun, the wind blows,
the rain pours, the fog hides everything around; or the sun shines and the
sky glows in blue. The atmosphere changes inside us as well, whatever
happens that may concern us, and it triggers emotions, from the mildest
ones to the most intense.*

*The amygdala, in our temporal lobe, detects and signals the relevance of
each experience; it gets activated by each signal of wellbeing, discomfort,
even more for every hint of danger. The cortex elaborates these signals and
generates those internal experiences that we call emotions.*

*They seem purely psychic phenomena, colors and harmonies – or
dissonances – of the soul. But they get to the heart, the stomach, the throat.*

*And even if we do not realize it, they invade the whole body, that expresses
them, trembling, paling, contracting or relaxing, pouring tears through the
eyes or opening the mouth in a smile, widening the eyes in terror or
making them glow with joy.*

It is the primordial form of communication.

*The brain is designed to read these expression of the Other's experience:
the amygdala guides our eyes to explore those of the others, to read them,
and already the newborn, whose image processing system is still
immature, has a circuit in the brain – between the occipital and
the temporal cortex – that recognizes the shape of a mouth below
two luminous points as a signal that directly evokes an experience
of being accepted, protected, reassured, of safety and wellbeing.*

*The newborn does not know that she is mum, yet. In fact, any image
reminiscent of a face will do – even a mere "smile", two dots on a half-
moon, in the crib – and they will be quiet. Newborns have no idea that the
smiling eyes that make them feel good and safe, and the breast from which*

they suck their milk, have anything to do with each-other, the same way they do not know that those strange things – which they will learn to be their own feet – belong to them.

But they already can read the emotions that the face of the mother sends them.
Not cognitively: simply, as the sun that tears apart the clouds suddenly brightens the atmosphere, so that smile suddenly lightens their soul. Because the smile embraces, reassures, protects. And the smile is a promise: a promise that one can be happy, can feel good, can succeed.

The smile is complicity. The smile is hope.
The smile is an invitation to walk together. To look at life with confidence. But the smile is also a hand offered by the one who can climb to us who slip, a hand offered by the one who can swim to us who do not see the coast and have no more breath to keep swimming.

Too often, in a society that asks, flickers a thousand perspectives without offering any safety, we forget hope.
We forget the possibility of finding a solution to the many problems, or at least a path to follow to go on.
If we rediscover the Other, if we can find again the capacity of smiling, and reading other people's smiles, it is a hope we can get back.

Too mellifluous?
But the question here is not to put nice words in a row to compose a sweet and idyllic tale for children: smile as solidarity, empathy, comprehension, for a better world…

Much more is at stake. Each moment of our life.

Dissonances, different perspectives, different needs, conflicts are there in every relation. And every time this distance appears, judgment inevitably comes about. Even in relations that are affectively important – especially in strongly affective relations – each sentence directly becomes an accusation or a defense, a verdict or a justification, a refusal or a request of being accepted. Too easily every confrontation becomes a conflict, every different perspective becomes a criticism, an offence, and makes one feel as a misjudged victim, stop, shut up, freeze in a situation with no way out: resentment, self-pity, unable to see a way to get out, to change.

But sometimes the magic works.
The magic that disarms the words.
It is a magic that is called SMILE.

The smile that tells affection, sharing, and transforms words from tools to attack and humiliate into an open proposal of a different perspective, into the offering of a ground of get-together, in the precious gift of a part of oneself.

The smile of a light, joyful irony, that destroys the tension, forces to take some distance and look at each-other from a little farther…

And magically, the wicked game of judgement and victimism melts down in the resonances of complicity.

Magics… The newborn does not know but can read the emotions in the face of the mother. The same way as the sun, tearing apart the clouds, suddenly brightens the air, so that smile suddenly illuminates the soul.

It is already like this for the newborn. It will be like this all one's life long.

Desired smiles. Smiles that change words' meaning and colors. Disarming smiles, smiles that dissolve the tension, unexpected smiles.

Smiles that force you to smile in turn, to not feel alone, to have faith. To feel bouts of joy, of warmth in your soul, even in moments of pain and grief. To find more energy, and discover the possibility, the strength, the hope to change, to get better, to keep growing.

* * *

In the second half of '900 a dynamic, sustainable perspective on the physiology of emotions has matured. Cognitive elaboration, our conscious thought, may autonomously generate conditions of satisfaction, frustration, expectation, fear, that are not directly reactive (to some sort of stimuli); these can generate emotions, that do not necessarily require visceral-somatic responses. Analogously, fear, anxiety, angst and gratification may persist well after visceral-somatic responses have ceased. Thus, the higher centers do not simply look down on the emotional turmoil in the viscera, and tell it, but they do contribute to generate, maintain and elaborate emotions.

* * *

Let's talk about something nice, let's talk about love.
Well, if one could really "talk" about love, using words to describe, to explain…

> *Kidnapped / in the mirror of your eyes / I breathe / your breath.*
> *I'm alive …   [Sappho?]*

No, this does not explain. When you talk about love, words don't tell, they may just suggest, evoke.

Ivano Fossati used to sing   'love… makes the water taste good'.

Exactly! because love is an exercise in imagination, that makes you live every sensation, every act, every moment, as if they were different.

They may well tell me that it is a question of pheromones.

Sure, you may be attracted due to pheromones. But it happens even for a single gesture, a way of smiling, a soft voice, a sentence that reveals irony and depth, possibly something somebody says about them.

Generally, it vanishes, or a feeling arises, you get friends, you have sex…

But falling in love is another thing: their image must find its way in your thought, fantasy must be captured around it, and keep falling there. Imagination must start spinning around their image, the idea of them, recalling intense moments to memory, and experiences full of emotion, prefiguring meetings, dates, gestures, words, smiles, caresses, sharing: pleasures to be savored. Fantasy and imagination fly and let you anticipate what may happen, in a game that sometimes is even more pleasurable than the actual experience manages to be.

Falling in love is an imagination job, forget pheromones.

It is an imagination job.
And this, may the animalists forgive me, is a human peculiarity.

One may climb the evolution staircase and ask where does consciousness appear: in insects? in reptiles, birds? in mammals, primates? in men? in women?

It may look like a clever question. It is not. All depends on what you mean by "consciousness". Is it the capability to react to stimuli? to feel emotions? to distinguish oneself from the rest? to recognize one is the owner and actor of their sensations, emotions and actions? to generate an internal image of reality? of oneself? is it the capacity of looking at oneself and feeling oneself living and thinking?
"Consciousness" is one of those words that can mean a thousand different things, depending on who is using them and in what context. Still, wonder of human language, you can use it freely, and most often the others pretend they understand what you are talking about.

Forget about "consciousness". The most human thing we possess is exactly the capacity to look at oneself, imagine oneself, TELL A STORY about oneself. And not only one's own past history, and present, but also prefiguring and savoring, imagining a history to come, in the future.

This is why an animal can be affectionate, can possibly love to absolute dedication, but cannot fall in love.

Falling in love, fantasizing on a person, a relation, coloring it with emotion one has felt or that may simply be possible, transforming it into an imaginary story even nicer and mor intense than it is in reality…
this is a pathology which is strictly human.

But, alas! what a nice disease! I hope you felt it, at least once in your life. That frenzy, the thought that keeps going there, the fantasy that runs, how everything changes its color, how intense every moment becomes, every act, every emotion…

* * *

Emotion is a two-way interaction, between corporeal responses and their interpretation, between the emotional value of cognitive elaborations and the cognitive relevance of emotional experience. Neurologically, this crossway corresponds to the so-called limbic system (a threshold, in between corporeal experience and cognitive elaboration). It is a system comprised of sub-cortical centers (hypothalamus, *amygdala*, *nucleus accumbens* and other structures) and by the most antique portions of the cortex, the innermost ones.

A whole system down there, integrated and complex, elaborates a true emotional LOGIC, though an implicit and non-verbal one, through the interaction among alarm regions (*amygdala*), areas of expectation and recognition of gratification (*n. accumbens*), a vegetative control center (hypothalamus), systems that favor adaptation to the situation and social relations (serotonergic raphe nuclei), and specific portions of the cortex (the most antique ones). In animals these areas perform some complex computation to attribute emotional relevance not only in an instinctive or associative way, but also based on some cognitive (albeit limitedly so) evaluation of possible onset of a situation of danger, discomfort or well-being.

In humans, the cortical regions involved are much more developed and broader, and even more relevant are the nearby regions committed to integration with other elaboration modalities. So, this implicit *emotional logic* can be put in bi-directional and complex relation with conscious cognitive systems. This makes it possible to read in a coherent way emotional experiences, that can be interpreted in an explicit and verbal way; conversely, this also permits to endow higher cerebral functions with emotional valence.

A complex aspect of this question is that the reading of the emotional picture by the limbic system is coherent and interpretable but – like the output of the visual cortex – it is not explicit and verbal, it does not follow the same logic as the regions that elaborate conscious thinking. Feature extraction, and detection of patterns, elements and relations can be tricked in the visual cortex, by optical illusions, and similarly in all other regions that elaborate information below the threshold of consciousness; among these, the limbic system itself.

In all cases, the errors are not intrinsic to the computation by dedicated cortical areas; they most frequently arise from misreading and misinterpretation. This is not particularly strange, as the attentive and conscious processes in multimodal regions of the cortex work on the overall experience as elaborated and contextualized by the hippocampus and follow rules and logical paths that are not the same that govern *unimodal* computation, and in particular emotional processing by the limbic system: thus, in our rational reading of emotions we often misread and misunderstand.

Given the strong predominance of verbal communication in humans, over other forms of communication, it is not strange that even the clearest emotional messages can be effectively contradicted by words, and that in such condition the rational (verbal) reading of emotional experience will be strongly influenced by verbal elaboration and forced into coherent interpretations that may actually violate emotional perception. In simple words, an implicit logic governs emotional perception – the *intelligence of the heart* – but its messages are read and often misinterpreted by rationality: they get lost in translation.

The other direction of this bi-directional communication, between limbic system and cognitive activity, is also intriguing: how purely cognitive activity can produce genuine emotions (bodily, visceral emotions).

On the one side, everybody knows that the simple thought of something frightening, or very embarrassing, or exciting, can reproduce a genuine emotion, with its accompanying heartbeat, breathlessness, redness, shivering, sweating, tangled guts, knotted throat... On the other hand, if nothing similar occurs, it is difficult to say we feel an emotion.

It happens sometimes in front of the news, looking at the last exodus of refugees, at the victims of the last war or terrorist act or natural calamity, to feel sorry for them but realize with some surprise that we do not feel such a strong emotion – be it habitude, or the fact that it happened so far away, or that the television shows us so many terrible fake things – and to feel somehow guilty and even more sorry for that.

But we do feel sorry, nobody could deny. How can we say the emotion is not so strong? simply because our body does not respond...

A way of looking at all this is to consider the process of identification and empathy. Bodily reactions that accompany emotions have a communicative function; for this communication to work, the lower centers of the nervous system that elaborate these 'messages' must be able to reproduce the same visceral-somatic reactions that are observed in another subject. This does occur, as we well know.

In humans, this also adds a further pleasant feeling to sharing emotions, the awareness of emotional sharing, the feeling of sympathy. This identification, and reproduction of the emotional status of another subject, also works with respects to our own past and future experiences: in remembering a moving experience we revive the feeling we lived then, and a similar process may occur in anticipating a future experience.

Thus, emotional identification consists in reproducing bodily reactions. And when the heart tells an emotion, it is difficult to neglect it. The fact is that emotions may well be perceived and elaborated in the brain, but the vital importance of an event or experience is estimated by the limbic system based on the presence of BODILY reactions typical of conditions of fear, happiness, angst, anticipation, joy, commotion, hilarity.

You sit at the theater and watch the play: the actors try to produce emotions in you; you do not miss their requests – here you are supposed to feel tense, or to sympathize, to feel sad or relieved. But sometimes you do feel like that, sometimes you do not. It is not a cognitive question; it is a visceral one. You feel the emotion when your body reacts the right way. What is intriguing is that your cognitive elaboration of what happens on the stage is sufficient to generate such bodily reactions: if that occurs, you decide that the play is moving, and the actors are good.

Anything in your intellectual activity that really moves you – be it generated by an experience you undergo, or by a memory or a desire – will produce changes in your vegetative conditions (changes in heartbeat, sweating, some kind of languor in your stomach, an increase or sudden release of muscular tension...).

Curiously enough, similar sensations can be produced by purely abstract experiences: the illumination when you finally understand something, the lightness and freedom when music embraces you, the relief and well-being that accompanies the right choice, and the ethical act...

All these cognitive experiences evoke the same bodily reactions that elementary and reactive emotions elicit, and one feels the associated pain, joy, sadness, and enthusiasm, angst or ecstasy as a result of the interpretation of such bodily reactions by the limbic system.

The brain is the one who interprets, the brain can generate its own emotions and read them back. Everything is in the brain. But if it does not manage to have your heart jump around, to strangle your throat and tangle your guts, you do not even realize that you are moved, that you desire, that you love.

Sadly, the reverse is also true. If you produce, by electrical stimulation of the appropriate neurons, or with the appropriate drug, the bodily reaction that accompanies fear, terror or pleasure, one feels exactly that emotion: depending on the way you produce it, it may feel it with slight or tremendous intensity. You may stimulate the reward pathway and produce intense pleasure; you may stimulate a portion of the insula (a hidden area of the occipito-parieto-temporal cortex) and produce disgust or irresistible hilarity...

And it is terribly easy to confound the ORIGINAL with a COPY.

It is terribly easy to confound the genuine pleasure of success, sympathy, love, enchantment, ethical pride, with the fake pleasure produced by a drug that reproduces bodily and cerebral activities associated with pleasure.

Perhaps, between the original and the copy the central question is, once more, multiplicity, what you cannot find in the copy: the story of the original, the emotion that has accompanied its gestation and birth, that part of the author that has remained permanently linked to it.

The question is very similar for emotions and for the possibility of reproducing them with an electrical stimulation or a drug: how many other cognitive aspects, intuitions, memories, desires and fantasies accompany genuine emotion! how many different aspects of interior life (and how many regions of the brain) are involved and vibrate in concert, or violently fight each other...

When you read, or listen, or study and try to understand, and finally you discover, understand; the moment you *get it!*, you *perceive*, and a new perspective opens in front of you... It is a deep pleasure that invades the whole of you.

In certain moments of wellbeing, in fantasizing a little detached from reality, it happens you prove something similar, and you get deceived... Sometimes it happens while you sleep: you cannot solve a problem, and *there!*, in your dreams you feel the wonderful relief of *having solved* it.

Then you wake up and realize that everything was so blurred in the dream, the problem was not exactly specified, the solution you found cannot be recalled, and possibly did not even exist: it was not an answer, just the impression, the emotion, that YOU GOT IT...

It is a *physical* feeling, the *visceral* impression of seeing, knowing, understanding, recalling... (*'recalling things that others have desired'*). As if rationality lost control of thought, and this were carried away by a stream of emotions that don't care of reality, of space, time, logics.

Well, nothing pathological, at all. But it helps to understand where the weak point of the soul is, in which point a wedge of pain and disease can penetrate to disjoint and dissociate the spirit: a split soul (schizophrenia), and therefore fool. Fool, yes, because of disease or of love, because of fanaticism or dismay, disoriented in space, in time, incapable of facing reality, disturbed in thought because that link has been lost that obliges THOUGHT to face visceral, affective experience; the link that keeps them interlaced, and does not let them split and depart from one another, because that would tear the soul apart.

Because quite a lot of our life moves out of our control.

And then, once more, who am *I*? Am I the one who feels and acts down there or the one who watches and tries to understand?

* * *

Words and Music

In talking of memory, we happened to compare it to language, in which every word takes on evocative, visual, musical, emotional, affective, personal value for each of us, increasingly varied and rich as time goes by and experiences accumulate.

Each of us like a language, then. But a personal, individual language. Each word has a different sound, emotion and color for each of us.

Maybe it is nicer and more appropriate to see each of us as two worlds, a language, but also a music, that meet each-other.

We are a flashing of fluctuating chords, a succession of possible words. And each harmony, each sentence is a moment of our life. Of ourselves. But not in the sense that each moment, each chord, leaves something written somewhere in us, so that it can be re-evoked. No. Each moment of our life remains in us, as a part of us, because that chord, that harmony has changed now, has become connected to new words and is enriched with new meaning. And those words are now different, colored by emotion, linked to new harmonies.

This will repeat over and over, and we might no longer be able to re-live any single moment of our life, that harmony and those words, by simply recalling them, because they are no longer there the way they used to be;

we shall 'live again' something possibly even richer, but different, because that harmony will now recall other words that it did not know at that time, each word will suggest harmonies that it had not heard yet, at that time.

We are a language and a music
a language which is not made of spoken sentences, but of possible sentences;
not a written music, but possible chords, sequences, harmonies (like jazz?);
a language and a music that change in talking and in playing.

Music lives in its tonality, in its rhythms, in its emotions, and follows the words, but cannot tell them.   And words cannot tell music.

We can grasp, understand, say, recall only an infinitesimal fraction of the combinations of words and music that chase each other and entwine in our life. Because only a part of the schemes of activity in the whole brain, which grinds needs, gratifications, emotions, fears, dreams, desires, readings, ideas, intuitions, projects, actions, is heard in the regions where consciousness arises and records aware memories. Only this small part is perceived, is fixed and understood, and this is what you think you are, what you feel you are.

But what does not surface is also recorded. And vague, fleeting memories reappear, that are not memories but vaguely familiar emotions.
Much of the music, that is your emotions and your life, plays muffled and only appears in the cadence of words you remember as moments of yourself.

You only realize this in a blurred way, like when the blues grabs you, and demands that you be sad because you just feel like weeping, not that you cry because you are sad...

* * *

Men and women.

There is a difference between music and words, between the emotion with which we live life and the gaze with which we look at life. Music keeps going, ever new. It can't stop, it permeates, expresses reality, it does not describe.

Curiously, in most languages there are two very different ways to express the meaning 'to understand': to grasp and to comprehend.

To clutch with clamps and pin down on the table, examine, dissect, violate.
To comprehend, identify with, take inside you (no problem if it becomes
allusive), let in, let yourself be pervaded, recreate inside you, tune with.

Words, and music, once again.
Words to grasp reality, to explain it, to violate it.
Music to comprehend reality, to live it, to care about.
Well, it may be a misconception, but everybody would agree that grasping
is the specialty of men, comprehending is that of women.

Words and music. Toward things, people, and towards other communities,
different cultures, alien worlds. Not only in looking at them.

Whether the question is of accepting reality, or actively intervening to
modify it, in both cases one can adopt two different approaches:
comprehensive-empathic or prevaricating.

It is Cassandra or the Greeks (sorry for those who do not know Christa
Wolf: it is their fault!). It is peace or war. It is love or control.
It is war against terrorism, gulf wars against the lost occasion of half of the
Islamic world that condemned 9.11, while the western world had not the
gut, or the strength, to open a dialog, or consciously refused and closed it.
It is the concept itself of 'just war', something that perhaps all of us can
conceive from the side of the weaker one, but only some of us can conceive
from the side of the stronger one: those – sadly it is not few of them – who
think that it is ok to try and understand the youngsters, and talk, and love
them, and counsel them... but sometimes a good slap resolves more than a
thousand words.

It is easy: ask one if in their opinion there are situations in which using
violence, or merely raising the voice, resolves something that love cannot
resolve, and if they say yes, you know that they have no problems in
conceiving the 'just war', and the rainbow flag of peace makes them
uncomfortable.

May it be accidental that women generally are on the side of peace?

We all hear the music. We all try and understand it and explain it.
But music, even YOUR OWN music... you cannot govern it, you may be
able to push it and guide it a little, perhaps, but you must eventually set it
free, and let it carry you.
You cannot direct it with words.

Music is played by sentiments, affects, emotions, perfumes, sensations,
dreams, desires, pain, pleasure.

Like a sax that enters with its solo, you can try to divert, to suggest a different rhythm, a new tone...
If it is the right one, the right moment, the other musicians may get along, follow you, and the music changes. But often, ...

Sometimes music starts soft, languid, moving, sad, triggered by a hidden melody, by an unrecognized chord.
It grasps you, colors your soul in blue, and as sad as it can be, still it gets you, it hugs, cuddles, soothes you: the quintessence of blues...

Sometimes instead it sounds joyful, fresh and inebriating.
And everything is colored and flourishes.

What is happiness? What is it?!
It is difficult to say, because one feels the answer should be made of words, one must describe it: what, how, why...
Instead, it is not difficult, happiness is when music plays within us, strong and inflaming. Trivial? But happiness is happiness and that is it!

There is no rule with which to combine tones and chords so that harmony and melody abruptly grasp you and take you away, stealing your soul.
There is no rule to create in yourself the right chord, the melody of happiness. There is no rule and often, too often, music drags you along its lanes while words would bring you somewhere else.

Who are you then? are you the words or the music?

Each of them follows its own logic; music asks for harmony, word for coherence. Music knows your needs, your rhythms, your secret dreams, and shows up in your gestures and modes, gets itself noticed and looks for harmonies and sends messages and requests; the words only see a portion of all that, and guide your conscious choices, pick your sentences; but often they cannot impose the tone and capture the reality that is around you; they send different messages and different requests.

The most concise and momentous definition of schizophrenia says 'dissociation between the affective and the cognitive sphere':
it may not be exhaustive, but it gets the point.

But then we are all a little 'schizo', men and women.

In a slightly different way, though, because women perceive better the music of the soul, they can give up explaining it – and getting it wrong – when it is better not to; they can follow it and live it and spread it around.

In saying this an old movie comes to my mind, 'Baghdad café', and that awkward, so sweet big woman, who emanates warmth, imagination, commitment and ingenuity, and manages in impregnating with this mood the rancid and sleepy place she happens to come about...

Or a lucky sentence in the movie 'The hours', that I once captured in pieces on the plane; mum: 'let's make a cake for daddy to let him know that we love him...'; the little girl: 'otherwise he wouldn't know?'...

It reminds me of how Lella Costa complains about how women can hurt themselves: 'thoughtless, ill-advised idea of trusting male intuition...'.

Yes, women often know how to live the music of emotions and sentiments, their words, and their acts, know how to interpret it, how not to violate it.

Maybe estrogens are needed to reach this syntony.
Maybe it is the two X chromosomes that have been talking to each-other since childhood, and communicate, get to know and understand each other, while our single one, with that crippled Y companion, talks by itself and gets dull. However, no doubt man is schizoed, because he rarely perceives the music as a part of himself: most times he ignores it, or studies and analyzes it like a strange insect, or cuddles and venerates it and abandons himself to it and loses his mind.

But honestly, women are also schizoed, at least a little so.
Ask a woman, the wisest you can find, what is she looking for, how much warmth, strength, and sweetness or hardness, availability, confidence, surprise, and protection and spirit and aggressiveness, in a man...
Then, look at whom she gets stuck with!

Perhaps, it is because music just looks for something that cannot be found, something that was not there in the past because it could not be there, could not be in those relations, and music looks for it precisely in people who resemble those who were not capable of that something, in people who cannot give it because they ARE NOT ABLE TO...

Music looks for that something, anxiously and passionately, because it does not and cannot find it... Because in the end not even women are so clever in reading the music. They can live it, true, and translate it in behavior, often coherent and confident, but they understand little of it themselves.

But then, how could they try and explain to us, men?
what do they hope we understand?

One thing, however, is clear to women, in general: that to complain, look back and denounce faults is useless. To live, you must follow the music.

Be it joyous or sad, exhilarating of moving.
Follow the music, without saving energy and calculating too much.

This is really something they should teach us men, also – especially – in politics: transforming the perception of what is missing, of what is not good, into an effort to build, with joy and commitment.
Rather than negating, analyzing, accusing, taking advantage of deficiencies,
perceiving them instead, recognizing them as a powerful motor to change.

In the seventies, for the first and last time in my life, I cuddled the illusion that people could get together and fight FOR something. It was kind of a feeling that many shared in Italy, at the time, and led them to fancy about 'hegemony of the working class'. But we were not able to give this aspiration the modes, the instruments, the objectives.

Thus, fighting FOR has become once more an exclusive patrimony of the healthy parts of the religious world, of nostalgic fringes of a different gauche, of juvenile associations, and of a few people committed in the world, in culture, in society.

And mostly of women, who still will not give up with music, with life.

* * *

Neurologically, we are visual beings. A great fraction of our brain is organized to elaborate information like the visual one: huge amounts of data that arrive simultaneously – not a perfume, a taste, a sound, but millions of colored dots. But data do not move nicely ordered as in a computer, all orderly written, one after the other, in a file: they do not even reach the brain as such: what gets there is pulverized at once, decomposed and recomposed again and again. No longer colored dots but lines, curves and combinations thereof, geometric figures, simple and complex patterns, each of them recognized by specific neurons, until we find neurons that are capable of recognizing very complex patterns, or any image where it is possible to detect a human face.

Each neuron focused on one aspect. A million explorers, each of them in search of specific hints: it seems they are there to *understand*, rather than to see. Each neuron an outlook, a thousand different readings and interpretations, simultaneous, there to be examined, compared, integrated, re-elaborated, and related with what has already been.

Thus, reality dematerializes in the brain: no photographs but elements, structures, relations, that expand beyond the information that is there to be examined and include emotional, operative, affective aspects.

In all this, links and analogies. And continuous and simultaneous re-interpretations in wider and wider domains.

We are visual beings in the sense that we can simultaneously analyze a simultaneous bunch of data in a thousand different ways: MULTIPLICITY, each aspect per se but also with respect to all it can be related to.

Internal rules and logic must be applied, but everything must also be examined from outside, in relation to any other possible logic. Thus, reading invades a wider domain, METAanalysis. Logic, and METALogic. Further and beyond. META: inside but also outside and above.

In examining the organization of the brain, one finds higher and higher systems, in continuous search of unified views and higher harmonies, even momentary ones. A kind of obsessive – and puzzling – search for harmony. But maybe not so puzzling, when one realizes that something more is there, more or less evident, in the brain, something neurobiology has not examined with sufficient attention: circuitries capable of producing the deepest pleasure – such as the pleasure a smile can generate, or an act of love – when an intuition, a new and unexpected glance, a set of sensations creates the harmony of a synthesis of multiplicity (the *BEAUTY*...).

The pleasure of BEAUTY... In between emotions and cognition, also this, deep there in neuronal circuits.

There, to be studied with much more care!

So, if it is true that emotions arise from the heart, and viscera and flesh, the brain is capable of combining them and drying them to extract their flavor, it is capable of distilling out of them a harmony, a music that continually accompanies brain activity and shows it the essence of life; and the brain is capable of translating this music itself, the music of beauty, into a novel and overwhelming emotion.

Maybe this way it becomes clear why emotions, and perfumes, suggest the soul: because few words make you think of the soul – and few fit to the soul – as 'harmony' and 'music' do.

* * *

I keep my countenance, I remain self-possessed
Except when a street-piano, mechanical and tired
Reiterates some worn-out common song
With the smell of hyacinths across the garden
Recalling things that other people have desired.

T. S. Eliot, 'Portrait of a Lady'

VIII

ME – Subjectivity, identity, agency

Most people would claim that the essence of consciousness lies in its capability to add the dimension of *identity* and *subjectivity* to the elaboration performed by neural circuits. If this were true, we might even achieve a clear and mechanistic knowledge of how the brain builds a precise, detailed and holistic, consistent internal representation of reality (the *epistemological* aspect of consciousness), but the question would still stand as to which circuits may ever generate some kind of 'conscious principle' that transforms such internal representation into a subjective 'perspective' on it; one may conclude that no neural mechanisms might ever do this, and some non-neural (possibly metaphysical) principle of *reflexive consciousness* must be involved.

So, let's try and examine how neuronal circuits process information and see whether this helps us in locating a source for the subjective and personal perspective.

* * *

THE OPERATING MODE OF THE NEURON

A common view of the function of a neuron suggests that it receives inputs (activation of the synapses on its dendritic tree and soma): the resulting electrical events on its membrane may generate a nerve impulse (spike, action potential) if their sum overcomes a certain threshold level.

This is true, in principle, but the situation for central neurons is much more complex and intriguing: the 'language' of the neuron is not the impulse (i.e. being *ON* or *OFF*), but a continuously varying *pattern* of impulse firing. The changing combination of momentary excitatory or inhibitory pulses that hit its synapses reflects the combined firing pattern of a large number of neurons in a cortical circuit (a 'complex pattern of neural activity'), and the response of the neuron does not reflect the overall synaptic activation, but the synchrony, consistency and interaction among the activities of all the neurons that synapse on it.

Cortical neurons examine the many inputs they receive with a degree of discrimination – precision, timing and selectivity – that depends on how narrow the time interval is for effective summation of the incoming signals; and such time window markedly changes, depending on the mode in which information reaches the cortex from the thalamus, so the dialogue between the thalamus and the cerebral cortex determines whether a circuit examines the incoming information in an approximate way – as it happens during inattentive processing – or in a more precise and discriminative manner.

Not data but relations – not sounds but music

It is as if the neuron listened to the melodies played simultaneously by many other neurons on its synapses. It would then elaborate, based on all this, an overall emerging melody (its own time-varying firing pattern). Depending on how each cortical circuit talks with the corresponding thalamic neurons, such melody would either produce a sophisticated ('discriminative') elaboration of all specific melodic and harmonic details in the concert the neuron is listening to, or reproduce the general tonality and rhythm of the incoming signals ('non-discriminative' mode).

Such a way of integrating incoming signals clearly indicates that no central neuron ever responds to a datum (be it sensory or endogenously generated). Each neuron detects specific *relations* among the *patterns* of activity of the neurons that connect to it and may thus attribute a consistent (either vague or specific) meaning to such complex.

The property of detecting patterns in the relations among sensory data is particularly well documented by recordings performed in central neurons positioned along the cortical paths that analyze visual information.

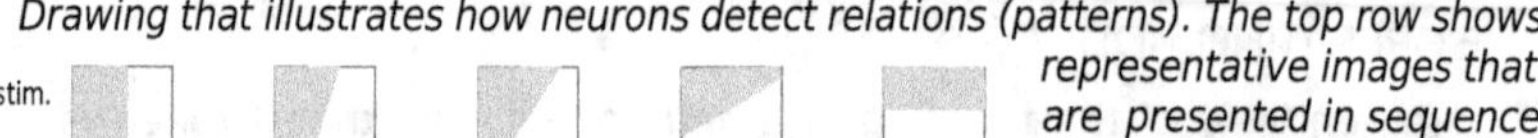
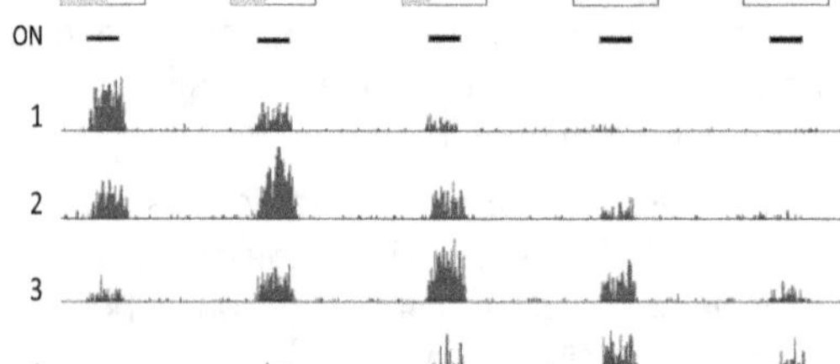

Drawing that illustrates how neurons detect relations (patterns). The top row shows representative images that are presented in sequence at the times indicated by the black bars (ON). Numbers 1 to 4 are histograms of spike frequencies recorded from neighboring neurons. Each neuron preferentially responds to a specific slant angle, but pattern detection is not crisp and absolute, but rather fuzzy, 'tentative'.

Neighboring neurons in occipital-temporal areas respond to patterns in the visual field, such as lines or borders with variable slant; the firing rate of each neuron reflects how closely the slant of the line/border approaches the angle it is designed to recognize, with neighboring neurons responding to slightly different angles, in an ordered way.

This occurs somewhat independently of the precise location of the line in the visual field, which indicates that these neurons signal the presence of a specific pattern in the incoming visual information, rather than precisely locating cues in the visual field. In more anterior areas of the temporal lobe, neurons display increasingly sophisticated elaboration of the incoming image and will fire in the presence of any visual pattern that may represent a relevant object, even a complex object like a hand or a face.

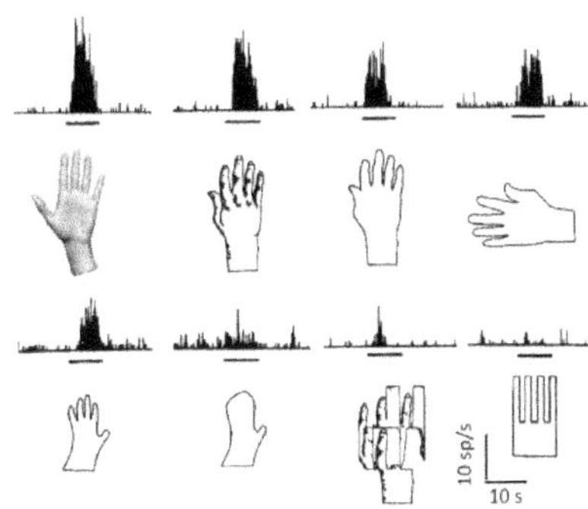

Object recognition by a single neuron. Responses (histograms of spike frequencies vs. time) of a single monkey neuron to the corresponding images, presented during the times indicated by the horizontal black bars. Many distinct elaboration paths clearly converge onto this neuron, which responds to many visual patterns, all related to the shape of a hand through a pictorial or a structural association or generalization. Object detection is tentative, and the discharge rate signals the likelihood that what is seen belongs to a certain conceptual category. [Modified from Gross, 1972]

In the above musical metaphor, if we were able to encode a complex pattern of neuronal activity into audible music, that music would indicate that something has been recognized, i.e. the 'awareness' of something has arisen. To refer to these rudimentary elements of awareness, observed in visual elaboration circuits, Semir Zeki coined the term 'micro-consciousnesses'. Note that if this same metaphor were applied to the auditory system, the "music" played by a neuron would not reproduce the sound that is being heard; it would rather signal a specific feature in the auditory input stream (a note, a chord, a melodic hint, phoneme, a specific sequence of phonemes, a word).

* * *

Detecting, recognizing, interpreting

The occipital-temporal path of visual elaboration is called the 'what pathway,' but elaborations of auditory, somatic and sensory-motor information also converge with this path to contribute to recognize 'objects,' and even to associate and memorize the sound of words (and the shape of written words) to objects. The recognition of objects arises from the capability of each neuron to generate a specific response when the complex activity patterns of many other neurons points to the possible presence of an object. This process of object recognition may be precise and reliable, when the neurons are in discriminative processing mode, or quite tentative and uncertain. In either case, an object is recognized if a neuron (or a set of neurons) specifically reacts to the pattern of neural activity elicited by the object, as if it were *designed to recognize it.*

Although there are neurons innately programmed to recognize specific relevant shapes (squares, circles) in the temporal lobe, for most of the objects that we recognize, this cannot occur by means of innately wired connections.

So, how does the brain become able to 'recognize' objects that the circuits are not initially wired to recognize? The amount of activity converging on a neuron is not as important as the precise way the combination of time-varying synaptic activations interact at each moment on each neuron; in fact, depending on the precise timing of converging synaptic inputs, distinct molecular events may occur and trigger biochemical modifications, in addition to the electrical events.

This may change the efficacy of the synaptic contacts (*long term potentiation* or *depression*) and consequently the way the neuron processes the incoming information. *Plastic* changes occur when specific sequences and time delays in the pattern of activation of neighboring synapses occur and will therefore make a neural circuit capable of recognizing a specific pattern of activity (an object) that it was not originally designed to recognize.

But recognizing objects and learning to identify novel ones means *attributing a meaning to them*. At every moment in our life, the ongoing activity of the cortex impinges on several deep subcortical structures (hypothalamus, amygdala, raphe, ventral tegmental area, nucleus accumbens, substantia nigra, basal forebrain) that evaluate the vital, emotional, hedonic, social and operational relevance of external cues and/or the current experience. The activation of these structures produces visceral-vegetative responses (change in heartbeat, sweating, weeping, shaking...) and changes in posture and facial expression (smiling, looking sad, frightened, angry...) and activates the limbic areas of the cortex that enable emotions (fear, pleasure, grief, rage, hope, disgust...) to be felt and cognitively elaborated by the areas of the cerebral cortex in charge.

Through neuronal plasticity, any novel pattern of neuronal activity, i.e., any unknown element of the current experience, can be associated to existing knowledge: it will receive a cognitive meaning (logical, causal, operational) based on its relations with known elements in the experience (similarity in neuronal activity patterns); it will be attributed a personal meaning (it will be connected with some vital value) based on the emotions associated with such known elements and with the current experience, with its cognitive, affective, social, operative implications (risks, opportunities, possible developments).

This way the circuitry gets to 'know' – and becomes able to detect – the novel elements in the experience, to attribute a meaning to them and to *re*-cognize them in the future. Once more, this process is totally based on the capability of neurons to examine relationships, consistencies, and reciprocal interactions.

A different perspective for each brain

The specific features of neuronal plasticity accounts for two quite relevant consequences: first, in general, the neural circuits change the way they process information in relation to the information itself they elaborate; second, the plastic modifications are intrinsically associative, in that they occur according to the precise spatial and temporal relations (association) among synaptic activations on the neuron.

All this accounts not only for all forms of associative learning (classical, aversive and operant conditioning, procedural learning, associative memory), but also for the fact that each brain elaborates the same information in a different, specific way, based on all the information it has processed up to this moment and – more relevant – the way it has elaborated such information. This is a strong basis for the emergence of *individuality* because of the operating mode itself of neural circuits.

Notice that depression and pruning of synaptic contacts are at least as relevant as long-term potentiation: the number of synapses in the brain markedly decreases in development, and especially so during adolescence. This trims the associative network and makes it so that from the childish generic and mythological perspective we develop the more precise, selective, rigorous and rational adult attitude.

This perspective on neural plasticity suggests a novel way to look not only at individuality but also at neuropsychological disorders.

Biological factors – genetic, developmental, pathological, iatrogenic, acute or chronic – may act directly on neuronal structure, viability, function and connectivity, affecting the function of computational modules in the brain and the higher functions that result from the interactions among such modules.

Conversely, experience influences all aspects of neuronal plasticity, so that most changes that can be produced by biological causes can also be produced by neuronal activity itself, i.e., by experience. This effectively blurs the border between the organic and biological 'Nature' of the self and the psychological 'Nurture' that shapes identity and possibly induces, through experience, psychic disorders that are traditionally considered 'endogenous' or 'organic'.

* * *

The self-centered brain

In addition to being processed along the 'what' pathway, all sensory data are examined in terms of spatial relations, both reciprocal and with respect to the sense organs that captured them. This is a particularly challenging process, because the location of a stimulus perceived by the eyes will be mapped according to gaze direction, auditory stimuli with respect to the head, and somatosensory stimuli with respect to the position of the limb that senses them.

The resulting sensory spatial maps, modality-specific, are collected by the superior colliculus of the midbrain and relayed to the parietal cortex, which puts in register these maps with each other and remaps the stimulus – whatever its sensory origin was – in terms of movement, i.e., the direction to which the gaze, the head, a hand or other appropriate parts of the body are to be directed in order to adequately encounter the stimulus. Such further mapping is bounced back to the superior colliculus, which controls reflex eye and head movement. These reflexes are extremely rapid and are brought about by subcortical structures (colliculus and tectospinal motor system): the cortex would be much slower in reacting.

This is why if a friend quietly comes to your left and touches your right shoulder you turn to the right, rather than toward them (and they think they are so clever…)

This remapping clearly occurs well below the level of consciousness, but it locates the external cues *with respect to the self* and based on mapping *one's own movements* to interact with them.

In the parietal cortex, higher processing of the spatial relations occurs, along the occipital-parietal path (the so-called 'where' pathway): spatial relations and the physical space, as well as any virtual spaces, are analyzed geometrically and mathematically: so, these circuits contribute to elaborate any complex sets of sensory or mental data and generate the idea itself of space, as a set of reciprocal relationships among elements that are simultaneously present.

While in the primary visual cortex the image coming from the retina is projected upside down but maintaining its spatial organization, in the neighboring, associative visual cortices the objects in the surrounding space are no more mapped along Cartesian coordinates (up/down, left/right), but rather according to a polar coordinate system (direction and distance from the origin), i.e., the space is represented *centered on the self*, in a *subjective* perspective.

The capability of the parietal cortex to remap all sensory inputs in the surrounding space, according to a motor map centered on the self, enables these circuits to directly activate premotor areas in charge of programming movements.

There, so-called *canonical neurons* prefigure the movements (reaching, grasping, rejecting) needed to appropriately interact with the identified object ('affordance').

Another set of premotor neurons (the so-called *mirror neurons*) are activated to prefigure an appropriate **aimed** action (a motor act with a purpose) that can be done with the object (moving it, bringing it to the mouth, throwing it away…).

Here, 'appropriate' refers to those interactions that have been positively reinforced during past experiences, since they were successful in achieving an operational aim, possibly producing pleasure or reducing discomfort.

By mapping the visual field according to a spherical coordinate system, the associative visual cortices essentially signal direction and extent of the movement to reach the identified objects, while the parietal cortex maps objects in space predicting possible behaviors to reach for them.

It appears therefore that brain circuits examine and interpret every cue not only in terms of their internal and reciprocal relations, but also in terms of their relations *with one's own body*, and of possible behavioral *interactions* with the cue itself.

* * *

The role of the hippocampus
In this process, the hippocampus plays a crucial role: this ancient structure, in the depth of the temporal lobe, elaborates information about objects and their spatial and functional relations, events and their sequence, according to many possible interpretive paradigms. This way the huge set of mutual spatial relations among objects is transformed into a sensible, contextualized perception of the environment (situation), and the temporal relations among events become connected sequences, possibly causally related (processes).

The result is an integrated, consistent, logically organized and dynamic internal image and interpretation of the external reality and of events and episodes.

Thanks to its great plastic properties, the hippocampus can save these readings and possibly recall them in the future to help analyze and interpret novel situations. In a sense, the hippocampus extracts interpretative paradigms, in analyzing the current sensory information, and saves such paradigms to profitably interpret future experiences. The hippocampus is strongly and bidirectionally connected to the limbic structures (*amygdala* in particular), designed to attribute a vital relevance to the current experience: the memorizing capability of the hippocampus is enhanced whenever the current experience is recognized as emotionally relevant; meanwhile, the hippocampus helps in correctly evaluating possibly relevant clues by contextualizing them into a sensible picture (a lion in a cage needn't elicit fear).

The input from emotion-related subcortical structures affectively colors the internal picture of reality and the current experience, generated by the hippocampus. Thus, the streams of data about objects, reciprocal spatial relations and emotional relevance becomes a comprehensive, integrated, emotionally tinted, vital experience, i.e. a properly *subjective* and *personal* perspective on the current moment of one's life.

This integrated *personal experience* of the current moment, rather than the raw sensory data it was built upon, is relayed back by the hippocampus to cortical areas involved in higher mental functions: we cognitively elaborate, and remember, the way we have (the hippocampus has) personally experienced reality and the episodes of our life, but not what was effectively there and occurring, or what was *objectively* perceived by our senses. In simple words, this integrated personal experience simultaneously constitutes a *state of mind* and an *internal image* of an object, a situation, an episode, a fact/concept.

* * *

And what about time?

Handling time-varying information is crucial for the survival of every organism. However, producing a response in the brain may require several tens of milliseconds (depending on the location in the body that receives the stimulus), and when intense processing is needed to extract significant information, neural circuits may take several hundred ms to perform complex feature extraction and attribute a meaning; similarly, programming and executing motor behaviors require at least tens of ms.

This may not seem particularly relevant, as in normal life one usually does not care about being late by possibly half a second... But if one sees how a lizard manages to catch a fly, it becomes clear that a huge problem for the nervous system is to be able to compute and compensate for the delay that separates sensing from acting: a fly typically flies at up to 5 mph, i.e., about 2 m/s, which means that a delay of 10 ms will make the lizard miss the fly by 2 cm: not much, but enough to never catch it. Independent of the complexity of the brain, an animal that can detect an object (e.g., a prey) and move to get in contact with it needs to be able to 'model' what is happening: it does not have information to reproduce what is actually occurring in this precise moment, due to the delay in receiving and elaborating sensory information, and any movement it might want to do must already have been programmed and commanded in advance, and will only be sensed and reported by proprioceptive circuits with a significant delay.

So, the neural circuits must be able to extrapolate available sensory information (which can only be processed with a delay) and anticipate movement, i.e., to build a model of the current instant that makes the animal capable of interfering with external objects – with external reality – in real time. A mathematical **model** of reality must be concocted, based on extrapolation and anticipation, rather than accurate knowledge and representation.

A clever machine

Imagine having to write a program to drive a tennis ball machine, which in addition to pitching must also be able to catch the ball hit back by the player.

The program will have to include an algorithm to record perceptual information (P-algorithm). With a video camera and reasonable several-gigaHertz CPU, there is no practical delay in the depiction of reality.

Still, a movement path must be designed to get the machine there in time to catch the ball, and this must be done sufficiently in advance to take into account delays due to the inertia of the machine; this also requires that the P-algorithm includes some predictive capability.

Even if a precise action computation (A-algorithm) is performed, some impediments might arise (or a small error, or some unpredicted or hidden factor might have not been considered).

It would be good to check the correctness of the predictions as well as the accuracy of the movement, on the fly.

The prediction can be corrected, as can the motor program, but corrections in the P domain do not imply actions while corrections in the A domain do.

It is therefore clear that the two algorithms must behave differently, so that a computational construct must emerge in the elaboration, which differentiates the P-algorithm, that maps onto a "R=reality" domain that cannot be controlled by the program, from the A-algorithm, that maps onto a "I=identity" domain on which it does have control.

A "P=perceptual" domain and an "A=agency" domain, as well as an "R=reality" domain and an "I=identity" domain emerge in the model with no need for any awareness.

If the machine were also to take note of what happens, nobody would claim that the machine is able to consciously *experience what is happening; still, something equivalent to the* cognitive *component of consciousness would take place – producing a representation of what is happening – and such representation would necessarily involve a distinction between the "P" and "A" algorithms, and between the "R" and "I" domains.*

This thought experiment could be made slightly more complex if instead of catching a ball the problem were to intercept an asteroid in space, say 3,000 km away: the task would be similar, but a delay would also be needed in the P algorithm (about 10 ms for the path the light has to travel).

This would reproduce what happens in a nervous system, which receives sensory information with a macroscopically relevant delay (20 ms correspond to an error >10 cm for an object that travels at 20 km/h).

In this framework, both the depiction of reality and the programming of actions require that delays be considered, but in this case as well the two domains must be treated differentially.

* * *

The emergence of 'identity'

Modeling is an intrinsic skill of nervous systems; it helps make sense of the external reality, by identifying objects, examining their mutual relations, and conjecturing their possible relevance. In addition to this, computational networks must be able to extract fundamental coherent rules about what happens out there, so that future positions of moving objects and the consequences of motor commands can be extrapolated.

Identity, as the capability of differentiating what is self from what is not, is based on two properties of living organisms: the richness of sensory receptors in the body of animals, and the somatic marker of emotions. Even unicellular organisms have receptors on the surface of their membrane; so, there is an objective distinction between anything that stays or occurs outside of the organism, and what gets in contact with it. The "self" is identically and inevitably distinct from the external reality, although sensory systems also produce internal changes in monitoring external ones. In multicellular organisms that can react with movement, an analytical system is needed to *realize* this distinction (and to *conceptualize* it): neural circuits must be intrinsically able to recognize whether some neural activity arises from external stimuli or from internal activities, and differentially handle information about external events or one's own movement. Notice that this must occur as a computational process, with no need for it to become a *mental construct*, unless a sufficiently complex neuronal network is there, sufficiently trained; in fact even human newborns cannot appropriately distinguish their own body parts from external objects, until they effectively learn this, exactly because the body generates sensations.

Every living system possesses biophysical and biochemical mechanisms that produce a response when something relevant to survival, to the maintenance of homeostasis, to well-being, occurs and is sensed. If the organism is endowed with a nervous system, any sensation that has this kind of relevance will produce a change in the mode of operation of the nervous system: an increase in vigilance, arousal, reactivity, to a variable extent; responses might be accelerated; freezing, escape, fight, or consummatory, aggressive, predatory behaviors might be elicited.

We may wish to call these changes in the mode of operation of the nervous system "pain", "fear", "rage", "pleasure", or prefer to preserve these words to indicate the emotions (*feelings*) of an animal with a sufficiently developed brain, but we must acknowledge their existence. To account for these phenomena, an implicit model must be built of the interaction of the self with the external objects: it ought to be the most consistent model of what is happening, and it is verified ex post, based on the result of behavior. Success or failure will train the computational modules, by producing plastic changes in the involved neurons and synapses. In building such model, however, two computational domains must be generated: a *perceptual* (P) domain, which accounts for the external reality, and is affected by a variable delay (lag); and a motor control, *action* (A) domain, which handles behavior, and must operate in advance by a variable time-lapse (lead).

The *perceptual* domain is characterized by the possible interaction among sensory modalities: if an animal can see its own body, visual and somatosensory concurrence will signal that something occurs when a part of the body of the animal encounters an external object, and something different occurs when it encounters another part of its own body. So, there exists a part of the world that has properties distinct from all the rest, because it gives rise to sensation, and a self vs. non-self distinction is required to model reality, even in the roughest mode.

One may still claim that such sophisticated modeling is not needed if no consciousness is there. However, even stronger need for a distinction between self and non-self arises from the computational requirement in dealing with the temporal dynamics of the two domains: what pertains to the former (*perceptual* domain) and is not static, must be processed to extrapolate from past information what may be the situation at this precise moment, whereas the elaboration in the latter (*action* domain) must consider the need to plan and give motor commands in advance.

Also, whatever is elaborated in the *action* domain will produce a reverberation in the *perceptual* domain, after an appropriate time delay, when one's own movement are perceived through proprioception and the action that is being performed and its consequences are observed.

Whether a brain has a 'consciousness' function that can tell it, or not, a time lag and a difference in the possibility of control separates the two domains of neuronal activity and must be considered to MODEL, and appropriately INTERACT with, the external world.

This constitutes a computational and logical basis of *identity*, which therefore emerges as a *computational construct*, necessary for any nervous system which is asked to interact with external reality in real time.

This construct must permeate the activity of any brain, even a bee's brain, whether *awareness* of such *identity* is there or not.

The emergence of 'agency'

Agency, as the capability of realizing that one is the subject of one's own sensations, emotions and thoughts, and the agent of one's own acts, is a much more complex function, but it must be present, at least in some rudimentary, implicit form, for any animal that is able to elaborate a behavioral strategy, in hunting, fighting and generally in interacting with other animals or objects. In fact, a further crucial consequence of the abovementioned computational duality consists in the fact that motor commands produce perceivable consequences.

Many neurotransmitters and mechanisms of potentiation or depression of synaptic contacts are associated with success or failure of the action; this results in either positive reinforcement or weakening, i.e., plastic changes in the neuronal networks that account for the capability of modifying behavior, based on success or failure of previous actions; this leads to the accumulation of heuristics that will guide behavior in a successful way. Computationally, this requires that an IMPLICIT CAUSAL CONNECTION be assumed between behavior (one's own actions) and the events and sensations that follow. The computational construct of *identity* combined with the detection of a causal connection between motor control and consequent changes in the outside reality generates another *computational construct*, *agency*, as a causal relation between the temporally separated domains of motor control and perception.

So, in modeling interaction with the external world neuronal networks display the capability of handling delays in sensory elaboration and time lead in motor programming. This way two computational domains must be dealt with (perception vs. motor control) on two distinct time scales. This, combined with somatosensory information, and with the proprioception that follows movement, gives rise to the emergence of *identity* as a computational construct. The heuristic selection of behaviors based on reinforcement and neuronal plasticity establishes causal relations between motor control and the results of actions. This gives rise in a similar way to the emergence of *agency* as a second computational construct.

All this comes about with no need for any form of *awareness*.

And this is quite curious, because one would naively think that *identity* and *agency* are cognitive dimensions that arise from – and certainly do not precede – consciousness.

Instead, the computational constructs of *identity* and *agency* must be there to build a working model of reality.

Only if a brain is capable to put together a sufficiently complex model of reality and the self may these computational constructs evolve into criteria to cognitively interpret reality and one's own sensations, emotions, actions, thus significantly contributing to the emergence of awareness and self-consciousness.

FROM COMA TO ECSTASY - Consciousness

Consciousness. What an uncertain and multiple word!
It is one of those things that all of us know, but that each of us knows and interprets in their own way.

The question here is not about conscience as an ethical compass (the word is the same in some languages), the interior voice, the perception of what is right, the spiritual version of Freud's super-ego, but about consciousness as awareness, seeing and feeling oneself living, thinking, acting.

Still, one may think of consciousness as a property of a creature – it is there or not; or as a state – awake as opposed to asleep or in a coma; or as a degree of alertness, vigilance, attention, responsiveness; or as a function – the process of transforming implicit impressions into a precise and lucid experience; or such lucid experience itself and the possibility of reporting it – *awareness*; finally, one may refer to "meta-awareness", the consciousness of being conscious.

We could try and measure the 'degree of consciousness'.

Some would propose it is a question of how awake, present we are, and therefore attentive, rapid and precise in our reactions. The point is not this: it may be a good answer for our unbearable high-school teacher, who believed that every time we abandoned him to his mumble-jumble we were falling asleep, whereas those were often the moments of most intense consciousness in the whole morning, immersed, swept by and carried away by memories, dreams and desires, betrayed love, sadness and joy of fight and reconciliation...

A more objective measure would be the degree of activation (electro-encephalographically measured activity) of the multimodal associative regions of the cerebral cortex. There, where different kinds of information converge, where the many readings of reality meet and are compared. Indeed, it should be so. What use is it to be aware of a color, shape, outline, object, of a relationship in the images we gather from the world, if not to put all this in relation with what we already know, recall, feel, wish, so that it resonates in many brain circuits, thereby acquiring a meaning, an interpretation, a possible role in our life?

On the other hand, most of this activity – relating, harmonizing, giving meaning, comparing, interpreting – continuously goes on in our brain, while it only occasionally emerges to consciousness. Below the surface, visible if you look for it, but not necessarily present, relevant, important.

So, though consciousness as measured by the EEG reflects mental activity, it may not be correlated with awareness and what we would consider properly 'conscious' processing. Or, we may consider that consciousness includes all our mental activities, independent of the degree of attention we dedicate to them, and therefore how 'aware' we are of them.

Associative regions can deal with information that comes from outside – images, sounds, objects, events, words – or with memories, emotions, feelings, projects, ideas that bubble in the brain. In all cases, the impression is that the degree of awareness is strictly linked to two specific aspects: on one hand how intense this re-elaboration activity is – whatever be its object – and on the other hand how much this frenetic activity is under 'our' control, how much 'we' look at it and guide it.

In spite of all we have said up to here, the fundamental fracture seems to stand up once more: who is this *we?* sure, the brain simmers with the most sophisticated elaborative capacities, and intellective mathematical logics, but there seems to be always an internal eye, an ego, a spirit, who watches, pays attention to what it is interested in, in all this activity; and we are 'aware' of what this eye is focused on...

A large gap seems to be there. We can accept that brain circuits have the elaborative capacity needed to recognize unity-multiplicity, before-after, cause-effect, greater-smaller, sequences, cardinality, order, periodicity and structures, to compute, to build meanings and symbols, to perceive space as a set of relationships even in the absence of objects among which to detect them, to generate virtual spaces and to perceive time as a flux, a story, a tale, even to speak.

Brain circuits perform most of the functions that Kant proposed to be the product of the transcendent activity of a metaphysical intellect. But it is more difficult to locate that internal conscious eye, which at any moment decides what 'we' want to care about.

So, let us look in better detail at how the cortex works.

* * *

The eye sends sequences of images to the cortex, and the latter analyzes them as such, but it also drives the eye to follow the outlines, to pause on details and trace and 'draw' the images; it links and coordinates sequences of images to recognize objects that move, or just change their shape, dimension, color...

The cortical circuitry can collect, analyze and synthesize, and re-elaborate, compare, follow in time: it is an unconscious and complicated process of focus shifting, approaching and moving back, changing angle and viewpoint.

This process is easy to deceive because it follows precise elaboration rules on which we do not intervene consciously: how many optical illusions have been created that make one see straight lines as bent, that deceive the observer on the relative size of objects, images that seem to move where nothing does, profiles that change meaning...

Similarly, the auditory cortex is capable of recognizing the presence of phonemes in the flow of sounds and continuously reorganizes such phonemes – often we even miss some of them because of other interfering noises and we do not even realize it – combining them in various ways to form possible words.

It proposes a verbal interpretation coherent with what has been perceived, and can rewind and change the whole interpretation in a moment, when the next phoneme is recognized: here the question is not the meaning of the sentence, it is just the recognition of the words; still, these regions keep talking with other ones that look for the meaning of what we hear, and suggestions arise about what may follow, which helps a lot to recognize – or, often, to misunderstand – the next incoming phonemes...

More 'elevated' or 'eclectic' cortical regions – composite and multimodal – combine these chunks of information (that are no longer merely 'sensory' but more abstract, conceptual), looking for assonances and dissonances, relationships with emotional feelings, physiological needs and motivational drives.

Once again the elaboration is based on examining these aspects of information one by one, and then all together, or again in a sequence, paying attention to one aspect or another, or to a precise combination, as if freely navigating in this sea of information, rather than orderly examining data; precisely this process, with all its aspects of uncertainty, multiplicity and variability, brings to the threshold of *consciousness* a bundle of perceptions that correspond to an event, a concept, an *idea*...

Consciousness blooms from this analysis, simultaneous and multiple, like a path in search of coherence and objectives that continually gets lost on single details and relations, and changes its way, attracted by unexpected evocations; it blooms as a glance, aware of oneself and of the world: once more a synthesis and unification of multiplicities.

There is no *spirituality* in recognizing – by examining several elements in succession and then all together – spatial relations, before/after links, order, hierarchies, or the confluence of events into a sequence, into a story, possibly with its own meaning and emotional valence.

Neither is there any *spirituality* in the capacity of a neuronal circuitry to examine an enormous amount of data altogether and shifting 'attention' (processing by higher circuits) now on one aspect and then on another one, to compare them and neglect what is not relevant, and to reconcile what has been elaborated with all other available information. But this is exactly the way consciousness works: perceiving, recognizing, and interpreting the results of the many elaborations that various cerebral regions simultaneously perform, examining them and reconciling them in groups, in a sequential and variable manner, until 'explanations' can be extracted or, even better, a single explanation arises, consistent albeit continually evolving. The general picture is that of a hierarchy of neuronal circuits: each system utilizes all elaborations produced at any moment by 'lower' systems and extracts relevant aspects and coherent readings by *navigating* among these partial elaborations.

This process of information evaluation is sophisticated and appears to follow the same general scheme all over: a specific relevance must be attributed to each piece of information, and each must be put in relation and conciliated with the other ones that are similarly relevant; the aim is to achieve at any moment the 'answer', or better the 'reading', that the system can offer to higher systems, which will have to relate it to the many readings proposed by other systems, so widening the perspective.

In this picture, the last step is a comprehensive 'reading' of reality, external and internal, of the world, of oneself, of history and the future, a reading that changes at any moment as the eye explores what is in front of it, by changing its viewpoint, focus, aim or interest. It really is an exploration, in the strictest sense, a continuous action, a story that evolves inside oneself, and consciousness is the development itself of this story. It is an exploration to which the enormous power of symbolic systems – gestures, tones, codes, internal or expressed languages, acting, speaking, drawing, writing, virtually or actually – adds the possibility of becoming a tale. A tale that one lives as an actor but also as the spectator and narrator, as an internal eye, as a spirit, as a consciousness.

* * *

Would you believe your own consciousness?

Can we ever fully believe what someone tells us about themselves?
Perhaps they are quite sincere, but how can we be sure their self-image is really accurate?
And why should we even believe that asking consciousness about itself would give credible and reliable answers?

Well, this is what Benjamin Libet attempted to find an answer to, forty years ago, pioneering a plethora of similar experiments, and provoking a never-ending debate on their interpretation, as well as whether they do or do not have any relevance to the question of free will.

Essentially, Libet reported that an electroencephalographic (EEG) signal could be recorded when a subject decided to push a button, and that this signal preceded the moment the subject was aware of their decision by a fraction of a second.

How is that possible? And how would you be able to measure that, anyway?

Libet's experiment was quite ingenious. Subjects were asked to push a button whenever they wished. The instant they decided to push the button (the "will time"), they would make a mental note of the position of a dot that was rapidly rotating in the face of a clock.

Meanwhile, an EEG was recorded. In the EEG, a preparatory signal (named "BP") could be recorded about 550 ms before the onset of the movement itself, indicating that the brain was initiating the activity to produce a movement. The time of the conscious decision to move, the "will-time" (W-time) as reported by the subjects, followed this signal by several hundred ms.

Libet's result was confirmed by many scientists who repeated the experiment, either identically or with some variations.

Much ado, then, ensued in the academic community: if one's brain makes an unconscious decision by itself, before a conscious decision is made, then the whole philosophical problem of free will must be revisited and reframed (that's if free will plays a part in this at all). The staunch reductionist scientists were overjoyed at finally being able to claim that the brain did all the work and consciousness just rocked up a few tenths of a second later to take the merit, but actually to just take note of something the brain had already decided on its own. Some pompous philosophers chose to look down on these 'technicians', mere measurers of electrical events, and who dared think this entitled them to speak about consciousness, or even free will. The neuroscientists, themselves, took to reproducing the experiment, changing some details in the hope that the result would be different.

And us mere mortals? Well, we simply puzzled and doubted as to whether those experiments had any true relevance with respect to free will, personal responsibility, and accountability.

Hence, back to our question: What would we expect from a self-report by our own consciousness? Could we really consider it remotely trustworthy?

First of all, we should use the word 'consciousness' with care. If we consider it the function of specifying and selecting unconscious, implicit mental activities and contents, to distill from them unambiguous, meaningful, explicit, and usable (possibly reportable) information, it can essentially be seen as the capability of building a consistent model of reality by putting together a coherent picture of what is around and of the current experience. But perhaps that's where the problem lies.

Because the information available to consciousness is far from consistent.

Imagine the action of hitting a baseball. The ball is travelling at more than 90 mph (about 40 m/s) and the delay with which we consciously perceive what we see is in the order of half a second, which is the time needed for the brain circuits to elaborate the visual information, identify and localize the objects out there, and generate an internal representation of what is going on. But this means that the moment the ball encounters the bat we still see it travelling about 20 m away!

Meanwhile, to be able to hit the ball, our movement must have started some 10 ms before the impact; but it must have been programmed even before that, as activity in the supplementary motor area, the region of the cortex that programs movements, typically starts some 100 ms before the initiation of movement. Following which, we must wait about half a second to consciously see the bat hitting the ball and to perceive (a) proprioceptive sensations that inform us about the muscle movements and (b) the somatosensory perception of the impact of the ball on the bat.

Given this set of inconsistencies, what would our consciousness tell Dr. Libet and his colleagues about this scenario?

If consciousness were a sincere creature, it would confess to being very confused, because in the moment it was hit, the ball seemed to be still travelling, some 20 meters away; it would say that it had decided to swing about a tenth of a second back, and initiated the movement right away, but that it was not feeling the muscles moving yet, although the cerebellum kept insisting everything was proceeding as programmed; and it would say that it was not surprised it did not see the ball being hit and did not feel the shock, but it knew what was going on, and at that precise time it had already issued the motor commands to refine the final part of the swing, to be sure to properly direct the ball...

No, consciousness cannot be sincere: it does not have the information in time; it must concoct a model of what may be going on and believe that the model exactly tells what is happening.

So, most probably consciousness would not tell the truth: it would claim that it decided to swing in the exact moment the brain gave the 'go' signal to the programmed movement and the swing started; and it would add that it saw the bat hitting the ball, and perceived the impact, in the same precise instant it occurred, while the bat was swinging. Although none of this is true.

We sometimes 'decide' to do something, but we may change our mind at the last moment. Wouldn't the true moment of the decision be that 'last moment', after which a movement cannot be aborted anymore? Interestingly, such a 'last moment' is close to the "will-time", suggesting that the preparatory activity recorded several ms earlier did not represent the moment of the final decision.

Hence, consciousness may be correct in locating the W-time, but the rest of its account is just hot air.

The point is that one of the main functions of consciousness as a process appears to consist in generating a mental construct - the concept of 'now' — as a totally arbitrary time coincidence between sensory information that must be extrapolated from a delayed recorder; intention to move (be it conscious or not) that must have preceded the event; the actual movement; and seeing oneself moving and perceiving the movement, which will occur a moment later.

Should we be surprised if, in reproducing Libet's experiment with some tricks that interfere with motor programming, or with sensory or proprioceptive feedback, the reports about the time of decision-to-move (will-time) were to change?

In conclusion, whatever Libet's experiment claims to measure, it relies on a subjective report by an information processing system – consciousness as we defined it above – that is designed to manipulate the times of sensory inputs, motor programming, movement initiation and movement monitoring to generate the illusional perception of a phantomatic 'now' moment in which intention, sensation and movement coincide.

Libet's experiment just measures how, under the particular conditions tested, consciousness does or does not manage to put in register the temporal tags of what it examines. It tells us nothing about free will and it tells us nothing about consciousness itself, except recording experimentally what the consciousness itself reports about the way it imagines it is working. Because the function of consciousness is exactly this: to imagine what reality is and deceive you into believing that it is true, just because this way it appears reasonably consistent…

Yet something does come to light: it confirms that the brain is an amazing machine that can precisely figure out what is happening out there, even though it has not yet received essential information.

Rest assured, the brain does happen to be wrong sometimes, and every so often it also misinterprets, but how can you blame it? You can only admire its tricks in playing with time, like a magician who pulls a rabbit out of a top hat which has yet to be put in the hat …

[from https://academic.oup.com/brain/article/147/3/740/7617475]

* * *

Still, even though the brain can be actor and spectator and narrator of our lives, so clever that it even understands what is going on in this magic way, this does not preclude thinking that something more is there, that there is another world beyond this, and the soul, over there, looks at this tale and lives it but also adds something else.

Something else, however; not this. Not the capacity of building and narrating our life, of suffering imagining dreaming, desiring, creating, getting committed, sacrificing oneself, loving. *Something else.*

* * *

By now we should agree that the activity of the nervous system is partly related to the generation of responses to stimuli – and this is perhaps the most material, the simplest part – but the continuous work of the brain mostly departs from this need of analyzing stimuli and producing responses; rather, it generates and maintains, it nourishes and develops other domains of life, logical, cognitive, affective, emotional, creative.

Thus, the whole approach to the study of the complex function of the nervous system must be revised. The relationship with the external world, with material reality, and the elaboration of appropriate responses to stimuli, is but an aspect of the multiple and extremely vast vital activity of our brain.

Interestingly enough, disengaging from elaborating the stimuli and responding to them is usually looked at as retiring and closing the psyche in itself. Rather than a closure, couldn't it be more appropriate to consider such disconnection an evasion from the narrow domain of a daily, biological, vegetative and ordinary burden? It is as if, by diverting from the humble job of elaborating adequate responses to stimuli, the soul could finally look out the window to see the world, its own world, reality as it appears in the soul, to the soul itself.

Sure, not a new idea, this one of a window that overlooks the world, and reality, from its own viewpoint, individual and irreproducible, specific for each thinking being. Looking at it this way, it appears there should be no possibility of communication or sharing, of any universal reality to agree on, because each one sees and elaborates a different portion of the world with a different glance.

An idea, this one of the incommunicability among monads, that certainly is not weakened by the difficulties we face every single day to have people who live near us understand what is important for us, *how* we would like to be appreciated and loved [*how*, yes, not only how much...], *how* we should like to be and to love.

But I really think that the metaphor should be overturned.

We are no monads who *look out* the window to see the world. We are connected to the outside world by stimuli, sensations and nerves, this is true, but the brain is traversed by innumerable complex activities that expand – partly by proceeding autonomously, partly by facing and conciliating one another – in a thousand material and immaterial domains: sensory information is only a small part of all this internal world. Sometimes the monad, the brain, can turn precisely to that small part, and open that particular window *within itself.* A window through which sensations that arrive from reality let us look at the world and this way *go back* to – into – the world.

It is not so far from reality, this overturned view. An interior life with infinite spaces and dimensions, of which the window that looks at the perceivable reality is only a small bit.

That window, in the brain, is the *thalamus*.

* * *

All sensory information, from the outside as well as from inside the body, must somehow arrive at the cerebral cortex. It gets there by two main pathways:
- the region where the spinal cord enters the skull (brainstem: medulla, pons and midbrain) displays a crowded network of neurons (the so-called reticular substance) where all sensory information is handled and bounced. This region produces many integrated responses, but through its direct connection with the cortex it also modulates the activation of the latter, rather than sending any specific information. Quite essential activity, though, as in its absence a coma ensues, a situation incompatible with the production of cognitive activities. Only in the presence of this diffuse stimulation by the reticular substance does the cortex work and elaborate
- precise information however does not reach the cortex through this path, but rather after being filtered, analyzed and integrated by all interposed processing stations, and after a final stage at the *thalamus*, which orderly distributes each specific sensory information – and in general each different kind of input – to the appropriate cortical areas.

Through the reticular substance of the brainstem all incoming stimuli maintain the cortex active; through the thalamus they offer the brain matter to be elaborated.

If the thalamus transmits the incoming signals, the cortex can assemble and live its readings, interpretations and metaphors, nourished by the information arriving from the senses; otherwise, it is 'free' to play with the products of its own activity, continuously and restlessly re-elaborated: in a sense, detached from the world. It is what happens when we sleep, and we dream. It partly happens in half-asleep states, when external stimuli arrive damped, deformed and contaminated by the unpredictable pathways of our fantasies; it is like when during a class we lose the thread, when facing a boring conference our mind involuntarily runs away, and having forgot what the matter is, almost half-asleep, we start following the infinite paths of our fantasy.

* * *

The thalamus then truly is a window. But it is a window that keeps us *in the world*, focused on reality, instead of letting us evade into the ether of our mental activities; and when it is closed, instead, it lets us *out*, carried away by all other dimensions and metaphors of reality and life that keep wandering around in our head. Like Peter Pan's window. His window is shut, and he is *out*, he can only care about himself, no contact with the world, he is confined to Neverland, *out* of the world...

The disconnection from the world, disconnection of cerebral processing from sensory information and influence, from the specific task of producing appropriate responses to external stimuli, is often referred to as 'closing within oneself'. Curiously enough, from the viewpoint of the brain this is rather closing oneself out. Or rather opening to the outside, where those that we call fools stay, and where poets wander. Out, where sailors are, who navigate offshore and do not long for wider horizons, but for monsters and storms horrible enough to make them forget the fear of coming back and possibly finding their windows closed...

Still, one can stay outside without remaining trapped.

When we are awake, when the window that leads back into the world is open, those cerebral activities that produce the many 'dimensions and metaphors of reality and life' that keep wandering around in our head are not switched off. They may occupy a larger or smaller portion of our conscious and rational activity, and one may happen to stay out *as well*, at least for a while, while one looks at the world and reacts to the stimuli.

The most fascinating aspect of consciousness is the fact that each of us not only perceives – and interprets – reality, but also clearly perceives their own perceiving reality and themselves. Meta... This is why the monad is an inadequate image: the world, reality, is only a small part of what we know, we can look at it from outside and from above, and we ourselves are so much greater, that we can see, from outside and above, ourselves watching reality from outside and above...

We are universes that also peep *into* the world. We may find it difficult to communicate in the world because of different viewpoints, glances and approaches, but we may also meet – and miss and find each other again – not only in the world but *outside the world*, in logical, creative, emotional, esthetic, affective harmonies and dialogues. We can connect with the artist through their colors, shapes and volumes, with the poet through the music and the rhythm of their words...

Maybe it is precisely because of this that we have such a clear perception that everyone of us is made of a body and of something else, which is not body, which may well be physically within the body, but in a thousand dimensions, other than the material one, is outside, is over, is *other* than and beyond the body.

Something that has always been called *soul*, something that communicates with worlds and metaphors that resemble itself and the staff it is made on, beyond the borders of matter, *such stuff as dreams are made on.*

X
WHAT IS IT LIKE TO SEE RED? – The 'hard problem'

So, it seems that after so much talking about neurons we have come back to the idea that something in us is *other* than and beyond the body.

David Chalmers seemed to pin down the problem by claiming that for neuroscientists there are two kinds of problems, about consciousness.

There is an 'easy' problem, that can be addressed through experimental approaches and may well lead to our precisely understanding which structures are involved in each step of the onset of conscious experiences, what informational processes account for the content of consciousness, what structures and transmitters are implied in sustaining each of its objective features and properties.

But a 'hard' problem would remain unsolved: how a physical system such as the brain can generate a conscious experience, transform the activation of sensory systems into a personal, private, subjective (in the end metaphysical) experience.

The question involves philosophical as well as neuroscientific aspects: on the one side we may speculate what consciousness is, how it arises, what is conscious and what it is not; on the other side we may investigate what neural activities underlie it, how its presence can be determined in a person, what is the role of the frontal areas and selective attention in gaining awareness of a sensory activation, and so on.

Most students accept the idea that a 'phenomenal' and an 'access' consciousness can be discerned; the former would refer to the genesis of the conscious activity, through the transformation of sensations into personal and private 'experiences'; the latter would instead concern the possibility for awareness to address such material and focus attention on it. Access consciousness functioning would be the object of the 'easy' problem, while phenomenal consciousness would constitute the 'hard' problem.

However, this distinction is not as neat as it is claimed to be.

The term 'phenomenal consciousness' comes from Husserl and his theory, phenomenology, in which the encounter between reality and a sentient subject was analyzed; it is somewhat of an oxymoron, because 'phenomenon' should refer to something (reality) showing itself (φαίνομαι), which suggests a passive spectator, while 'consciousness' intrinsically implies an active, conscious subject elaborating it.

The oxymoron is powerful in suggesting that such a prodigy stems from the clash between the *physical* stimulus (generated by *physical* reality) that acts *physically* on the perceiving subject, and the *active metaphysical* response of the subject's consciousness.

In this perspective it is not at all clear whether consciousness was there a priori, as an empty vessel to be filled with content, a spotlight to be pointed to some target, or it arises during the process, in the form of phenomenal consciousness: in phenomenology, consciousness is an 'intentional' act (in the strict sense of in-tending, tending toward), so necessarily oriented toward an object: the point was that there cannot be consciousness that is not 'consciousness OF' something.

Whether a philosophical standpoint is chosen or a neuroscientific one, consciousness cannot be looked at as a black-or-white story: the philosopher should differentially classify, epistemologically, the distinct degrees of awareness, accessibility, and precision of mental contents, while the neuroscientist should try and determine the corresponding sites, modes and properties of neural activity.

The hard problem and Descartes' heredity.

Chalmer's approach obviously arises from a dualistic philosophical perspective, i.e., from the idea that thought, consciousness, subjectivity, necessarily pertain to a metaphysical domain, separated from the mechanistic properties of matter and physical systems.

On the other hand, neuroscience has done little to dismount this perspective.

In fact, in the face of this argument, most neuroscientists have dismissed it, as a product of an untenable dualistic perspective – untenable because there is no reasonable way to explain how an immaterial entity could communicate with the brain. To bypass this aspect some students have been calling into play quantum mechanics and the possibility of an action at distance with no contact, or electromagnetic fields generated by the rapid and ordered rearrangement of large polymeric proteins, as if introducing something we do not understand could recreate the halo of mystery that scientific discoveries keep thinning.

Other neuroscientist simply concluded that no such 'hard problem' exists, because once we manage to explain how consciousness WORKS, no conceptual gap remains to be filled.

It seems that something stands in the way of a solid scientific approach to the question. Dennet gave a name to this obstacle: Cartesian materialism.

Though many scientists reject Descartes' idea of an immaterial soul interacting with the body, in most cases they suggest that unconscious mental contents are transformed into conscious material by the 'working memory system', or by a 'higher order thought', or by 'being broadcasted in the global neuronal workspace'. In other words, the idea of a thinking entity – be it some physical system or process instead of a metaphysical thing – that observes what the brain projects on a screen, and issues commands, still constitutes a powerful image in common thought.

One may ask why this image is still so powerful. The main reason probably is that we keep thinking of the brain as a system that depicts, represents, or reproduces reality... and this sentence inevitably end in: ... so that we (a consciousness, a higher order thought) can grasp it, interpret it, react to it.

As long as the brain is seen as a system that depicts and represents reality, the epistemological and ontological conundrum of consciousness is not going to be solved.

In fact, there will always be the need for someone or something (a physical homunculus looking at the sensory cortices, an immaterial entity located in the pineal gland, or the central executive of working memory in the frontal lobe) that looks at this representation, interprets it and experiences it: this is the Cartesian heredity we seem unable to shed, as denounced by Dennet.

In nineteen-ninety-eight, neuroscientist Christof Koch took on Chalmers' challenge to solve the 'hard problem' of consciousness and bet that in 25 years the problem would have been solved. A few months back – 25 years gone by – he had to bring Chalmers a carton of champagne. This is because neuroscience did make a lot of progress in the meanwhile, and several interesting theories have been put forward about the neural substrate of consciousness, but even the most appreciated ones seem to essentially explain what kind of activity must be there for the brain to produce consciousness, rather than why and how such activity would produce consciousness.

The Global Workspace Theory (GWT) proposes that a neural content is made conscious when it is broadcasted in the 'global neuronal workspace' (GNW). But why would that make it *conscious*?

The alternative theory, Integrated Information Theory (IIT) pushes this perspective further in a rigorous conceptual frame: the presence and the intensity of consciousness depend on the complexity of the information elaboration process, which in turn depends on the interplay and integration between local processing and global elaboration.

Consciousness identically is complex, integrated information: the more complex and integrated (and information rich), the more conscious.

However, neither theory goes beyond the description of how a content of brain processing becomes conscious, or explain *why* this produces a conscious, personal, private experience.

A simple translation of the 'hard problem' is expressed by the question 'what is it like to experience something?': what is it like to see red? you cannot explain it to a blind person, you cannot communicate the feeling, you can only have the other person undergo the same experience (which by the way may not be possible), and even if you do so you are not certain that they would feel exactly what you feel…

The first step in facing Chalmers challenge should be to disentangle the sequential steps involved in the generation of a conscious experience, that Chalmers lumped into a mere process of cognitive representation of reality – the 'easy' problem of consciousness – separated from the mystery of the ultimate step, 'the hard problem', the transformation of such representation into a personal, private and qualitative experience.

In this perspective, introducing some immaterial entity that reads the conscious representation and feels, judges and reacts seems inevitable.

But a misconception is hidden in this entire line of thought, as in Chalmers' view such immaterial entity is involved from the first step of sensation – and so is phenomenal consciousness.

* * *

The specificity of living systems

A machine can _SENSE_: it may have *sensors* and signal processing devices that detect and carry information from the outside to the central processing unit. This process is called 'SENSING'; it does not imply consciousness; let's refer to this strict meaning with small capitals: SENSATION; no consciousness needed to SENSE.

A machine can _ENCODE_: if the machine has a computational capability, the *sensed* stimulus can be translated to an internal code (e.g. binary code for a computer) that makes it possible to analyze it, extract features, detect similarities, and essentially interpret it; no consciousness needed to ENCODE.

A machine can _RESPOND_: the machine may produce a direct reaction when it *senses* a stimulus, through a direct mechanical or electronic connection, the same way as the spinal circuitry generates the myotatic reflex when the neurologist hits the patellar tendon; no consciousness needed to RESPOND.

A machine can identify (_PERCEIVE_): a machine may have mechanisms, memory banks and algorithms that allow it to detect and interpret relations and patterns, so that it can recognize and identify specific entities by analyzing the stream of _sensed_ and _encoded_ data; it might therefore signal the presence of specific objects or events (for example detect a bolt on a treadmill and check whether it is correctly built and undamaged); in a sense the machine _perceives_ the presence / occurrence of a specific object, although the process does not imply consciousness.

The small capital term PERCEPTION will be used in this restricted meaning: detecting, interpreting, identifying; no consciousness needed to PERCEIVE.

A machine cannot _EXPERIENCE_.

At least as far as currently available machines are concerned, they do not have the capability of generating a private, personal EXPERIENCE based on these processes of SENSING and PERCEIVING. They cannot perform the step that the term 'phenomenal consciousness' refers to. This is the reason we believe that 'consciousness' does not apply to a machine (at least as of now); thus, _sensing_, encoding and PERCEIVING, as defined here, do occur, but they precede the possible onset of consciousness. In particular (this is where Chalmer's is misled) phenomenal consciousness has no role in SENSING or PERCEIVING.

From SENSING to EXPERIENCE

The way the perception of painful stimuli is discussed in physiology clearly illustrates the usefulness of employing distinct terms, with clearly different meanings, for the various processes in this sequence.

Many factors can be noxious, i.e., they are able to damage living tissues: excessive heat or cold, excessively high or low pH, excessive pressure, stretch or strain, chemicals that signal cell death or inflammation.

Nerve terminals that detect such noxious conditions are called *nociceptors* and the activation of nociceptors is referred to as _nociception_ (not _pain_).

The central, supraspinal elaboration of nociceptive information, which may give rise to visceral-somatic reactions, suffering, and conscious re-elaboration of related emotions, is referred to as pain. Therefore, the activation of a sensory receptor, and sensory ascending paths in the spine (nociception), is considered as a SENSATION, while pain is considered as the suffering and distress that may accompany such sensation, and therefore constitutes an EXPERIENCE (a subjective, personal, private experience).

Some Authors even distinguish pain, as an _emotion_, from _suffering_, as a _feeling_ (an EXPERIENCE), which may not be there in rudimentary brains.

The term 'perception' seems to imply awareness and consciousness, and possibly be the key to explain phenomenal consciousness. However, an animal (or a person) can be conditioned to respond to a particular combination or sequence of stimuli while still being unaware of having elaborated, recognized, and reacted to a complex set of stimuli that needed sophisticated analysis, recognition, and attribution of meaning. It would therefore be important to reserve the term PERCEPTION to the process of recognition and attribution of meaning, that may lead to a variable degree of awareness but does not necessarily generate a conscious experience.

* * *

With this terminological approach, the SENSATION process can be equated with the function of sensors and signal handling devices in a machine, the PERCEPTION process is equivalent to computational analysis by a machine to detect and identify known patterns / objects. This would suggest employing the term (phenomenal) _consciousness_ to indicate the subsequent step: the function of transforming a PERCEPTION into an EXPERIENCE (generating awareness).

In the following, CONSCIOUSNESS will therefore be used to indicate such **function**, not the mental state (level of consciousness) or the conscious realization/knowledge (awareness) of something.

Such function can be imagined as a lamp that sheds light on information elaborated by neuronal circuit, and can do it in a dim, diffuse way, or in a more and more concentrated manner, thus generating an uncertain interplay of shadows or a clear picture with bright colors; a vague, ambiguous and imprecise impression or the well-defined and verbally reportable awareness of the ongoing mental activity. Thus, the experience generated by consciousness can be blurred or sharp, showing variable scale of precision and verbal reportability (_explicitness_) of the EXPERIENCE.

This way we precisely reserve the term EXPERIENCE to the generation of a consciously perceived, first-person, qualitatively specific, and personal, experience (what it is like to...), variably explicit; this 'phenomenal' aspect would be clearly distinct from the steps of SENSING and PERCEIVING. It must arise from other processes, be they metaphysical, inexplicable, events, or neuronal activities, amenable to scientific exploration.

EXPERIENCE will refer to being aware of the moment one is living, whether such experience arises from an external stimulus, an internal sensation, an emotion, a memory, a feeling, or a thought.

* * *

So, how happens that a machine can have sensors and computational devices so it can *SENSE, DETECT* and *RECOGNIZE*, but cannot *EXPERIENCE*?

The answer – "because it does not have a phenomenal consciousness" – is simple and effective but is obviously tautologic and certainly does not explain why a living organism would instead possess such a thing. Still, the question is useful, because it restates the 'hard problem' in slightly different terms and, luckily, the problem in this form can be addressed scientifically.

There is in fact a crucial difference between a living organism and computational machines (at least in their standard current form).

A living system is a dynamic, unstable equilibrium, that must continuously interact with the outside to gather the energy and the substrates needed to continually renew its own components and its state, in addition to perform complex programs of growth, development and reproduction. Interaction is inevitable and useful, but a bad stimulus, a faulty interaction, the wrong response, will produce damage, possibly death. Thus, any living organism needs to be endowed with mechanisms that allow it to evaluate the relevance for survival and well-being of whatever happens and of all interactions with the environment, to appropriately react.

Even unicellular organisms tend to move towards a source of nourishment and escape noxious stimuli. This process does not require any consciousness, not even a brain. If a central nervous system is there, the detection of vital relevance produces vegetative and visceral adaptations that prepare to best face the situation, somatic responses with preparatory and communicative function, and, if a sufficiently complex nervous system is there, changes in its overall mode of operation: the 'somatic marker' of emotions.

So, anything relevant that happens to a living organism with a brain will either elicit an innate emotional response or resonate with previous experiences and derive its own emotional color from the emotional frame that characterized the past experiences it resonates with.

The inevitable emotional characterization is intertwined with the cognitive elaboration of the incoming information and leads to the attribution of *MEANING* to incoming information (here *MEANING* indicates a cognitive, emotional and/or operational valence for the individual, rather than a mere semantic reference). Attribution of *MEANING* appears therefore linked to the capability of reproducing (reviving) global neural activities correlated to past experiences; in other words, to the capability of re-enacting patterns of neuronal firing and synaptic activity that have been experienced and learned, in the past.

The brain would reproduce (IMAGINE) something similar to what is being perceived and attribute a MEANING, based on reviving the corresponding emotions, to the current experience.

Thus, a living system cannot be *indifferent* to what happens.

It is *necessarily concerned*, it cannot help *evaluating* (physiologically, not consciously) the relevance to survival and wellbeing of anything that occurs, it is inevitably AFFECTED by whatever happens. A doom, which we may refer to as PATHOS (capability of being affected).

It would be hard to claim that 'phenomenal consciousness', as the capability of eliciting a private and personal experience, has nothing to do with such PATHOS …

The phenomenal dimension seems therefore to be an inevitable property of living organisms, of the reactivity of their body.
It is a *property of life itself*, not of consciousness.
PHENOMENAL PATHOS, not *consciousness*.

PHENOMENAL PATHOS might be an important ingredient of consciousness, but it is there even if no brain is there, and no sites or structures able to give rise to consciousness. This may be a hard problem for scientists to explain, but if so, it is the *'hard problem' of life*, not of consciousness.

Notice that this poses a terminological question: if we use words such as sense, perceive, emotions, in their common meaning, implying presence of a consciousness, we are led to attribute a consciousness to an amoeba; in particular a 'phenomenal consciousness', which would therefore be a property of life, rather than of nervous systems or animals with a brain (or even with a soul).

So, SENSING and PERCEIVING should be viewed as merely computational activities; *emotion* and PATHOS are instead intrinsic properties of life, independent of consciousness, that arise from to the fact that every SENSATION is inevitably emotionally colored (if it is relevant), even in those organisms that do not have a nervous system sufficiently complex to produce a subjective EXPERIENCE (or consciousness) of the emotion.

* * *

The inevitability of PATHOS as an affective component of any experience raises an interesting question: are emotions states of the body or states of mind? Before Damasio proposed his analysis of the neurophysiology of emotions – *emotions* as bodily reactions, distinct from conscious *feelings* – an emotion was generally thought of as a 'state of mind'. Now, we would say that a *feeling* is a state of mind, but an *emotion* is a specific state of the body.

This is easily accepted as regards basic emotions such as pain and pleasure, but most other emotions share this biological nature. If pain and pleasure, and fear, joy, sadness, anger, and disgust, are seen as specific states of activation of the body and specific modes of operating by the nervous system, their existence, origin, and elaboration pertain to the domain of the 'easy problem', i.e. accounting for the mechanisms through which information is elaborated by the brain in giving rise to consciousness (not accounting for how and why consciousness arises).

A mind is needed to produce and elaborate *suffering*, the misery and distress dimensions of pain, but no mind is needed for the body to produce a 'state of pain' (more accurately, a state of reaction to nociception). Thus, the question of phenomenal consciousness can be clearly specified as the mechanism/process/mystery through which the bodily state (body marker, _emotion_) gives rise to the EXPERIENCE (_feeling_).

Still, we haven't said anything about how this step takes place.

* * *

The inevitable property of nervous circuits: endogenous neuronal activity

In considering living systems that possess a nervous system another key factor, another inevitable feature, must be considered: all neural circuits share the intrinsic property of being spontaneously active.

If neurons are extracted from a mouse brain and plated in a Petri dish, they will initially appear as round cells, having lost their neurites in the extraction process. In a few days, they will start emitting neurites, will polarize and produce dendrites and an axon. After two-three weeks in culture, the neurons will have formed effective synapses and display electrical and synaptic activity. Therefore, if an organism has a brain, the latter will inevitably sustain a continuous activity, which is not necessarily guided by external stimuli.

The endogenous activity of the brain at rest (neuronal spiking and network correlations, and specific patterns of electric activity) has started to be analyzed in the last 20 years, after two 'default mode networks' (DMN) were identified in the EEG of the brain at rest, i.e., in the absence of stimuli or cognitive tasks. These neuronal networks, involving various areas of the cortex, displayed a consistent, slow oscillation in their level of activity: one set of structures, more related to cenesthetic perceptions and mental wandering, alternates in its activity with a second set of structures, more oriented to the exploration of the external realty. If you sit in the subway, in the drowsy mood of the end of a long working day, you may be able to experience this alternance: your mind wanders and you do not even see what is around, but once every minute of so you involuntarily raise your head and give an exploratory glance around...

Subsequent network analysis of human brain connectivity has identified several other sets of regions (hubs) that are critically important for efficient neuronal signaling and communication, during perceptual or cognitive tasks.

It therefore appears that the normal operation of the brain arises from the interaction between the networks that sustain endogenous (spontaneous) activity ('default' networks), and those involved in task- or stimulus-related operation.

Consequently, stimuli produce specific responses in the brain, but such responses *will necessarily interfere with the endogenous activity*, so that both the responses and the spontaneous activity get modified.

The endogenous, spontaneous activity in a brain will produce mental contents, even in the absence of any external input. Let us define such phenomenon as IMAGINATIVE ACTIVITY.

To describe the genesis of the EXPERIENCE, the property of the living organism of being affected, PATHOS, and the property of the brain of displaying a continuous endogenous, IMAGINATIVE ACTIVITY must be taken into consideration. It is then tempting to suggest that any organism, at difference with any machine, is capable of PATHOS, but if it also has a central nervous system that produces such endogenous, continuous activity, PATHOS will color the endogenous, continuous IMAGINATIVE ACTIVITY in a way that begins to look pretty close to something that we can call a personal, qualitative, private EXPERIENCE, i.e. the onset of phenomenal consciousness. Notice that this clarifies that *phenomenal consciousness* is not related to the capability of explicitly reporting such experience, so it is in no way a specific property of humans.

* * *

The neural correlates of consciousness (NCC)

The processes through which the brain detects, recognizes features and identifies objects, patterns, events, situations have often been referred to as 'neural correlates of consciousness' (NCC), indicating that the onset of certain neural activity patterns at specific sites of the cortex is directly correlated with the conscious realization of the presence of certain patterns (e.g., color, movement) or objects. This constitutes an impressive progress toward clarifying how an EXPERIENCE is generated but these activations do not reflect the onset of such EXPERIENCE. The specific activities in defined locations in associative cortices, evoked by features and patterns in sensory stimuli and referred to as NCC, precede reportable awareness by several hundred ms; they represent the *content* of the (conscious to be) EXPERIENCE, which will come about only later:

they are not correlates of the *onset* of awareness, but of *future* awareness.

NCCs have been proposed to give rise to awareness when they interact in higher processing areas of the cortex. Here we directly face the main terminological conundrum about consciousness. We PERCEIVE, and do, things without being fully aware of them. Often, we can focus on them, and they can become fully conscious EXPERIENCES; in other cases, we are totally unable to recall them and realize we PERCEIVED, or did, them.

Should we define as conscious all mental activities that we could be aware of, if we focused on them, or only those that we are fully aware of? in other words, all the potentially accessible information or the minority of information that can actually be reported at any given time?

Notice that this question carries with it another problematic aspect: apparently, such "focusing", needed to bring mental activities under the spotlight of consciousness and make us aware of them requires some tens of a second. So, either 'phenomenal consciousness' has nothing to do with SENSATION and PERCEPTION, or it is an unconscious activity (!?...) that precedes by a significant time lag the onset of consciousness.

The term 'perceptual consciousness' has been proposed, to indicate all the potentially accessible information. The NCC would be the neural correlates of such perceptual consciousness, preconscious material that may be broadcast to brain general circuits to become conscious (to become target of 'access consciousness'). Broadcasting would occur for material that is judged relevant by the limbic structures (bottom-up control of selective attention) or on which our working memory needs to focus to perform its ongoing cognitive task (top-down control).

This suggests that both the accessibility of material and the actual access and reportability are the result of a graded and fuzzy process, and not clear-cut yes-or-no questions.

Freud's famous iceberg metaphor for the psyche nicely applies here: only a minimum part of mind's content emerging to the surface of the conscious, most of the rest submerged in the depth of the ocean; but also many contents that may be reached by diving below the surface.

Again, this may explain why, and partly how, a mental content manages to travel all the way and become conscious mental activity – this is nice – but still, it is not clear what "becoming conscious mental activity" means.

* * *

Imagination, the dawn of consciousness

What becoming conscious mental activity means, how a neural activity turns into an EXPERIENCE, is exactly the issue of Chalmers' argument on phenomenal consciousness.

In Husserl's view, the 'phenomenon' consists in the encounter between reality that reveals itself and consciousness that actively elaborates it: consciousness is an intentional activity (in + tension, tending to) oriented toward its object, and phenomenal consciousness is not a mere cognitive function, but an active interaction. This reading of the word phenomenal somewhat violates its etymology (reality shows itself, but the subject _grasps_ it).

Actually, in reference to consciousness it is even paradoxical. In fact, the main difference between a machine and a living organism, in the face of something that 'reveals itself', is that a machine is not affected by it, whereas a living organism is inevitably AFFECTED, to an extent that depends on how relevant it is for the survival, the wellbeing, the needs and the (possibly unconscious) purposes of the organism.

A machine may actively elaborate the event, if it is programmed to do so, and the living organism may or may not actively consider it, but contrary to the classical implication of the 'phenomenon', the main difference between a machine and an organism is not in their *active* response (processing it), but in the *passive* one, being AFFECTED or not.

Being AFFECTED is what transforms a cold, analytical interpretation of a sensory input or an event into a something meaningful, which may ask for a defense, or require a reaction, or offer an opportunity; in all these cases it will tend to accordingly modify the reactivity of the organism and change the operating mode of the nervous system (if one is there). But being affected (which sounds quite passive) does not mean that there are no *active* aspects in phenomenal consciousness. Two active aspects arise from 'being affected': attributing meaning and relevance for wellbeing to the event transforms any possible reaction from an automatic response to a purposeful act; furthermore, the whole path from SENSATION and PERCEPTION to EXPERIENCE is pervaded by an active, endogenous component.

> When sensory information is processed by analyzing patterns to identify objects (the 'what' pathway) and examine the general spatial relations among them, and their affordance (the 'where' pathway), the resulting neuronal activity necessarily interferes with the endogenous imaginative activity and guides it, through associative paths, to recall experiences (cognitive, or possibly affective) that resonate with what is being elaborated.

This mutual interference between the neural activity evoked by sensory stimuli and the endogenously generated imaginative activity helps to _attribute a meaning_ to what is being experienced: a cognitive meaning, through analogy with the resonating past experiences and known facts, and an affective meaning, based on the responses – to what is perceived and to what the resonance has recalled – in the subcortical structures that detect possible vital relevance (*amygdala*), hedonic valence (dopaminergic nuclei of the midbrain) and specific relevance for social interactions (serotonergic nuclei of the raphe).

Given this capability of _imaginative activity_ to dialogue and resonate with sensory information, the brain must be able to distinguish whether activation of the associative cortices arises from an actual sensory input or from imagination; this is a crucial role of serotonergic projections from the raphe: serotonin can influence the exam of reality and the intensity/depth of the experience, as indicated by the hallucinogenic (or anti-) effects of ligands to serotonin receptors, such as LSD or atypical antipsychotic drugs.

Every cortical circuit might be invaded, at any moment, by inputs that represent the result of processing sensory stimuli, but also by information endogenously generated from elaboration of memories, simulation or prefiguration of possible situations, projects, etc. The more significant the emotional, vital, operational valence that is associated to each of these inputs, the more the projections from subcortical structures and limbic areas will enhance the activity they produce and the related elaboration. Acquired patterns of activity in other areas that tend to resonate with them may be triggered and recruited.

This way many (possibly unrelated) activities simultaneously go on in the brain; in terms of access to awareness, they compete to gain attention; each is sustained by its emotional and operative valence; each tries to recruit other circuits, and may obtain various degrees of 'expansion', 'alignment' with other circuitries and 'globalization'. This constitutes a multifarious, inconsistent, ambiguous and possibly contradictory set of mental contents, which cannot be addressed by lucid cognitive elaboration unless a process of filtering, of selective attention, focusses some content that can be clearly specified, translated into words and possibly reported.

The abovementioned theories, about how a mental content can be broadcasted in the 'global neuronal workspace' and involve many semi-independent circuits to give rise to a complex and integrated elaboration, seem to refer to such process of filtering and selective attention toward mental contents, rather than explaining how these mental contents become personal _EXPERIENCES_, whether they do o do not gain the focus of awareness.

Also, this suggests that a whole shade of intermediate situations can occur, for a mental content, and an *EXPERIENCE*, between remaining confined to a limited cortical circuit, vague and hidden, or taking the stage of conscious, explicit elaboration; and we experience how mental content can shift between these two conditions every time somebody speaks to us: we may be concentrated on something else, and we just hear noise coming from a mouth that moves; or we may pay attention to them and turn on auditory elaboration circuits to a variable level (again, not a yes-or-no), and we shall vaguely perceive what they are talking about, or clearly understand what they are saying.

* * *

If consciousness is regarded as a function, rather than the tip of the iceberg, the question is no more about whether a mental content is accessible or not, but whether it gives rise to an experience and the degrees of discrimination and precision with which it is dealt with.

Obviously, the less discriminative the elaboration of a content, the more difficult it will be to address it and report it precisely and explicitly as a conscious content.

We may merely *SENSE* something – activate the sensory receptors and ascending pathways – or *PERCEIVE* it through cortical elaboration and attribute it a *MEANING* through the _pathos_ and _imagination_ it elicits; we may pay it a variable degree of _attention_, based on its relevance and consistency, and how related it is to current cognitive elaboration; eventually, we may analyze it in a precise and discriminative way, transforming a vague mental content into a clearcut, unambiguous concept, _explicitly_ transparent in our mind, verbally reportable.

The so-called 'perceptual consciousness' may possibly include everything from *PERCEIVING* to attributing a *MEANING*; phenomenal consciousness would permit *EXPERIENCING*; this would account for all contents of which we have even the slightest impression of being vaguely conscious: contents that may be outside the reach of our lucid awareness, but may possibly be accessed, at least in some cases, and examined and explicitly reported. This actually is the central assumption in treatments based on psychodynamic approaches.

* * *

So, sensory information is interpreted through its interaction with *IMAGINATIVE ACTIVITY*, by letting it guide imagination through memories and past experiences in search for resonances, to assemble a cognitive and emotional *MEANING* by reviving them and generate _EXPERIENCES_.

This process has the crucial properties of Husserl's *phenomenon*, in its being simultaneously a passive and an active event, a mechanistic (neural) reaction to physical stimuli that assumes a meaning through the way the endogenous imaginative activity of the brain is influenced, i.e. the way the *conscious* subject actively meets it.

This description of the recognition process highlights how the attribution of MEANING requires an active and global involvement of subcortical centers (emotional) as well as cortical (limbic and cognitive) systems: these traits – being an active process and involving a global, oriented activity – are the fundamental features of consciousness as a function.

The integration of emotional coloring with cognitive elaboration, strongly based on the recall of past experiences, transforms the detection process (PERCEPTION) into the *endogenous* generation of a subjective, private, and personal EXPERIENCE, which does reflect the incoming information, but in a way heavily filtered by the personality, the mindset, the values, the opinions, the purposes of the subject, and the luggage of one's memories and past experiences.

Phenomenal consciousness arises this way in the encounter and resonance of an endogenous IMAGINATIVE ACTIVITY, with its strictly personal content, with incoming information.

So *phenomenal consciousness* is not elicited by the stimulus; rather, we *experience* the stimuli because they interfere with an imaginative activity that is continuously going on in the brain, and possibly force it to pay attention. Such IMAGINATIVE ACTIVITY may seem a metaphysical function, but it is necessary and present, at least in a rudimentary form, in any animal who needs to actively, intentionally, regulate its behavior. Thus, to approach Chalmer's 'hard problem of consciousness' in a scientific way, we should probably turn our efforts to clarify how the spontaneous, endogenous activity of the brain produces *imaginative activity*, rather than merely looking for the neuronal process(es) involved in transforming a sensation into an 'experience'.

The accuracy of the resonance of the neural activity elicited by a sensory stimulus with *known* patterns suggests the likelihood of a MEANING, so that the attribution of meaning is tentative, based on such likelihood: it is the result of an *endogenous production of patterns*, in search for the ones that best match those produced by incoming information.

In simple words, recognition *is the result of imagining the reality that best matches what we are perceiving.*

It is a work based on analogy and resonance: recognizing an object, an event, a situation, means being able to produce an endogenous activity that resonates with the patterns elicited by the incoming information, being able to imagine a reality that fits the external reality, as guessed from the incoming information.

Phenomenal consciousness is the result of endogenous imaginative activity and its encounter with reality, perceived in a subjective way; it *is the way reality is imagined*, and the way the self is imagined, helped by the computational constructs of IDENTITY and AGENCY.

This is not playing with words: describing brain function as <u>imagining a reasonable reality</u> that fits sensory information, and not <u>depicting</u> or <u>representing</u> the external reality, escapes the trap of 'Cartesian materialism', because a spectator may be needed to interpret what the brain depicts, but none is needed to interpret what the brain IMAGINES.

Possibly the most intriguing consequence of this observation is that not only sensory information, but also every mental content produced by the brain, in its incessant activity, whether it is produced in response to a stimulus or endogenously, is bound to undergo the same processing, interact with imagination, recollect related concepts, revive affective reactions: in other words, the cognitive and emotional resonances, elicited by each and every activity in the brain, add an affective color, a personal perspective and a subjective meaning to the neurological activity, which gets transformed into a private experience.

This precisely addresses the question of phenomenal consciousness, because in asking 'what it is like' to experience something, we are precisely asking what mental images and past experiences arise in our brain to interpret and color the current experience with personally relevant cognitive, emotional, operative details.

So, can we explain what it is like to see red to a person who cannot see?

No, we cannot, Chalmers is right.

The experience is private and cannot be shared. But apart from the activity in the retina (*sensation*) and the occipital cortex (*perception*), the personal (metaphysical, not merely neurological) <u>experience</u> of seeing red consists, for each of us, in reviving images and emotions related to whatever is red: blood, fire, heat, anger for most people. For me and those who shared some of my experiences, red is also the mood associated to red flags waving on the wind, the dedication and enthusiasm of marching for peace, for justice, for solidarity, for freedom from tyrannies...

Memories, connections, emotions, the energy of red as opposed to the peace of green – the relaxing feeling of laying down on the grass and hearing the wind whispering between the leaves – or the stillness, silence, possible fear of black – nothing, the vacuum, a hole with no bottom…

'It has done me good,' said the fox, 'because of the color of the wheat fields.'

Thus, it is not possible to share with another person our own neurological response, but it is possible to elicit in them a very similar cognitive and emotional *experience*, if we have enough common references in our culture, history, knowledge and past experiences.

Phenomenal consciousness is not what happens in the neural circuits but what we do experience. But then, it does not blossom from nowhere in a magical way: it simply consists in how our imagination is carried around by what happens to enter our brain or autonomously wanders in it.

WHY DO WE CARE - Consistency

Spontaneous activities in the brain, cognitive and emotional, as well as incoming sensory information, recall, revive and interact with memories and past emotions; an affectively colored imaginative activity ensues, that reads reality and the events from a personal perspective, giving it a subjective meaning and transforming all this into a private experience.

So, this seems exactly what Chalmers was talking about in defining the 'hard problem' of consciousness. The only step in this process that cannot be clarified scientifically, however, is not so much "awareness" as it is the abovementioned *pathos*, i.e. the ability of every living system to be affected by sensory inputs, evaluate the relevance for survival and wellbeing, change operating mode and – if a brain is there – *suffer*. The 'hard problem' not so much of *consciousness*, but rather of *life*.

* * *

But if explaining what it is like to have a feeling, and understanding why it is like that, constitutes a difficult problem for neuroscientists, an even harder problem is explaining why one should share other people's feelings, and understanding why, if one in looks at this child, so terribly sad, either they smile to minimize the emotion, or their mouth tends to bend downward, making them feel at least a little bit miserable.

Imagine baby deer.
It goes with the herd to the river, to drink.
It does not know anything about wolves. But when the more experienced doe snores and changes her posture, because she captured the scent of the wolf, the fawn gets the message, rapidly becomes equally scared and flees.

So that is why we empathize; it is an evolutionary advantage, run away three times and you learn to associate the scent of the wolf with danger and the need to run away.

But that is the purpose of this ability, it does not explain how it works and from where it comes – the cause.

One evening Fadiga, a researcher in Rizzolatti's lab, was cleaning up at the end of an experiment. He had been recording the activity of a neuron, in the lateral frontal cortex of a monkey, which fired spikes at high frequency whenever the monkey grasped a peanut to bring it to the mouth. The electric signal from the neuron was fed to a speaker, so that when the neuron was active one could hear a burst of knocks.

In resetting the lab, he grasped a peanut that had remained on the table, and the neuron started to burst.

The experiment was supposed to be ended, but it was actually beginning, and led to the identification of neurons that fire not only when an animal makes a move (the same story was later confirmed in humans as well), but also when it sees another subject doing the same, or if it simply hears a sound (the cracking of the peanut shell) suggesting that the action will be performed.

These neurons were called mirror neurons. Their activation was named by Gallese *embodied simulation*: he explains that we do not just 'see' another person acting, or feeling a sensation or emotion, but we unconsciously elicit an "internal representations of the body states associated with actions, emotions, and sensations", as if we were having the same experience.

In generating this 'embodied simulation' mirror neurons reproduce in the observer at least part of the neural experience of the observed subject; thus, they are important in learning by imitation, and even more so in understanding the purpose of other people's actions, by evoking in one's own brain a similar activity.

This kind of neurons are present in the medial part of the cortex as well, in areas that control mimic and emotional facial expressions and postures. One may involuntarily reproduce the expression, but even if they don't, and the activation of mirror neurons remains covert, the observer is experiencing a subconscious imaginative activation similar to the one of the observed subject. The sensory and perceptive components of the experience are lacking, so it is not possible to fully share the emotion, but it is at least partly reproduced, and this way correctly interpreted and empathically felt.

Thinking of this phenomenon, and of the similar, strong emotions that reviving memories can produce, the power of imaginative activity in producing conscious experience should appear quite clearly.

Still, there is something in this story that we would prefer if it were not there.

The degree of activation of mirror neurons depends on how familiar we are with the action we are observing. They may be activated in seeing a monkey grasping a piece of food and bringing it to its mouth, but they are not when the same monkey does its fancy trick with its lips.

If you are a capoeira dancer, seeing somebody dancing activates your mirror neurons more than mine. So, mirror neurons and empathy are related to familiarity and affinity with the other person.

If we want to joke, we can suggest that this is at least one of the reasons why men will never understand women and their emotions, but if try to be serious we must realize that the tendency to feel empathy is much weaker for people who we don't feel affine to, because of the color of the skin, the physiognomic traits, the habits and the way they behave…

Far from justifying racism, this may contribute to explain why so many people, often even normal and nice people, can sometimes display unexpected receptivity to demagogic, aggressive and essentially racist propaganda.

* * *

An interesting role of mirror neurons is that of letting you understand what other people do, and why, by putting yourself in their shoes. Thus, it helps us understand that other people see things from their own point of view and act based on what they see and know. Attributing a *mind* like ours to other people is often referred to as the capacity to create in our brain a *theory of mind*. This is not an innate property; children younger than 4-5 years old do not realize that other people have their own knowledge, thoughts and feelings; children in the autistic spectrum develop this capacity later and incompletely and this contributes to their problems in handling the subtlety of interpersonal communication.

The capability of understanding other people's thoughts and feelings is crucial in pursuing a behavior that makes us accepted socially. This is one role of the ascending serotonin projections from the raphe to the prefrontal cortex, the area that develops behavioral strategies. Thus, activation of these projections tends to reduce active aggressiveness (though *reactive* aggressiveness persists) and to make us worry about doing the right thing; so, the collateral serotonin projections to the limbic system tend to generate anxiety, the concern of being rejected, and depression if we cannot find the behavior that makes us socially accepted.

This is a curious observation, because people generally think of serotonin as 'the neurotransmitter of happiness', which is far from true. What is true is that drugs that act on serotonin receptors or on its reuptake (and its persistence in the synaptic cleft) can interfere with the exam of reality and produce (or counteract) hallucinations, but they can also treat major depression, with prolonged administration. This is not because serotonin improves mood the same way as sugar makes your tea sweeter; this happens because those drugs can enhance neural plasticity and trophism: endogenously depressed patients (but not healthy people who have been dumped by their partner) show a decreased thickness of the cerebral cortex, in several areas, when examined by neuroimaging techniques such as CAT scan, PET scan or MRI; treatment is often able to restore the normal anatomical appearance in the long term.

Actually, some drugs such as ketamine appear to be able to produce this same effect – a "neuroplastogenic" effect – even after a single or a few administrations. This has brought back to centerstage hallucinogenic drugs – quite loved by the beat generation as a means of evading reality and stimulating creativity – as possibly effective drugs for depression.

Intense research is going on in the attempt to separate the hallucinogenic from the neuroplastogenic/antidepressant action.

* * *

Serotonin truly is the most fascinating neurotransmitter.

Interfere with its activity and you will interfere with mood, sleeping rhythms, feeding behavior, aggressiveness, judgment, relational and social attitude, behavioral strategies and the exam of reality. It seems such a complex set of actions that it almost does not make sense…

Still, there is a curious analogy between the roles of serotonin and what appears to be the most central property of consciousness: whatever we mean with the latter term, it certainly has to do with a modeling function the brain has. Depicting, representing, reproducing reality is not the crucial aspect, because it would anyway require somebody/something that looks at such representation and interprets it; the crucial aspect is modeling, i.e. interpreting, attributing a possible function to objects, giving a meaning to events, reading interactions and sequences as processes in which causes and effects can be identified, and which can be interacted with. In two words, modeling reality.

* * *

Information processing by the brain displays one key property in order to model: the unrelenting attempt at finding consistency in the incoming information.

Much attention has been paid, in cognitive neuroscience, to the role of the anterior cingulate cortex: it has been considered as a difficulty, error, or novelty detector, as it is activated in the presence of conflicting information. This elicits alertness and stimulates cognitive re-elaboration of information in search of a consistent reading of reality (or a successful strategy).

When information is incomplete, gap-filling mechanisms intervene to generate a complete and consistent picture. Experiments on split-brain patients (in whom the left and right hemispheres cannot communicate) have showed that when they are fed different information to the right and left hemisphere, they are always able to produce a consistent verbal explanation (which comes from their left, verbal hemisphere) for actions of their left hand (controlled by the right hemisphere), actions that only make sense based on what the right hemisphere knows, but the left ignores: in the face of difficulty, error, novelty, inconsistency, and incompleteness, the brain however tries to build a complete and consistent internal image, using the information available to it.

As the child grows up, the story of the white-haired, bearded, old and fat guy climbing down the chimney in his red coat to bring gifts, a story that used to be consistent with the little they used to know about real life and the constraints of physics, becomes unbelievable, because it 'does not make real sense' (sorry if some of you still thought that Santa was the one bringing them their Christmas gifts...).

It may be interesting to consider a number of aspects of this process of refining the model of reality, aimed at building a consistent picture:
- the process is accompanied by synaptic pruning: we become more discriminative and rational by dropping loose (possibly misleading) associative connections and privileging precise and solid ones
- it essentially consists in developing an exam of reality
- it gives rise to behavioral rules and moral constraints that help to behave in such a way as to be socially accepted
- it limits our freedom and forces us to repress some instincts
- it corresponds to the process of development of the *Ego* as proposed by Freud in his psychanalytic theory
- it may generate anxiety, exactly because of the need to repress and the fear of being rejected
- it may generate depression, if we do not manage to cope with social requirements

Curiously enough, these are exactly the functions of serotonin projections, that therefore appear to exert a crucial role in the genesis of the *Ego*, in building a rational and consistent perspective on reality, in consciously regulating behavior: favoring the generation of an exam of reality based on consistency of sensory data, previous knowledge and logics, favoring compliance with social requirements, favoring some anxiety and depressive reactions.

Also curious is how all these aspects are strongly relaxed when dreaming: we can feel very strong emotions, but we lose the capability of being afflicted by inconsistencies. Impossible things happen, beloved people may appear in disguise as unknown characters, sequences may be interrupted or illogical, but we do not care, we do not wake up, bothered by the nonsense. And in dreaming serotonin projections to pontine cholinergic nuclei are switched off, and serotonin-dependent exam of reality if suspended; this suggests that the functions of the *Ego* might be attenuated when dreaming, and aspects of the *Id* and its subconscious processes may transpire or emerge in their incoherence, unreality and conflictuality (as suggested by Freud theory on the interpretation of dreams); this is also consistent with the perception that drugs that interfere with serotonin, hallucinogens, may let one reveal and explore unknown territories of the soul, may have a psychedelic effect, by showing (δηλόω) the soul (ψυχή).

In the face of all this, it seems that consciousness (as a function) does indeed rely on an imaginative activity that fills the gaps and fixes the inconsistencies, thus building a personal experience in resonance with the exogenously and endogenously generated sensory, emotional and cognitive neuronal activities.

The 'pre-consciousness' thus generated must clearly be redundant and semantically pleiotropic, in that innumerable resonances compete in every moment to propose possible 'meanings' for every single aspect of the experience. But consciousness (the function) aims at consistency. So, at each level of the search for a meaning, in rearranging suggestions of tentative 'meanings' to generate a unitary experience, selective mechanisms intervene: emotional relevance on one side (bottom-up); consistency and relatedness to current focus on the other (top-down).

Each reading, each imaginative aspect, each detail receives a higher or lower weight and relevance in the search for a tentative 'meaning'; as a consequence, the internal EXPERIENCE gradually becomes more precise and defined, but also necessarily impoverished of possible evocative connections and collateral 'meanings'.

Through this filtering process we end up with a single, unambiguous reading – an explicit reading – that can be reported in words and used for logical and strategical computation by the working memory system.

It is therefore clear that active processes – imaginative activity – play the main role in interpreting sensory inputs and mental contents: these are initially evanescent, ambiguous and rich of possible meanings and connections and need to be pruned, shriveled and polished to become explicit, reportable content. This view points to a domain of pre-verbal awareness (pre- or sub-consciousness) characterized by vagueness, multiplicity of 'meanings', excess of associative interconnections, and prevalence of emotional links on cognitive ones, which has nurtured the story and evolution of psychoanalytic and psychodynamic theories.

This domain – which could be referred to as 'implicit awareness' – has been investigated by Freud using the analysis of lapsus and free associations in a relaxed condition, by Jung with his active imagination, by Desoille with his rêve éveillé dirigé, and by several other researchers and schools using other imaginative procedures or daydreaming.

This domain of the psyche – implicit consciousness, or 'the imaginary' – is a fluid turmoil of images and emotions, characterized by semantic pleiotropy: each image simultaneously contains several associative and evocative links, and therefore has a high and multiple symbolic (σύμβολω = throw together) content.

In this perspective, the domain of what we are perfectly aware of ('access consciousness') would no longer be a mere selection of preconscious contents, which are broadcasted in the global neuronal workspace and become the object of awareness, but rather the explicit, verbal translation of selected meanings from the redundant symbolic production of *IMAGINATIVE ACTIVITY*. This selection translates the vague and fluid production of the imaginary into explicit concepts and chunks of information that can be handled by the working memory system to produce lucid, conscious, cognitive elaboration (thought).

However, verbal translation requires choosing words and thus filtering, eliminating vagueness, ambiguities, and canceling redundant symbolic links; in this process, meanings and associations that would generate discomfort and anxiety can be dropped (a simple interpretation of the mechanism of removal), but they may possibly be retrieved and revived by the exploration of the imaginary, which is therefore an ideal domain to investigate deep psychic processes, create a therapeutic space, and handle transference in psychotherapy.

In conclusion, consciousness as a function can be defined as the active interaction of the continuous, endogenously generated neural activity (*IMAGINATIVE ACTIVITY*) with mental contents produced by stimuli, internal events, or other results of brain elaboration.

Such interaction is based on the evaluation of the vital, emotional and operative valence of the mental content and a more or less intense effort to attribute a personal, private MEANING. Such MEANING is attributed through the active generation of a consistent internal image; in this process, IMAGINATIVE ACTIVITY produces many vague and ambiguous hints, rich of symbolic links, that constitute an implicit, emotionally colored and semantically pleiotropic, internal EXPERIENCE (presumably coincident with what some refer to as 'phenomenal consciousness').

The last step in this process comes about in the name of consistency: in general, this multifarious and redundant imaginative activity will not be reportable, unless selective attention mechanisms bring specific aspects it in the focus of cognitive activity and reduces the fuss to a defined, univocal, complete and consistent, explicit experience, that can be expressed in words.

XII

TIMES AND CHOICES – Motor control and behavior

Eventually, let's stop looking for meta-spaces in the brain, and get back to the classical approach: the brain is not there to think, it is there to act. Indeed, even frogs have it, and they do not think so much, do they?

A crucial aspect of evolution is the appearance of organisms with a body divided into segments and – even more crucial – of organisms in which, during development, after the segmentation of the embryo each segment gives rise to a different portion, anatomically, structurally and functionally different. So, there come cephalic segments, with eyes, and antennas, thoracic segments, with legs, or wings, and so on to the tail – for those who have it.

When each portion of the organism develops different functions and must originate organs and structures with distinct organizations and functions, two kinds of problems arise. The first, which has fascinated and occupied scientists and has been clarified quite well in its general lines, is how such differences can be generated and refined in a coordinated and organized way during the development of the embryo, which after all originates from a single cell, not at all divided into segments. The second problem is how the different segments and the different organs can work in a concerted way so that each one makes its constructive contribution to the survival of the organism.

The development of an organism is a complex but fascinating topic. The general mechanisms, variegated and sophisticated, can be related to a common and ingenious general scheme. To understand it is necessary to realize that a cell is a complex equilibrium; its structure is determined, and its functioning is regulated by proteins. These are large molecules that perform many functions: structural support functions, thereby determining cell shape; control functions, thereby regulating all chemical reactions that occur in the cell (and in its numerous specialized organelles); and functions of transport and exchange across cell membranes, to maintain the different concentrations of electrolytes and biologically relevant molecules between the exterior and the interior of the cell (and of its organelles).

The presence, quantity and localization of the various proteins in the cell – and in particular the differences between one cell type and another – make it possible for the diverse cells to display different shapes, structures, organizations and functions, and to interact in a different way among them and with the extra-cellular matrix.

Here is the trick! Though everything is written in DNA, the sublime library of recipes to build any protein that the cell may wish to produce, the question is to decide today's menu. It is a vicious (virtuous?) circle: who decides what to read in the DNA, which genes to turn on or off and which proteins to produce? Always and anyway proteins, other proteins (transcription factors) or small substances whose production is again regulated by cellular proteins. Then, it is sufficient that a cell starts to produce a specific protein, that controls, by binding to specific sites in the DNA chain, the production of certain other proteins, some of them useful for specific cellular functions, some other capable of turning on or off the synthesis of other additional proteins...

Anything is sufficient: take a small molecule, for example, say retinoic acid, that is produced at a specific location in the cell, that is not exactly in the center. When the cell divides, one of the two daughter cells will have more retinoic acid, the other will have less. Mr. Retinoic regulates some genes, and the two cells will produce several proteins, and transcription factors, in different amounts; they grow up different, and may in turn generate daughter cells even more different, with diverse destinies. If you sit back and think of it for a moment, you realize that something like that must happen: otherwise, the egg cell would become two, then four, eight, sixteen, and a balloon would come out instead of an embryo.

If an egg-cell is capable of generating an organism, it is not only because it possesses all the genes that let it produce all the proteins that will be necessary for each cell in the organism, but also because a fine, complex, fascinating game links proteins and genes, which regulate each-other in a sophisticated minuet, generating complex and diverse figures and choreographies, taking divergent development pathways, apparently unpredictable, but implicitly designed in the complex biochemical relations between DNA and proteins. Notice that once more we see a picture that reaches a much higher degree of complexity because of the mutual interaction between distinct systems: DNA even a hundred times longer, containing a hundred times as much information, would not be able, by itself, to generate the *degree* of complexity that arises from the interplay between DNA and proteins.

In this picture, some proteins – the products of the so-called *homeotic genes* or 'master' genes – can orchestrate long term programs. Their differential expression in distinct regions of the embryo determines divergent fates for similar cells, which will therefore generate different organs, or portions of the body – a wing rather than a leg or an antenna, for example – depending on their localization in the axis of the embryo.

In an organism that displays well differentiated body structures and organs, the problem of communication arises. Specific cells can recognize precise stimuli from the external environment, but it is likely that the response of the organism requires the activation of other cells, presumably different, possibly positioned in a remote region of the body.

The cell that recognizes the stimulus may produce substances that, when released in the extracellular space – or in the blood of organisms that have a heart and circulatory system, – reach all the other cells, and therefore also those that produce the correct response. This is the principle that underlies hormone production.

On the other hand, it would be much more efficient to be able to transfer the signals specifically and precisely from one site to another in the organism, especially when the kinds and intensities of the stimuli to be distinguished become more numerous, and similarly the variety, specificity and tuning of the possible responses grow; being able to add, compare, elaborate the signals, before leading them to the site where the response is to be generated, would be even better. This is the function of the nervous system. And the greater the complexity and richness of the information the organism obtains from the environment, and the variety of the possible behavioral responses, the greater is the necessity that the elaboration of signals be centralized, and therefore that a *central* nervous system be there to correctly analyze and correlate all information.

Here we are. The classical, neat vision of neurophysiology: thousands of diverse and refined sensors, a system of signal elaboration capable of computing the most appropriate response by the organism to the momentary external reality, and systems that produce such response, by controlling internal vegetative and visceral activities as well as all the elements in the organism that can produce movement, and therefore a *behavioral* response.

We got lost in noticing how, in this process, the elaborative elephantiasis of our brain escapes and goes astray in abstractions, among symbols, sentiments and existential wishes, instead of studying, like good scientists, how external reality, stimuli and their interpretation, determine our behavior.

Let's take care of this, then, straight ahead.

* * *

Warning: skip! hop! jump! here is another bunch of neurophysiology pills...

NEUROPHYSIOLOGY OF MOTOR CONTROL

Muscle movement is controlled by nervous cells (motor neurons) that are positioned in the anterior part of the spinal cord, close to the point where the spinal nerve leaves the spine to reach the peripheral organs.

Motor neurons receive many synaptic signals that control their electrical activity and determine the frequency with which the motor neuron itself will discharge 'spikes', electrical impulses capable of propagating down to the nerve terminal. When the impulse reaches the terminal, a neurotransmitter (acetylcholine) is released, which produces an electrical response in the muscular fiber and a twitch of contraction. Typically, to produce the contraction of a muscle, the group of motor neurons that innervate its fibers discharge spikes in an alternate and coordinated way so that the asynchronous twitches of the single fibers merge into a smooth contraction of the whole muscle: the more motor neurons active simultaneously at any moment (the higher the frequency of discharge of the neurons), the stronger will be the contraction of the muscle.

In the muscles there are small structures (the "muscle spindles") made of modified fibers which do not contribute much to contraction but host nervous sensory terminals, activated by stretching the fiber itself. The sensory neurons that capture this signal – the length, and changes in length, of the muscle – deliver it to neurons in the spine, involved in local control networks, and to nuclei in the brainstem, which will relay it to the cortex so that it is informed of the length of muscles and position of the limbs. Locally, one process of the axon directly reaches the motor neurons that innervate the muscle itself from which the information arrives: try and stretch a muscle and the motor neurons are activated directly, through a simple reflex arch, and contract it back. Hit the tendon, just below the knee, this stretches a bit the quadriceps muscle of the thigh and the reflex arch produces a contraction of this muscle and a forward movement of the leg. Trivial circuit. Little fascinating and little interesting as well, at first sight.

But let us think for a moment what this stupid circuit produces. I decide I want to put my leg in a certain position; because of a shock, a change in weight distribution, an involuntary contraction of another muscle, an acceleration of the bus, a change in pitch of the ship, the position I wanted to maintain changes a little; a muscle gets stretched, the reflex arc stimulates it, it contracts and gains back the original length, the limb resumes its position. So, the circuit is not so stupid: though trivial, it is sufficient to help maintaining the position of a body segment without any need of continuously re-computing and modulating the degree of nervous stimulation that is needed to maintain the chosen position.

Generally speaking, most of the circuitries in the spine are organized along these same criteria, though they may contain much more complex and sophisticated circuits: networks of neurons stabilize the position of body segments by comparing, computing and balancing the levels of activation of motor neurons; they help a muscle to contract by avoiding that muscles with an opposed action be simultaneously activated; they regulate positioning of muscles and joints to assume comfortable or effective postures; they facilitate the coordinated, alternate and oscillating activations of opposing muscles that constitute the basic design of complex motor behavior such as perambulation (hey! here the most sophisticated one is not us: if it is complex for us to walk, just think what a mess it must be for a millipede...).

As you ascend in the central nervous system you find ever more complex networks – the so-called *central pattern generators* – that coordinate and integrate complex but standardized motor behaviors. For example, in order to control posture, and simply stand still, you need all circuitries in the spinal cord up to the brainstem, where vestibular information, from the inner ear, joins the central nervous system and tells it what the position of the head is – and indirectly of the body – with respect to the gravitational axis. These axial circuitries sustain several complex reflex behaviors: if you suspend a newborn by holding their thorax with your hands, they will extend all four limbs in an 'anti-gravitational' reflex (the "parachute" reflex); if you hold them with your hand under their shoulders, let their feet touch the table and slide them forward, they will coordinately move their leg as if they were walking; if you touch their cheek they will turn their head, open their mouth and start sucking – this works better if there is something to suck, but is not a specific response elicited by the happy realization that mum (a wonderful object with breasts) is there, it is simply a reflex activity. Some quite complex behaviors are therefore interpretable as pure reflex responses, sustained by pre-wired circuitry in our lower nervous system. Pre-wired circuitries may also involve higher, possibly cortical, structures to sustain quite complex and sophisticated behaviors. These behaviors might be defined as 'instinctive', and together with reflex responses constitute a rich set of '*innate*' behaviors.

We have already discussed the role of *cerebellum* in controlling and assisting voluntary movements, and its great learning capability, such that after assisting for several times a specific sequence of movements the cerebellum becomes capable of realizing it all by itself, with no need for conscious supervision to control the movement: indeed, more precisely and markedly more rapidly. This is the most important kind of procedural memory and underlies the execution of many automatic behaviors.

Curiously enough, we tend to think of 'spontaneous' movements, reactions and behaviors as something that is more strictly *ours*, inborn and personal; still, most of our 'spontaneous' responses – rapid and not intentionally controlled – are automatic rather than pre-wired and are therefore acquired by repetition. They represent (who is going to accept this?) the result of conditioning.

Truly voluntary, intentional behavior is regulated by even higher centers, mostly the motor cortex.

Notice that, with the hierarchical organization of motor control we have discussed, an incredible number of reflexes, counter-movements and balancing reactions must be controlled, inhibited or modulated to execute any movement the cortex may wish to command. Thus, something in our head must keep track of all lower control systems and tell the cortex which muscular groups must be stimulated and which inhibited in order to execute even the simplest intentional movement without being contrasted by all reflex circuitries. This is one of the roles of the **BASAL GANGLIA** (striatum and related structures). They receive information on motor commands the cortex wishes to output and return to the cortex all necessary indications about which muscles must be facilitated or inhibited to properly execute the desired movement. Dopaminergic projections from the *substantia nigra* reach the striatum and modulate its circuits in such a way that they help to execute the actions that are most relevant, and have been positively reinforced in the past, and inhibit all the other actions that may interfere with them.

The basal ganglia also receive input from pre-motor areas of the cortex, regions where movements are studied and prepared before execution; thus, they can modulate all commands from the motor cortex in such a way that future movements are also favored. This makes it possible to execute complex sequences of movements with great fluidity, to harmonize different motor tasks that must be performed simultaneously, and to reconcile behavioral programs on different temporal scales. This explains why dysfunctions of the basal ganglia – such as are encountered in Parkinson's disease – interfere so heavily with the initiation and the performance of motor tasks.

Once again, we might recall here the general observation that a circuitry capable of performing a specific cognitive elaboration will generally perform such elaboration on all the material that is fed to it. Thus, the cerebellum is not used only for motor learning, but also for any form of procedural learning, such as for example repeating multiplication table results, a poem or a prayer, or performing grammatical and syntactic checks on sentences while we speak, and any other purely automatic procedure in cognitive performance.

Similarly, the basal ganglia not only choose the appropriate actions and help in harmonizing complex sequences of movements – and display a relevant learning capability in that respect – but also apply the same computational scheme to the control of cognitive activity and thought (driving it as an autopilot among possible associations, when purposeful reasoning leaves space for mind wandering), and help processing visual, auditory and cognitive information in a seamless way.

Thus, thanks to the dialogue between the posterior part of the basal ganglia and the occipital (visual) cortex, an interrupted sequence of images can be filled in, in observing relevant scenes while awake (we can 'see' a person while he walks behind a column) and in generating dreams while asleep, or visual hallucinations in the presence of psychiatric disorders or in response to administration of drugs.

The most relevant aspect of all this story is that each stimulus may produce many different responses, from the simplest and fastest one (reflex) to the slowest and most complex one (intentional behavior), and any *response which implies a more complex elaboration to be executed requires that simpler responses be inhibited.*

* * *

The question, in discussing human behavior with the aim of being scientific, is that science is required to maintain a purely deterministic approach (and this has been pretty wrong in the last fifty years, in my opinion): the nervous system is a machine made to produce appropriate responses to stimuli, so that the conditions of the organism are maintained stable – when everything is ok – and are brought back to balance when something goes wrong. It is the 'black box' idea: signals enter, something happens, a result comes out. Science's job is to argue how the box works. The difficulties arise when drives, motivations, or purposes among which one must choose are equivalent: in that case the intellect – taken as a black box – does not offer any indication, the will remains undecided, the choice does not occur and one ends up like Buridano's donkey, who dies of starvation because it cannot CHOOSE between two equal and opposing stimuli.

Furthermore, something else intervenes in moving our behavior: desires are there, and ambitions, sentiments, emotions and values: what is all that? is it the *Spirit* that somehow tickles the neurons?

Anyway, how do these abstract drives get translated into motivational forces, capable of moving the neuronal network?

At every moment a thousand forces, reflex, inborn, instinctive, learnt, visceral, rational, affective, ethical, ideal, face each other in the brain to decide your acts, your words.

The soul is measured by the result that this turmoil of opposing forces produces.

But the forces are not immutable. Each of your choices confirms, negates, or retouches the equilibrium that you – your history, your past choices – have established among the forces that guide your spirit.

Each choice retouches your soul. YOU retouch your soul, at every moment, by every choice you make, that marks a new – or partly so, or not at all new – notch in the balances that guide your choices: this way you write your own life, your future. A future that is written as a note, to be reread and reformulated – possibly equal, or almost such, or different – in a moment or a day, a month, a year, when you make another choice, when you DECIDE to choose different balances, because of a new experience, or a thousand of them; or, better, because of how you have lived such experiences, how you have decided to live them.

Nothing is written.
But what is not written is not CHANCE.
Sure, fate can push you, here or there.
But at any moment a slight gust decides, in the uproar of contrasting winds, your direction, and brings you somewhere else, where the game of the winds is different.
Your story may well be the game of these winds, but perhaps precisely that slight gust, that beat of wings of a butterfly, at any moment decides the future tornadoes of your life.

The wings, the butterfly, are not 'chance'. No. It is the soul.
It is the soul, that gets formed and grows through details and nuances.
If a daimon is there, a guiding spirit that governs your choices and needs, it is you the one who build it, a bit at a time, in every moment of your life.

The slight gust, the hissing of wings, are clearly perceived.
Similarly, you can perceive when souls are immobile: you feel the stale air.
But what an enthusiasm, when you encounter untamed souls that can change, evolve, grow.
Souls that are capable of being.
Curious, attentive, multiple, mobile, alive.
You can feel the aroma, from the eyes, the gaze, the gestures, the emotion.

* * *

The idea of a computation, of behavior as an accounting balance, is unacceptable: in looking inside oneself one finds something more than cold, detached evaluations, because passion is there, sentiments, angst, commitment, doubt, fear of blundering.

In the black box of neuroscientists there is a multiplicity that is too often underestimated – 'there are more things...', how was that? ...
Yes, and there are many more than we can dream of in our nervous system as well.

True: sensory stimuli can produce responses. But, more importantly, they do more than that. Each input to our nervous system influences the activity of thousands of neurons and in each of them it gets combined and integrated with different data. Each neuron and each neuronal system computes, elaborates and recognizes different elements and relations within the set of input it receives; this is partially coincident with that of other neurons and circuits. It is called 'parallel processing': a thousand systems that elaborate information in different ways, simultaneously, each of them with its own criteria, purposes and logics, each one focused on what it is interested in recognizing.

The stimuli do produce responses, then, but the responses are not computed by a machine: they are always the result of the interplay among many possible responses, among many elaborations that proceed concurrently.

Let us analyze some adjectives that we use in referring to behavior: *reflex, instinctive, inborn, automatic, spontaneous, conscious, voluntary, intentional, rational, ethical.*

REFLEX is almost inevitable: a neural circuit, they hit you below the knee, the muscle gets stretched, the nerve brings the signal to the spine, the neuron that controls the muscle is activated, and you kick; only if you take care, and if you know it in advance, you can avoid it.

INSTINCTIVE is more complex, but it still tastes neural circuits, reflexes, something already written there: hold a newborn baby by the thorax and they will extend arms and legs, as if they wished to attenuate the crash... hold them standing on a table and let them slide forward, they will move the legs as if they walked; it is complex behaviors, such as sucking and swallowing as soon as you touch the corner of the mouth, but still it is something already predisposed in the nervous system. And it accounts for most animal behaviors.

INBORN may be less defined, it suggests individual differences, somebody may think of fates, destinies and *daimones*, in addition to genes and circuits... But certainly, still no flavor of free will.

AUTOMATIC, you can learn it. We begin to escape the domain of behaviors that are pre-written in neural circuits. It can be very complex; it even lets us perform sophisticated and efficient behaviors in such a clever and quick way that we could not do intentionally... You can repeat a poem in an automatic fashion, play a very difficult piece at the piano, but you must not think about it, otherwise you get stuck... You can play the play-station automatically: my sons taught me, never try and understand or explain what you must do, in a rational way, only learn to rapidly press the keys, and let your fingers do it.

SPONTANEOUS is somehow the sum of instinctive, inborn and automatic, partly already written and partly learned, complex but rapid, without thinking, unintentional, possibly unconscious, sometimes even unaware. Here genes and *daimones* have already lost control: what we see and live as spontaneous, in most part is *LEARNT* rather than innate.

Then there is *CONSCIOUS*, looking at oneself acting, comparing different reaction schemes, recognizing what we are doing and what guides us.

And finally, choice appears: *VOLUNTARY* (strictly speaking, *INTENTIONAL*, because *physiologically* any muscle that you may move voluntarily is called a voluntary muscle, even though it may move without our even noticing it, like respiratory muscles): *intentional* is no longer being carried, no longer autopilot, it is acting, intervening.

At each of these steps new possibilities are added, and greater complexity, and growing multiplicity.

RATIONAL is all this, plus attentive analysis and synthesis, in addition, and logics and harmony.

One thing is crucial in this escalation: *TIME*. Reflex responses in milliseconds, more complex inborn circuits may need a few tens of milliseconds, demanding automatic responses a bit more. A voluntary act requires tenths of second – the structure and the complexity of the neuronal circuits demand these 'long' (on the timescale of neuronal activity) times – and a rational response may ask for seconds, minutes sometimes, or a good sleeping night.

Finally, *ETHICAL*. If one watches closely, this *only* adds beauty. Harmony, capacity of reconciling different needs, considering reality, and the others, and love, good, right, just. Taking care of everything. And for an ethical choice, sometimes an entire life is not long enough.

The more you ascend this staircase, the stronger the flavor of soul.

* * *

Identity – me

Strange ambiguities and paradoxes.
Sweet, bitter, tasty, spicy, acid, flavorless, tasteless... The most efficacious 'sensorial' adjectives, those that appear to grasp the essence of things and their emotional relevance, are gustative – the most visceral sense. Sure. The part of the brain that elaborates emotions is strictly linked to the regions that control visceral functions; but is it there, then, the deepest part of us, is that the way to the soul?

Let us go back to behavior: it seems that what is spontaneous tells more about us as we really are, the deepest and truest part of us.
Baloney! It tells more about a part of us, the fastest and simplest one, the most biological, least multiple, least beautiful part of us.
Least beautiful: it is not ugly, but it is trivial, ordinary, it does not scent multiplicity, complexity, freedom, it has no flavor of soul.

Flavor, scent, perfume.
Sure, perfume: perfumed lily of the valley, and cold, beautiful and scentless orchids. Like people, one would say, some of them handsome, gorgeous but with no hidden treasures, others like timid, but scented rosemary.

Easy, maybe too easy, the parallel between perfume and soul. Nothing strange: the part of the brain that analyzes odors is among the first ones that developed in evolution; almost all animals have an olfactory cortex, more developed than ours. This is obvious: the nose lets you localize enemies, prey, food, fire, toxic substances, partners and their sexual accessibility.

Lower animals, that swallow whatever moves, may do without much cortex, but differential identification of a smell is a complex question and requires sophisticated processing: this justifies the development of the archi/paleo-cortex, which is mostly organized about olfactory input. And this region of the cortex, the most antique one, is intertwined with the areas that elaborate visceral information and move emotional life.

Perhaps this is why what smells seem to talk to us more directly from deep inside, and to more deeply mark our memories.

Because that which moves the ancestral, visceral, emotional part of the brain leaves the most profound marks (should we mention Marcel's madeleinettes?).

Perfume, visceral, emotional...
Damn! we look for the soul, what should be the most true, deep,
uncontaminated, ineffable part of ourselves, and we end up on the
instinctive and visceral part!

The most biological, corporeal and fleshy among the sublime games of
neurons, something much less spiritual than logical abstractions,
reasoning, fantasies, dreams, desires, ideals, commitment, sensibility to
beauty and justice and right...

In the end, it appears that the deepest individuality, far from being pure
spirit, be rooted and entangled in the strictest and deepest way with our
viscerality, with our flesh, with our cells, nerves, with biology, with
matter.

Still, who would not see all this as a part – a deep, indispensable part – of
the soul?

* * *

We must change our perspective.

The brain cannot be considered as a machine that generates responses and guides behaviors based on the stimuli the organism receives.

One cannot even get close to understanding how the brain rules behavior without initially being surprised, astonished and enchanted in front of the richness and multiplicity of the facets of each activity of the nervous system, from simple perception of sounds, odors, images, to emotional and affective coloring of each experience, thought, word.

Let us talk about choices, then, and doubts; but true questions, serious doubts, say 'to be or not to be?'...

It is so evident that here one escapes the domain of pure calculus, that science can explain. But it would be nice to try and show that science can say something about this as well.

Once more the question is that of multiplicity, and integrity. The choice becomes INDIVIDUAL when all components participate in it, cognition, emotion, affectivity, esthetics and ethics, and knowledge, memory, desires, affects, fantasies, dreams, passions, commitment...

Under such conditions the choice, and doubt, is ours, individual, whether the instinct or the reason guides us.

Such choice must consider the 'world out there', and that the answers may change. The problem often is that choices and acts, once they have been made, cannot be erased...

But nothing is dictated by the 'world out there', by the necessity of things and events. Here is the essence of free will: the possibility of choosing by combining a hundred distinct procedures of evaluation and motivation, which are confronted and faced in the centers that guide acts, actions, behaviors, projects.

No calculus holds here. It is a complex mechanism, the intersection of a thousand processes, and a simple nuance might lead to totally different choices and results.

A scientific approach has been developed to face systems like this one; it is the mathematics of nonlinear systems, and the theory of CHAOS – which has nothing to do with disorder, randomness or chance. It is a powerful approach that makes it possible to describe, and partially understand, the behavior of unpredictable systems, by identifying 'attraction basins' (types of behavior into which the system tends to fall back) and crests, from which the system will tumble toward one or the other – possibly totally opposite – evolution for the slightest, imperceptible difference in any one of the internal or external parameters, like a ball placed on the blade of a razor.

This approach lets us describe, UNDERSTAND – if one likes overstatements – a chaotic system, but never PREDICT it. A thread, a nothing that was imprecisely measured, or neglected, and the system will change in an unpredicted way.

For human behavior, this unpredictability tastes freedom, individuality, uniqueness and creativity.

* * *

Thus, what is truly individual is the combination of all our ways of reacting, from the reflexes, and spontaneous and visceral responses, to all that we have learnt as automatic, to our rational and ethical evaluations.

The doubt, the choice, the act, is then ours, *INDIVIDUAL*, whether instinct is guiding us, or emotion, or rationality. Many analyses and evaluations simultaneously arise within the nervous system: they consider distinct aspects with different gazes; it is a concurrent and tumultuous proceeding of independent elaborations, as in a badly governed assembly, or an evening among friends: one starts talking, another one interrupts and starts talking about something else...

The most interesting aspect is that this is exactly our way of elaborating, the way our brain works. It is so for memories, emotions, desires, it is so for thinking, reasoning, dreaming.

In response to each stimulus – be it external or internal (images, ideas, spoken words or simply the thought of) – each system proposes its own associations – be they sensations, emotions, memories and images of past episodes, associations to other concepts, evocation of other words.

And one ends up following a new, often unexpected pathway, the same way as *thought* follows a thread as long as it can, to finds itself displaced as soon as a word or an image produces a strong evocation; the same way as a tourist abandons the tour proposed by the guide, distracted by an unexpected sight.

Each brain is distracted / attracted by different perspectives...

Primary cortical areas (visual auditory, somesthetic, motor) are rather invariable. In the face of a trompe-l'oeil, of an optic illusion, we are all deceived in the same way, because we all elaborate the image in the same way, no one has a cortex cleverer that the others.

But when we consider the parts of the cortex that elaborate, when we reason on it, then each of us reasons and interprets their own way. Because each one of us, in the pathway of thought, of evaluation and of choice, evokes different associations, images, memories, emotions, desires, stories.

This is why our choices cannot be predicted, there is no constraint, predestination, automatism, or trivial computation determined by genes and experience. Human choices cannot be predicted, the same way as the value a stock will have tomorrow cannot be predicted, even though the mechanisms that determine stock value fluctuations are perfectly clear, and even if no hazardous or unpredictable events occur (wars, or prime ministers who have financial involvements passing on their suggestions to their friends...); because the stock exchange trends are the result of many many heads, each one with its own criterion.

Experts teach you that if you wish to take a decision in a rational way you must fetch pen and paper, write down pros and cons, possibly with scores, for the different hypotheses, and build a table that lets you see everything there, together.

But why would doing so be useful? Obvious! because the brain does not do that, it is not able to do that: the same way as thought follows a thread, but any evocation can deviate and enrich it, so we also perform our evaluations: it seems we follow a thread, but there isn't a single thread. It is many threads, and now one aspect prevails, now another, now an emotion weights a perspective and unbalances towards 'pro', now a memory brings back to other considerations...

It is not the arithmetical sum of a hundred simultaneous evaluations, a hundred forces – motivations – that pull in favor or against, a hundred numbers with a *RESULT OF THE COMPUTATION* that determines whether it is yes or not.

No. Each evaluation evolves in time, the intensity of its motivational force changes, while the spotlight of attention points to one of them now, to another one in the next moment.

We have seen that already in sensory cortices the neuronal circuitry can collect and analyze, and then re-elaborate, compare, follow in time: an unconscious and complicated process of displacing the focus, getting closer and stepping back, changing view, angle and perspective.

The same process occurs in multimodal regions, where various kinds of information are combined in search of resonances and dissonances, relations with emotional impulses, physiological needs, motivational drives. The exam is performed by focusing on single pieces of information, or combinations thereof, again and again, with different sequences; the experience is narrated, bringing to the threshold of *consciousness* events, concepts, ideas, and the awareness of reality and of oneself.

Similar processes produce the choice: in the hierarchy of the neuronal circuits, each system exploits all elaborations produced by simpler systems and extracts relevant aspects and coherent readings by cruising this sea of elaborations. Each piece of information is weighted, attributed a specific relevance; each one must be confronted, put in relation and merged with the other similarly relevant bits of information, to yield at any moment the best 'response', or better, the best 'reading'.

But this is not a computation. The many analyses and evaluations, which simultaneously consider different aspects with different gazes and move around in the nervous system, may push us to choose exactly now, and say *YES*, or wait just a little, and end up saying *NO* just an instant later.

It is not the result of a calculus, once and for all. Not only each evaluation may yield a result that varies in time; the centers that control motivation consider and analyze one of them now, and in a moment focus on another.

Innumerable distinct procedures of evaluation and motivation are concurrently generated, alternated, compared; they face each other in the nervous centers that guide gestures, actions, behaviors, projects. Thus, one more instant may be enough to let a new evaluation prevail, often a more complex one, sometimes a more valid one.

Here is the unpredictability of human behavior. Unpredictability of our choices even for ourselves. Yes, there are mathematics that describe processes like this, complex and mutable – the fascinating mathematics of chaos theory – mathematics that can portray such systems, and define probabilities, edges, bifurcations and attraction basins, but cannot *predict* behavior. Because behavior can be totally different due to a single, imperceptible, infinitesimal difference in whatever detail.

Still, if you precisely knew each single irrelevant detail....

* * *

No. You cannot.

This is one of the most important cultural progresses of the twentieth century. Heisenberg's indeterminacy principle – or uncertainty principle – assures us that even in an apparently simple system such as an atom you cannot know where exactly an electron is in a particular instant, and the more precisely you get to know that, the less precisely you will be able to tell its momentary velocity. It is not a mere problem of accuracy of the available measurement instrumentation – maybe tomorrow we shall be able to... – no, each electron has a precise probability of being at each location in each moment, this can be computed, but its precise position cannot be known. Better, it cannot be defined.

This is certain. One of the few things we can rely on.
The certainty of our uncertainty.

And if the position of a simple electron CANNOT BE EXACTLY DEFINED, the same principle should grant that there is no way of DEFINING (notice, it is not even a problem of 'knowing') WITH INFINITE PRECISION all the drives and motivations that fight in a brain, and their strength, and the sequence with which they are evaluated, and which will be the exact moment of the decision and what will be the way each drive and motivation is considered and weighted at that precise moment.

When I was young, and catholic, the thing that used to irritate me most in the whole story was 'Mysteries' (capital M).

Actually, I am not disturbed at all by mysteries, the unknown, difficulties. No, the problem was that those 'Mysteries' could not be understood.

To be honest, the relativity theory is not easy, either. But those 'Mysteries', you WERE NOT ALLOWED TO understand them, it was FORBIDDEN. 'Human mind cannot...' – they contradict logic, to say it flat.

But this is absurd! Precisely: it is a MYSTERY, you believe it — faith — and that is all.

Deep in my heart, I always wished I would be able to demolish at least one of these mysteries. Now, the MYSTERY OF FREE WILL looks like the right one to be dismantled.

Actually, free will is a tricky subject per se, but what is so 'Mysterious' in it is not well apparent at first sight: you might need to be catholic to understand it.

The question (the 'Mystery') is:

a) you are free to act following your 'free will'

b) God knows everything, and

c) though your body might be considered as the natural product of procreation by your parents, God CREATED your soul, thus

d) God obviously knows what you will do on any occasion

e) if He (notice, absolutely not "She", if you are a good Catholic) had wished you did something different He would have created your soul different

f) still, it is right that you be considered responsible, and rewarded or punished, for your acts, because they are the consequence of your FREE choices

g) here is the MYSTERY — what defies human logic: how can you be responsible for how God made you, and how can God know what you will do if you can change your mind at any moment.

But we just said it is not possible to DEFINE WITH INFINITE PRECISION the motivational interplay and therefore to predict human choice, that is therefore intrinsically, constitutively unpredictable. God may well know everything, but it would be no use, even to Him, to know something that cannot be DEFINED.

So, there is nothing to know. And you are FREE.

No MYSTERY there, whatsoever. Here is one of my preferred aspects of the wonderful power of the uncertainty principle.

* * *

So, it is not possible to precisely know all the details, and human choice is intrinsically unpredictable. Like a nonlinear, chaotic system.

You may tell how likely it is to behave in this or that way, in a certain condition, but you will not be able to predict with any certainty. And it is not a matter of chance, it is a 'deterministic' process (cause → effect), although it is so complex that the outcome appears to be influenced, or even determined, by chance. Choice is unpredictable. Genes and facts are not sufficient to predict it, but chance has nothing to do with it...

All this has the flavor of uniqueness, individuality, freedom, creativity. 'But what if I...', then, is not a futile game, the impossible history that different choices would have produced.

It is doubt, regret, remorse. It is a possible truth, another possible story, if a detail had not escaped our attention, if an imperceptible instant of delay had permitted more complex and slower neural circuits to add some other evaluation criteria before we made an important choice.

* * *

There are three axes, along which the various levels of behavior move.

1. TIME:
- pre-written circuits respond in milliseconds;
- automatic behaviors are almost as rapid: if you try and construct your dance steps, the movements of your fingers on the piano, the words of a poem or prayer learnt by heart, you stagger and hesitate;
- voluntary acts require tenths of a second;
- rational choices at least seconds – better an overnight sleep
- for an ethical act an entire life may not be enough.

2. MULTIPLICITY:
the more time you allow for your reaction, the more numerous approaches are confronted; instinct does not necessarily succumb, but it is no longer the only or the main factor. Multiplicity – each aspect per se but also with regard to all that it can be put in relation with: rules and internal logics, yes, but looked at from outside as well, and in relation with any other possible logic. And analysis, re-reading in a wider perspective – metanalysis – and higher systems always in search of unifying views, of HARMONIES, although momentary.

3. BEAUTY:
even an automatic act can become perfect – under the athletic and formal aspects – but there is a kind of higher beauty in the ethical act, a beauty that comes from the synthesis of all aspects and dimensions: ethics, in the end, is nothing but being able to look at oneself, and choosing the most beautiful act, absolutely, the choice that reflects the most comprehensive harmonies, in all possible aspects and domains.

The pleasure of beauty... this as well in brain circuits, to be studied more carefully.

If all this is in the nervous system – and it is there – one cannot look at the brain as an input-output control system only, studied to optimize the response to incoming stimuli.

But – one would say – if the evaluations are performed by a computing system, complex as it may be; if it is so awkward that it cannot evaluate everything together, but continues to change perspectives; if it is true that a moment of hesitation is sufficient to react in a different way...

Well, this way it seems it is simply chance, it is not ME who decides, it is only a flow of evaluations and who knows how, one of them suddenly wins and... zac! The choice is made.

Where has all the poetry gone? and angst, and enthusiasm?

No, it is not a chance. It will rather be the way *YOU* have come to move among the different evaluations, the weight *YOU* attribute to their affective relevance, to self-assertive aspects, to fear, stability, need of protection, and social, political, ideal aspects; it will be the way *YOU* have learnt to find your way in this labyrinth; it will be *YOUR TIMES*; all this determines what your final choice will be.

All this and not your genes. Neither is it the experiences you have lived (the '*ENVIRONMENT*').

Rather, it is *THE WAY YOU* have lived them. How *YOU* – with the genes you happen to have, sure, and all the experiences you have gone through – how *YOU* have gradually modified, moment by moment, *YOUR OWN WAYS* of elaborating, by modifying connections and circuitries among your neurons; how *YOU* have performed each of your choices, thereby progressively modifying *YOUR WAY* itself of performing your choices, and *YOUR TIMES*, *YOUR* criteria.

> *"We start by being made by others, and then we remake ourselves, starting out from what others have made of us".*
>
> *"We are what we do", thus "We are what we make of what others have made of us", and "What is important is not what happens to us, but how we respond to what happens to us"*   *Jean Paul Sartre*

* * *

We have got to know many cellular processes that make neurons modify their connections and their way of elaborating the signals they exchange, in consequence of the information itself they are elaborating.

Each experience changes the circuits that analyze it, the brain is modified by elaborating, the same way as the language evolves in speaking: each relation that is identified, each analogy and evocation, becomes a paradigm and a new perspective in future data elaboration, the same way as each word that is used in a different context assumes new color, meaning and evocative power. The circuits change, are modulated and continuously retouched in each of us, at each moment; they are different today from how they used to be yesterday, or they will be tomorrow. So, each of us is not their genes, their interactions with the environment and their acts: each of us is THE WAY we have lived our experiences, have made our choices, and the TIMES, the EQUILIBRIUMS, the HARMONIES according to which we have learnt to think and act.

Here, in this fluctuation among a thousand evaluations, is the origin of free will. This is the reason why our choices cannot be predicted.

There is no constraint, predestination, automatism, trivial computation determined by genes and experience.

Not even our own choices can we predict...

The origin of all this is in that part of our brain that explores, cruises among evaluations, motivations, possible choices, and unpredictably fluctuates, unpredictably but not randomly, guided by the finest details that we ourselves have built in our own brain, in performing each act we have performed up to now, in interpreting each experience we have lived and interpreted, in judging every event we have judged up to now.

That internal spotlight illuminates one or the other of the areas that suggest possible behaviors and elicit motivational drives, in the attempt to follow a logical path in reasoning as well as in making an ethical choice. The crucial characteristic of our choices is this fluctuation.

Rarely do we change our opinion gradually, a little step at a time...
Rather, we keep changing perspective.

If in a precise moment they commanded us to decide, exactly in that moment, we might decide in a certain way, but if they asked us to do it just 10 seconds later, our choice might be quite different; because the picture we are examining keeps changing, our attention is caught by different aspects at any moment, now it is more focused on emotional aspects, then it cares more about rationality, or is guided by dreams, memories, desires...

Here, in this swinging among a thousand evaluations, lies the origin of free will, in the way developed by each of us, in our history, to navigate in this storm of opposed winds.

This is why one cannot predict our choices.

It is free will, and simultaneously it is the doom of remorse and regret. Because in the end what wears us out is conflict. In front of hard choices only this we may ask, that the conflict ends – that the thousand forces that quiver in our soul agree, calm down, stop once and for all redrawing lights and shades that change all the time, generating doubts.

* * *

The dud for a whole generation of parents, exposed with no forewarning to dr. Spock's revolutionary theories (Benjamin Spock, not the other one, with pointed ears – or maybe he had pointed ears, too, but nobody told us, or perhaps I am confusing names, his name was not even Spock...): "you must understand and explain, the child must understand".

For many of us this came to mean, simply, stop with NO's, no more prohibitions, no more duties for these poor creatures. Only freedom.

Now, the problem is not whether they grew up better or worse – sure, in general they are less respectful, they do not say 'good morning, sir', 'good evening madam', they do not give way or cede their seat on the bus...

No, the problem is that with no prohibition and duties it has become a terribly demanding task! for them!

I mean, give them a break! give a break to this child, give them some certainties! some rules based on authority, that freed them from conflict. Let them get angry at you, sometimes, instead of fighting within themselves, between desires and rationality.

Not always, sure. Do let them have something to mull over, some interior struggle to fight... But, at least every once in a while, give them a break!

Vittorio Alfieri knew well how difficult it is to decide – every single moment – what to do, what is right. He used to be presented as a model, in Italian schools, a model of strong will – 'volli, fortissimamente volli' (I wanted, extremely strongly wanted) – and instead he was merely able to oblige himself to study, tied to the chair, otherwise he would not do it at all.

If only Hamlet could ask somebody to tie his sword to his hand and guide it to perform the act that had to be performed!

deciding once and for all: here!, decided!, I do it!, done!

and in that same moment – not an instant later, when a new doubt, uninvited, might appear – everything is done, finished, nothing more to say about it...

Because the soul is like the tide
now a few isolated rocks on the golden burning sand,
now only water, everywhere,
now rocks that sink and emerge,
and waves that stubbornly slap them and shatter and come back,
over and over again,
as if they really thought they could change the world.

How nice would it be, instead, to know that nothing will change,
to decide now, here, and to know that somewhere else, tomorrow,
the soul will be the same, every choice will certainly be confirmed,
there will be nothing to regret or to be sorry about.

But in our soul a thousand drives, weak or strong,
ask and scream at every moment, and face each other;
now one seems to prevail, now another...

And regret is hiding there, ready to show up tomorrow...

* * *

Will, wanting. It is not a choice, it is a storm, a babbling of voices, requests and calls. Will is not deciding, making statements, screaming – it is persevering, resisting to circumstances, fatigue, doubts, desires – it is not setting a course, but being able to maintain it.

So, how you have faced each choice in the past; how you have learnt to make choices, and changed your way of making them; what each of your choices has etched in you, in your neurons and in the connections of your brain; how you have lived each experience, each instant, each choice...

This, all this indeed IS YOUR HISTORY – not what happened to you but HOW you lived it, and how you have been changing because of this, moment by moment, and building your ego, yourself.

* * *

An interesting aspect of all this is that in making choices we surely are not particularly clever. Because when we finally decide, it generally happens that in the end we have overvalued some aspects and neglected some others. But when the question is to be able to consider higher values, and to compress some of our needs – possibly strong ones – in the name of something more important (higher harmony, beauty of the choice), then our 'decision making' procedure, based on examining many subsystems of the problem under many different points of view, is the best one, and make us able of true ethical choices.

Still, in order to really consider most aspects, and to make an ethical choice, one must remain in trouble for a while. And forget the hurry and the simple, easy and rapid ways...

A collateral but crucial aspect is that about half of our brain (the frontal part) is in charge of planning behavior, and its major contribution to decisions consists in simulating and IMAGINING the execution of the act and predicting its consequences. This SUBJECTIVE rehearsing often contributes to delays, uncertainty, angst. Especially when we are faced with choices which imply unpleasant aspects on either arm.

Did you ever hear about that test "if you push that button you kill 10 people, if you do not push it 300 will die"? most people honestly tell they would not have the courage to push the button... and the linguistic trick is perfectly correct, here, because when your forebrain simulates pushing the button, that precise act produces the death of 10 people, and you actually KILL them, whereas if you do not do anything your forebrain has nothing to simulate and the 300 WILL SIMPLY DIE.

YOU KILL some, or many *DIE.*

The terrible thing is that this attitude becomes a diffuse ethical-political attitude (there would be many examples): it is always easier not to do anything than stand up and intervene, it is always easier not to assume any responsibility...

Once more we find ourselves talking of extremely elevated aspects, ethical aspects, altruism, assuming responsibilities, aspects that go well beyond the dimension of our own personal life. We may not name the soul, but all this bring us in a social, ideal domain that departs from what one normally associates to brain and its functioning, to behavior in a neurological sense. Still, these things rumble precisely there, together with emotions, and memories, and dreams. It is curious, it often seems to us they bubble somewhere else, in some ethereal domain we feel some need for. Because the brain, if nobody tells us, we do not even realize it is there. Possibly, this comes from the intriguing fact that the only part of our body which does not have any sensory receptors, for pain or anything else, is the brain.

On the other hand, this may be obvious: what use could the brain do of receptors that tell it what is going on within the brain?

Well, this might be exactly why it is so difficult for us to locate in a part of our body, or brain, all these emotional, affective, evocative, esthetic, social and ethic aspects, and we end up looking for a soul, somewhere outside the body, to accommodate them.

XIII
MOTIVATION – Needs and pleasure

After all this talking about the wandering of our mind in search of the best choice, the question comes to my mind 'why should our brain undergo this heavy burden of continually changing its perspective, examining things from a thousand different angles, trying to consider all possible aspects?', what in the world pushes it not to content itself of a sufficiently strong drive...

Think of a sudden desire for chocolate – we could take a more complex, or noble choice as an example, but this one will do: why one does not simply go for it, why should one wonder whether there are other aspects to be considered, calories, sugar, self-control, lack of food in the Third World (sorry, I know it is no longer politically correct to say 'Third')...

One may think this built-in mechanism of doubt, and reconsideration, helps in making the best choice. In my opinion this is a quite optimistic view: generally, our way of making choices is not the best one, or at least not the most efficient. The best approach would probably be to select the significant aspects, weigh them simultaneously and decide, rather than continuing to cruise among different views and perspectives.

From the physiological point of view, the question is twofold: what pushes our brain to follow this procedure, and what is the advantage of all this (in particular the evolutionary advantage).

The first one is a tricky question: as we have seen, the brain appears to work this way, in general, it need not be *pushed* to do it; this is the way sensory data are analyzed by unimodal associative areas, which *cruise* in the mass of information by focalizing single aspects or combining them in various ways, changing perspectives, considering and comparing different interpretations. This is the way multimodal areas operate, to generate awareness and produce consciousness. Nothing strange if motivational areas also use the same approach. On the other hand, a fundamental difference exists between cognitive processing and motivational elaboration: the former can go on forever, in principle, whether new interpretations emerge or the brain loops again and again around the same ideas; the latter, instead, must soon or late converge to a choice. Thus, this may be the best way of exploring reality, but it does not seem to be the best way to make a choice. Indeed, to keep questioning is not even pleasurable: if cognitive speculation is an enjoyable game, putting doubt to an end is often a blessed relief.

The same way as procedural and behavioral learning is strongly affected, if not ruled, by the motivational power of pleasure/pain, the continuous search for alternative possibilities and better, more comprehensive and coherent syntheses, the continuous re-examination of behavioral choices (but if, and if instead...), postponing the relief of choice, must be reinforced by some kind of gratification, a motivational drive capable of counteracting both the anticipated result of the appropriate behavior and the impatience itself of overcoming doubts.

The circuits that make us waste time and energies in fantasizing, that load any choice with doubts and re-examinations and revisions, for the sake of research and discovery of more complex equilibriums and more round harmonies must have some capacity of producing pleasure, of generating a motivational drive by activating deep centers linked to pleasure, capable of producing a diffuse sensation of well-being.

Indeed, each intuition, understanding, each new unifying perspective, each unexpectedly found – or sought for – harmony, all this generates the same kind of pleasure as a smile, a hug, as social appreciation and success...

The trick that the brain has enacted, to have us search for better solutions, and never be satisfied but pursue something better, is that we manage in enjoying, PROVING PLEASURE in beauty, in harmony.

While I am revising these notes a paper comes out on *Neuron* that shows how the ventral striatum (that *n. accumbens* which fires when we expect a gratification and to announce pleasure) is activated by novel stimuli, simply because they are novel. Is this too trivial?...

> *"You were not made to live your lives as brutes,*
> [you got this drive in your own accumbens, dullards!]
> *but to be followers of worth and knowledge".*   *[Dante]*

Thus, what pushes us to look for a better choice are two aspects: the general operating mode of the cerebral cortex on one side; the 'pleasure' of looking for a more comprehensive analysis and a higher synthesis on the other side, the pleasure of *achieving* it, the pleasure of harmony.

But why should humans develop the capability of proving pleasure, in front of harmony, of a synthetic coalescence of incoherent data?

Well, once you do have the capability (read, sufficient number of neurons) to interpret the same data in many ways, and to find several solutions to the same problem, you offer the nature a marvelous possibility to pursue its objective of multiplying survival strategies within one and the same organism...

Why then should not nature change this potentiality into reality?

It would be no use to be able to offer many solutions to the same problem, if one were not pushed in some way to find another solution after having found the first, sufficiently good, one. Thus, there must be a prize, a gratification, if you manage in suspending the choice to find a better solution; a gratification to be compared and measured against the possible usefulness, gratification or relief of accelerating the choice.

Still, though speculative attitude may be an evolutional advantage, why do we follow that clumsy procedure? Actually, when we face a difficult question it seems that we are not able to simultaneously consider all the aspects; it seems that we use a spotlight that is only capable of illuminating single subsets of the reality we must examine, and we cannot but move around the spotlight, changing perspectives and judgments, in the hope that sooner or later we shall have explored the whole matter.

Well, probably our wonderful brain, with all its computational power, is much more skillful in decomposing reality and examining subsystems than in putting everything together: actually, it appears that human mind cannot 'compute' (interpret, explain) systems and processes where more than a fixed number (seven?) of independent factors interact. To take care of that, it seems that we did a good job in building computers...

* * *

Neurophysiology of motivation

In the absence of external stimuli, many sensory systems are nonetheless active:

- 'proprioceptive' systems, that report the length, movement and tension of muscles, and the position of the joints;
- 'enteroceptive' systems, that gauge the degree of filling and tension of viscera, arterial and venous pressure, plasma pH (acidity), electrolyte concentrations, oxygen saturation and carbon dioxide level in plasma, glycemia and anything else that may bear some relevance to the survival of the organism;
- 'thermoceptive' systems, that measure the temperature of the skin and the interior of the body, and of the skull

All this information is elaborated and integrated, at various levels in the brainstem (the extension of the spinal cord into the skull), by circuits and control centers that determine specific responses – such as an increase of respiratory activity if the oxygen/carbon dioxide ratio is altered, or a stimulation of the heart and vascular constriction if blood pressure falls...

These medullar centers send the results of their control activity to higher centers. At the top of this hierarchical organization sits the hypothalamus, a nervous structure positioned centrally at the base of the brain; the hypothalamus conciliates and rules all these functions of vegetative control, by coordinating hormonal responses (it directly controls the pituitary gland, that is located just below it) and neural responses. It produces the necessary activations to re-establish blood pressure, if it has been altered; it governs renal activity if the volume or composition of the plasma are abnormal; it controls body temperature by producing vasoconstriction, to avoid heath dispersion, and shivers, in the cold, or by inducing vasodilatation and sweating when the temperature is too high; it intervenes on the regulation of respiration if the pH, or oxygen saturation, or carbon dioxide, are abnormal...

Ok. Wonderful. But it is so obvious that all this is not enough!... Not even to merely survive. If it is really cold, you can vasoconstrict, and shiver, but if you do not fetch something to put on, or find a warmer site, you end up frozen.

If the glycemia falls, you can use up all glucose stocks in the liver, and burn perhaps some more lipids, or even the precious proteins of your muscles, but if you do not eat you end up like a skeleton... And if water is missing in the organism, one can certainly stop urinating, and sweating, but if one does not drink, they will certainly die.

Thus, even for mere and simple vegetative survival it is necessary to perform active behaviors – dressing up, moving, fetching food, eating it, fetching water and drinking it... The brain, the cortex must enact these behaviors. Otherwise, it is necessary that somebody else does these things for us, by shrouding us, feeding us, hydrating us...

The area in the cortex that starts movements (primary motor areas, in the posterior part of the frontal lobe), however, is not sufficient: it is an output area from the brain, those neurons are not the ones that DECIDE what to do, they are merely refined executors.

Performing a 'behavior' – a sequence of ordered movements – requires the activation of areas near to the base of the frontal lobes, in regions near the median line; these are regions that can be considered as the promoters of any movement, those which actually do decide, among the thousands of possible behaviors, which ones are to be enacted. In trying to understand the role of various cortical regions in cerebral functions, it is instructive to consider how the various functions are altered in the presence of localized injuries (traumatic, tumoral, vascular lesions) to specific regions of the cortex, and to this purpose language possibly is the most informative function, as it can be altered in quite many ways: cognitive, logical, affective, syntactic, motor, motivational aspects.

A lesion in these 'prefrontal ventral medial' regions produces an almost total *aphasia* (general term that indicates a disturbance of language), with demoralizing features: it is essentially a form of mutism, due to the fact that the subject has absolutely no drive, motivation to speak. It is not that they can't or don't know how to do it: they could speak correctly but they would only do it in response to a particularly strong stimulus.

These regions of behavior 'triggering' need not program movements in any detail, they simply activate the appropriate areas – in the frontal lobe, 'premotor' areas – that elaborate, design and program the precise movements, by integrating them at several levels of complexity, in the various regions, and over time scales that range from seconds to years.

Here, the point is not to define in detail how premotor areas translate these programs into specific movements: we have seen elsewhere how they also use the cerebellum and basal ganglia to control the precision of movements, to produce learnt 'automatic' movements and to be able to fluidly and harmonically perform complex sequences of movements.

Let us make some steps backward: these regions trigger the behaviors, 'decide' *WHETHER* and *WHAT* to do. But who or what in turn moves these regions, pushes them, orients them in their choice?

Some aspects of this process are clear, others are less so.

A structure of fundamental importance in this interplay is the *nucleus accumbens*. As previously mentioned, this nucleus contains, among others, two populations of neurons with clear-cut functions: one of the two populations discharges each time it is possible to obtain a gratification (feel pleasure or stop a discomfort) – we might define them neurons of 'anticipation' of gratification; the other population of neurons discharges when the pleasure comes or the condition of discomfort is resolved ('reward neurons'). Suppose you are thirsty: the hypothalamus notes the vegetative imbalance, that asks for a behavior (drinking); the *anticipation neurons* will be activated if the hypothalamus points out the need of drinking and the sensory and elaborative structures recognize that there is the possibility of fulfill such need (we are offered a nice glass of iced water), and this results in a very strong stimulation of the centers that 'trigger' the appropriate behavior. It is easy to delay drinking, it can be done even when thirst becomes burning, but if in such conditions somebody shows us a glass of water, then resisting becomes really hard... A less poetical example, but maybe even more convincing, is when the bladder is overfilled and asks for attention: when we finally get to the bathroom the need suddenly and greatly grows, and if an impediment arises at the last minute, unpleasant accidents might happen...

The activation of 'reward neurons', on the other hand, produces a sensation of PLEASURE, pleasure in the strictest sense, no adjectives. But in the meantime it strengthens the related *anticipation neurons* and 'reinforces' the behavior that has permitted this situation to happen, by stabilizing the synaptic connections that have produced such behavior and making it more straightforward and easily executable in the future.

* * *

The dark side of it

It may be worth considering how expectation, anticipation of pleasure, is itself pervaded of pleasure. In many cases, that is the real good part of the whole thing: 'I look forward to, I cannot wait for', it is not simple, anxious or sad impatience, it is the pure pleasure of anticipation.

Perhaps the most difficult thing in growing up is precisely to tune the perception of the relationship between anticipation and achievement of pleasure to a new condition of independence and autonomy.

As young children, expectations of gratification are mostly satisfied – as far as elementary needs are concerned (at least in our privileged society); for the rest, it is the parents who realize the magic, the fulfillment of desire. Conquering gratification simply implies developing the appropriate strategies to OBTAIN it from the parents; indeed, parental approval itself becomes the greatest gratification, an implicit promise of all future gratifications (like the clicker for trained dogs…).

With adolescence, existential needs change: desire has now turned to conquering appreciation, to self-assertion, to the satisfaction of creativity, of projects, to the consideration and admiration by the group of the peers. This creates a situation of dissatisfaction towards the whole world, because it does not fulfill these desires on simple request, as our parents have taught us, and it is not sufficient to well behave to be rewarded with what we desire, or to cry desperately enough to obtain it; in addition, a feeling of inadequacy arises, for the incapability of fulfilling one's desires on one's own initiative, and a drive to look for behavioral and adaptation strategies to conquer other people's benevolence.

If requests, 'good behavior' and strategies fail, the possibility remains of researching one's own autonomous way to self-affirmation; but this is mostly turned inwards, and concentrates on seeing/feeling oneself acting: the value of the GESTURE grows abnormally, of the bravery act in particular, often self-damaging, because of the intensity of the associated feeling of self-sufficiency, and of being able to face and overcome pain.

If you wander around the network, among blogs, you stumble with incredible frequency on narrations of self-damaging acts by youngsters, conscious, programmed, anticipated. What strikes most is the explicit anticipation, a kind of emotional rehearsal, of the act, the declared love for the blade, the ritual, closing oneself in the bathroom, the pleasure of seeing oneself doing it, the pain, the blood that flows...

Get around some more, and you will find other young bloggers describing, with the same rhythms, with the same words, making holes in their own brains...

The fact is that these gestures only depend on you, on your 'nerve' to do them, and you get excited to the idea of seeing yourself performing them and recalling 'I have had the courage'.

Here is a terrible paradox.

This has nothing to do with the original meaning – message – of the act ('cutting one's own veins').

No! here one must turn psychoanalysis upside down: it is not desire of death, a question of auto-destructiveness, of 'lapsus', or of biting one's nails.

No! this apparent auto-destructiveness is not death, it is life – distorted as its interpretation may be – it is assertiveness, it is shouting 'look at me, here I am', it is shouting 'this, at least, this which depends on me, this I can do!'.

* * *

The nervous pathway that most specifically and intensely activates 'pleasure' neurons originates from deep regions in the midbrain, the uppermost portion of the brainstem, in a region called 'ventro-tegmental area' (VTA).

This area originates two most important paths, that both employ dopamine as a transmitter; one of them proceeds towards the *nucleus accumbens*, and from here on to the 'limbic' regions that elaborate emotions (meso-limbic pathway): its activation produces a sensation of pleasure and in the meanwhile reinforces the behavior that has produced the present (pleasant) situation. This is said 'reward pathway'. The second pathway originating from the VTA goes to the prefrontal regions, precisely those that have been described above as implied in choosing, programming and enacting behaviors, and thus in the modulation of voluntary, intentional behavior (this is called meso-cortical pathway). Dopamine is the transmitter in this pathway as well.

Balance between the activities of the two paths, mesolimbic and mesocortical, is crucial to maintain the correct relationship between cognitive activities (and voluntary behavior) and emotional experience. A strong unbalance, that can be generated or sometimes 'treated' by using drugs interfering with dopamine activity, produces 'dissociation' between the two spheres – cognitive and emotional – and gives rise to thought and behavior disturbances of a psychotic type, up to the well-defined clinical picture of schizophrenia (break, rupture if the soul).

The reward pathway is not involved only in vegetative imbalances (cold, heat, need of drinking, eating, sexual desire) and their resolution, but also in emotional aspects, in valuing affective and social interactions, even in strictly cognitive tasks: the possibility of encounter the beloved person and the pleasure of having them close by; anticipating social appreciation and actually obtaining it; realizing that a problem can be solved, a difficult question can be understood, and feeling the pleasure of solving it, of understanding. The nucleus accumbens responds to all these anticipations of gratification – and to the achievement of them – exactly in the same way as it responds to the possibility of stopping a pain or a vegetative discomfort, and to its effective discontinuation.

Obviously, the neurons of the reward systems do not constitute a homogeneous population, that responds unanimously like a well-disciplined army in response to any situation that may resolve a discomfort, or prelude to a pleasure or signal a gratification.

Distinct groups of neurons are involved in each case, and their activation elicits one specific anticipation and motivates or reinforces a specific behavior.

Not everything is already written in the VTA and *nucleus accumbens*: there are neurons originally destined to discharge when water is presented or thirst is quenched, but most others are prepared to acquire through experience the capability of tuning on recognizing any possible gratification that one might ever encounter, it if occurs repetitively, and signaling it. It is not fully clear how wide is neuronal plasticity in the VTA and accumbens, or in other words whether the circuitry of the accumbens itself 'learns', or learning is demanded to the cortical regions that, directly or indirectly, project on these structures. What is clear is that, if a specific form of gratification repetitively occurs in a certain situation, then some neurons in the accumbens will learn to discharge each time that same situation occurs again, to initiate the behavior that may lead to the gratification; and other neurons in the accumbens will discharge when the gratification is realized, thereby reinforcing the behavior.

Behavior is guided by motivational drives. When these arise from biological factors (thirst, hunger, sexual drive), the source of the drive is generally the hypothalamus, according to the paradigm of negative feed-back; responses are graded as a function of the distance between actual and desired values. In this respect, there are major reward centers in the hypothalamus, that elicit fighting and rage when strongly stimulated, and punishment centers (in the hypothalamus and in other regions) that elicit fear and punishment reactions and can inhibit reward and pleasure centers.

On the other hand, motivational drives may arise from personal and social motivations (either innate or acquired/learned); they may be related either to danger, fear, survival – in which case the *amygdala* is the main motor – or to hedonic aspects (pleasure), either direct or indirect: escape pain, pursue well-being, love and care, social acceptance, preserve self-image ...

Newly experienced sensory stimuli excite multiple areas in the cerebral cortex: if no reward or punishment reaction is elicited, repetition leads to extinction of cortical response (habituation); but if a reward or punishment is produced, the cortical response becomes more and more intense upon repetition. This generates, or strengthens, motivational drives towards behaviors related to the situation.

Motivational drives (both homoeostatic and not) are influenced also by the circadian clock and by environmental factors, such as food availability, or clues suggesting the possibility of obtaining pleasure; this latter aspect makes it so that motivational drives can be generated and controlled through conditioning.

Classical (Pavlovian) conditioning consists in generating an association between two events, so that one becomes able to produce the typical response to the other: the sound of a bell, associated repetitively to offering food to a dog, will become able to produce salivation (the response to the offer of food) on its own. This is a purely associative process, is mostly based on cerebellar learning and therefore remains unconscious.

A positive hedonic value (pleasure) or a negative one (fear, pain) can be associated to an initially neutral stimulus, situation or action, through precisely the same mechanism. Conditioning with a fearful or painful stimulus is defined as *aversive (fear) conditioning*. On the other hand, the reward may consist in an actual pleasure (*positive reinforcement*) or in the removal or interruption of a painful or uncomfortable factor/situation (*negative reinforcement*). In all these cases the learning mechanism is different from classical conditioning, as systems that evaluate vital and hedonic relevance are involved.

However, the detection and recognition of alarm signals (whether instinctual or learned) or the association between a gesture and a prize do not justify, per se, modifications in behavior. It is necessary that there be structures and circuits, in the nervous system, capable of both learning and intervening as *motivational forces (drives)*, thereby modifying instinctual responses or generating autonomous behaviors, even without awareness.

If a situation or the result of a behavior are painful or threatening, as in aversive conditioning, the *amygdala* is involved: it triggers emotional responses, enhance memory formation, alerts the cortex to accelerate and improve responsiveness. Avoiding or escaping harm or punishment triggers a hurry, and behavior will be driven by urge and **NEED**.

Anxiety and stress play a similar role with negative reinforcement, and push to act in a hurry, by eliciting instinctual responses, like in aversive conditioning, rather than favoring the calm and rational evaluation of behavioral strategies. Behavior is again guided by the **NEED** to escape. Conversely, a positive reinforcement favors discovering and learning new behaviors: in the absence of stressing factors it is normal to explore the environment and tryout novel interactions with the surrounding objects and novel behaviors (e.g. pressing a lever in a cage for the mouse to receive food): acting can be **POSTPONED**, the prefrontal cortex is given enough time to intervene and to look for rational, possibly novel, strategies to achieve a possible positive result (food, or simply a nice word). Behavioral flexibility – and learning – are strongly favored if to drive us is not **NEED** but by **DESIRE**.

Consistently, conditioning is very effective in molding motivational drives and modifying behavior, but anyone who has tried to educate a dog knows well that through punishment you might be able to teach the animal NOT to do something, but if you wish it to learn a new behavior you need to reward it. You can teach a person to do something, through punishing them if they do not do it, but you need to explain to them what to do; it is conscious and explicit learning, and it is not so easy to do with an animal.

* * *

In few words, behavior driven by need tend to be instinctual, repetitive, while behavior driven by desire favors behavioral flexibility and may be creative. Something learned in *pursuing a desire* (attracted by a reward) involves strategical *programming* and favors the search for *alternative solutions* in case of failure, while something learned to avoid pain or fear, pushed by discomfort, by *a need*, tends to reproduce a *stereotyped response, accelerated and strengthened by anxiety and hurry.*

This is an important distinction in the evolution of many habits, that may start as something pleasurable, done because of the pleasure to do it – recreational activities driven by *desire* – and gradually transform into a *need*, often not even so pleasurable when fulfilled.

Why does this happen?

One factor is that release of dopamine to produce pleasure and motivation does not exactly parallel the hedonic value of an experience (how good it is in absolute terms): a component of *habituation* tends to reduce the pleasure of an experience if one gets used to it as a repeated experience. A second factor is that the pleasurableness of an experience is more related to whether it is better or worse than expected, rather than to its being good or bad per se: *dopamine* release constitutes more of a *prediction error detector* than a signal of absolute hedonic value.

So, a pleasurable habit may lose its capability of producing pleasure; still, the association that was established – following the unconscious tricks of conditioning – between it and the original pleasure survives, and revives the expectation, prefiguring the pleasure and worsening the disappointment when dopamine falls because the result is not the expected one. And the failed expectation can only strengthen the desire.

Even most important, in many cases a habit that arose as recreational may become a consolatory "refuge" in a situation of difficulty it (a way of escaping suffering and pain, a generic *coping strategy*): it will not help to solve the real problems, but it will tend to be pursued, repeatedly tough uselessly, as the only known strategy to escape *anxiety, distress* and *need*, and will become the stereotyped response, that promises rewards and fails to deliver.

A useless, ineffective response, that boosts discomfort and anxiety, intensifies the *need*, and imprisons the *addict* in the hopeless loop of a compulsive behavior.

All drugs that facilitate dopamine release (or potentiate its action) in the reward pathway produce some pleasure (nicotine, marijuana, alcohol, amphetamine, ecstasy, opiates, cocaine, possibly even chocolate and sugar, though more mildly).

Consequently, one 'learns' to look for the drug as a source of pleasure.

More subtle, and equally crucial, is learning by 'anticipatory' neurons, which learn to signal the possibility of obtaining pleasure from the drug whenever a situation occurs that recalls those in which the drug has been obtained in the past – places, people, situations.

Because of this learning, the activation of 'anticipatory' neurons can give rise to a violent motivational drive, which explains why the risk of relapse into drug addiction remains so high even for people who have 'definitely' abandoned the habit: being exposed to places, people, situations that were previously associated to taking drugs triggers 'craving', a violent desire, a strong motivational drive towards searching for the drug and taking it, a drive resisting to which is real hard.

If the habit is using a drug, in particular, tolerance may ensue, and possibly physical dependence (a withdrawal syndrome comes about if the drug is not taken) so that the loop becomes totally unescapable.

However, any initially purposeful pleasurable activity (shopping, playing cards, gambling, drinking, smoking a joint, even a sexual relation or a romantic story), may undergo the same transformation if it becomes the preferred way of evading everyday problems – which will persist unchanged, by the way – and becomes a *habit* that no longer produces any pleasure as a result.

Still, anticipation of a pleasurable experience keeps activating the *reward pathway*; such expectancy has been etched in the circuits by past positive reinforcement and will keep inducing dopamine release and eliciting the motivational drive to repeat the behavior. Only a bout of dopamine, thus, but no more reward. Only discomfort. And **NEED**.

* * *

Consumer society and commodification and monetization of everything makes us lose perspective.

Everything is shown to us, and the message is clear: you can have everything, you can buy everything: a cheaper soap or a trip to the Caribes. The question simply becomes: can I afford it?

If I can, no need to desire, I can have it, right away; if I can't, don't even think about it.

It is as if a glass wall, invisible and unsurmountable, were splitting reality – and life – in two: on one side all that we can afford, no problem, you do not even need to write a check any more, you just click a button in internet; and on the other side of the glass what we can look at, but not touch, what we shall never have, what we can only dream of.

We find ourselves deprived of all the room in between, the terrain where humans have the opportunity of realizing their specific nature of special and different animals, because they are capable of pursuing a project, modify the external reality and even themselves.

We find ourselves deprived of the terrain of DESIRE *and the room for* HOPE.

One can play with dreams. Or with memories. "Memory is not a sin as long as it helps" [Eugenio Montale]. It can give you reassurance, or regret, provided it is sweet, and make you think, grow, act. The same is true for dreams: they are not a sin, as long as they help.

You can play with them, sure, but if they remain dreams, if they have nothing, and nothing will ever have, to do with reality, how do they help?

The brain does not record reality, objects, events; it imagines a reality reasonably likely. It may be an adequate and faithful image and lead us to success. Or may depart and become fantasy, dream: nothing terrible, as long as everything works ok, and we know that it is a dream. One can dream, one can imagine a different reality, be it a possible reality or not, and sit there and just watch; or one can prune the imagination, so that it fits reality as much as possible, and act.

Animals also interpret reality, imagine, dream. The big difference between us and them consists in WHAT *we can imagine, in how we use this capacity to imagine. We can simulate, prefigure, invent; we can concoct a tale and tell it. A tale in which we are active subjects, capable of modifying reality, capable of modifying ourselves.*

This is an enormous expansion of the terrain that lies between life and dreams. Between life — reality that must be accepted the way it is — and dreams, that unrealistic reality that we long for but we can only imagine. It is the terrain of a possible different reality, that we can imagine but we can also create. It is the terrain of DESIRE.

Time keeps contracting, everything becomes faster. It is no longer necessary to move, you are there, instantly, in internet, in teleconference.

And you can have what you "desire" in an instant, until the word "desire" itself dries up, empty of any meaning. It does no longer make sense to "desire", you can simply choose: anything you may have is already there, on the tray, to be picked up, right away.
The rest, unless you can postpone, elaborate a plan, get committed…
No point in desiring it, you can only dream of it.

A glass wall, between objectivity and dream, that has invaded and is eroding the terrain of desire. That room in which imagination, neither forced step by step by reality, nor lost in dreams, can design a possible different reality, a path to get there, a plan to commit to change it.

We are not talking about revolution. We are talking about everyday life.

It is a drift that gets us used, day by day, to sitting comfortably and choose, pointing (with our finger or with the mouse) at what we prefer in the menu of life. No effort is needed: changing the menu, or inventing new recipes, is not up to us.

No effort is needed.

The contrast is sharp. What is possible is easy, the rest is impossible.

It is a drift toward impotence, that starts from the domain of objects, commodities and services, and gradually invades all other domains of our life, relations, self-image, one's role in the world.

The contrast is sharp. What is possible is easy, the rest is impossible.

A working or social situation is difficult or painful? Just take note and look for an easier one. If none is there you take note and soothe yourself: "it is other people's fault, reality's fault, it is bad luck tormenting me". Maybe one dreams of a different reality, impotent victim, ever more frustrated because reality keeps moving away from one's dreams.

A relation does not work? Just take note and look for an easy solution; or defend yourself: "it is not my fault", "I cannot do anything". Maybe one dreams that the relation were different – impotent victim – ever more frustrated because reality is so far away from one's dreams; or one may even believe to their own dream, negate reality and the other person's right to reality, and stalking comes about, and violence in the family.

Am I not the way I would like to be? I just take note – impotent – and cuddle the image of how I would like to be, knowing it is only a dream, reality is what it is and cannot be changed.

One does not need to be a therapist to encounter these arguments and attitudes.

The "impotent victim of reality" syndrome is spreading around, paralizes, hits like a contagious pest.

Where does this novel suffering come from?

Possibly, from the contraction of time: a lot to choose from, here and now, why bother, why would one renounce to what can please us now, to look for something far away, maybe, god knows when?

It is frightening: this incapacity of looking far away is what you observe in subjects who have a lesion of the ventromedial frontal cortex, the region that is crucial for the comprehensive evaluation of strategies on various time scales, the region that endows us with "judgment".

Similar problems are observed in individuals with compulsive behaviors (pathological gamblers) and many drug addicts. These people gradually lose the capacity to postpone a gratification: satisfaction, here and now – adrenaline, for the gambler, drug for the addict – is worth more than any reward or punishment, tomorrow.

One can understand that a lesion to the cerebral cortex produces such a disturbance, losing the capacity of judging; but how is it possible that the spiral of compulsive behavior, slavery to videogames, to drugs, can bring to that same situation?

We saw it: in our brain something bad gradually happens: the motivational system, that initially attributed a value of gratification to that activity, now attributes it a value of relief and escape from discomfort, whatever its origin.

Even without being compulsive or vicious, the shortening of the temporal perspective, the need to decide as quickly as possible, the availability of so many immediate choices, many of them pleasurable, everything contributes to impair the onset of a quiet evaluation, a rational and strategical consideration of the consequences of each choice in time.

This way the ability to be the conscious authors of one's choice, of one's aims is shrinking: one gradually drifts toward the sensation of being a victim of the circumstances, forced to choose instead of desiring, to take instead of building, to react rather than act.

But if there is no room to build projects, were does DESIRE end up?

There is no more room to desire. There is no more room because desire can only be cuddled if there is a possibility of realizing it, changing reality or changing ourselves. And only this possibility opens the space for hope.

When a dream rises above the horizon, and our commitment manages to create the conditions for a possibility to realize it, even a remote one, and to design a plan, then HOPE is born.

But hope is not a product of dreams. No, it is a product of the capacity to IMAGINE, to PREFIGURE a way, a path, a COMMITMENT.

The way and the path will depend on the external reality, and in part on the others, but commitment will not. Commitment is our own stuff.

Prefiguration, strategy, commitment are born and grow inside us, They depend on us. They can turn a dream into a desire. And let us nurture it, see it grow, become realizable, become a project, give us hope.

Hope, a unique energy that multiplies our forces, our skills, our possibilities.

We have a capacity other animals lack: prefiguring strategies, paths and solutions, enjoy the anticipation, transform it into motivation. And the capacity to prefigure and to prefer the pleasure of savoring a future success, though merely imagined, to satisfying an immediate need or whim, allows us to delay the gratification, to give up the immediate good for a greater future one, to develop strategies, which may even imply suffering, for a higher reward, to sacrifice our interest to pursue what is right and sacred. And will make us feel good about ourselves.

This is why the drift of society and culture toward an exasperation of the immediate availability is so depressing: if I can have it, I must have it right away; and if I can't have it now, I simply cannot have it.

The diffusion of drugs, gambling, compulsive shopping, internet and videogame and phone dependence, highlight this need of immediate satisfaction, the incapacity of postponing, or neglecting it, in name of something more important, but less near and incumbent.

The complement to this incapacity to face reality is the growing incapacity to relate to oneself: the diffuse narcissism, insane narcissism. Because loving oneself is nothing bad. But certainly bad is losing the capacity of looking inside oneself, misled by the image in the mirror – constantly feeling as a victim of circumstances and other people, hiding our own responsibility in what happens, not being able to imagine what we might do to change, and to change reality.

It is a form of training to give up imagining, training to unlearn to evaluate costs and benefits, present as well as future, to consider the risks, the commitment and the distress that are required and the future rewards, material, personal, social, ethical.

It is a training to give up desiring, with all the corollaries – effort, uncertainty, fatigue, but also sweet anxiety, expectation, anticipation – that accompany desire.

But it is also a training to feel like impotent victims, to give up hope.

* * *

Any behavior that can bring discomfort to an end, or produce a gratification, is demanded – MOTIVATED – when *the possibility* of enacting it, and obtaining its positive outcome, comes about.

The associative regions of the cortex perform a continuous activity of elaboration and evaluation of the real situation, simulation of behaviors and assessment of their consequences; this translates every strategy – even the most complex – that can earn us a gratification into *prefiguring* the reward and *exploring the possibility* of performing the appropriate behavior, and this way MOTIVATES the possible strategies.

At every moment the prefrontal areas in charge of behavioral control are assailed by requests from each associative region, proposing different behaviors aimed to obtain positive outcomes, be they vegetative, emotional, affective, social or cognitive. So, these regions must evaluate the compatibility of the various behaviors and strategies in question, considering the intensity of the MOTIVATION associated to each of them.

This is not a mere static computation, a score for each motivational force and the strongest one simply wins... It is a continuous re-evaluation of alternative hypotheses, in the attempt at reconciling or excluding them; complex paths, alternative plannings, interior simulations of behavior are proposed. And the whole process is interfered by reflex, instinctive and automatic responses, that are generated at low levels of the nervous system: these sometimes prevent a complex behavioral planning; in other cases, they can be anticipated and inhibited, so that the complex behavioral strategies elaborated by higher centers can be pursued.

* * *

The picture we just finished drawing is quite disconcerting: prefrontal associative areas of the cerebral cortex incessantly elaborate strategies and behavioral plans, that are evaluated based on the pleasure they can secure and the *possibility* of achieving it. When a sufficient motivational force sustains a strategy, the behavior is initiated.

This is totally disheartening.

Where did the soul go?

Weren't we supposed to talk about the soul, here?

True. If you tell it this way, it appears it is only a hideous materialistic calculus *(NOOOO! how many times must I say that it is not a computation, but an evaluation, which is continually evolving, of alternative strategies, a continuous re-examination in the light of ever-new proposals of integration, reconciliation, exclusion...).*

Ok, it is not calculus. But it is materialistic, isn't it?
I have only talked of gratification, discomfort, pain and pleasure.

Well, ok, should we pretend we didn't know this already?

Kant himself had a depressive crisis when he finished his "Critique of practical reason" and realized that his *categorical imperative*, that metaphysical force that drives us to act irrespective of any personal interest, pursuing what is RIGHT only and exclusively BECAUSE IT IS RIGHT, does not actually occur in life: the motivation is never exclusively ethical, the satisfaction of having behaved well is anyway there, pride, the feeling that we deserve approval by ourselves, by others, by those who do not know but if they knew…, possibly even the expectation of a prize in another life, and freedom from remorse, and the feeling of superiority that comes from not having to thank but rather to be thanked, and we could go on for some pages along this line…

But here, if we wish to understand what mechanisms sustain such behavior, as it would be expected from a treatise about the PHYSIOLOGY of the soul, the question is not whether there is a spiritual force that overcomes the motivational storm in the frontal cortex – fully taken by earthy pleasures.

The question is how can superior values, supra-personal, social, ethical, ideal values, *enter* that motivational storm in the brain, being sustained by a currency of equal worth, so that the cortex might consider and evaluate them in a 'homogeneous' and fair way, with respect to the other motivational drives described so far.

Here, once more, some limits and borders seem to magically disappear.

Because if we consider these supra-personal values one by one, we see that they have precise correlates into specific cerebral activities, and therefore they can be translated into 'neuronal' motivational forces, not different (from a biological point of view) from vegetative motivation, and from those aimed at avoiding pain and pursuing pleasure.

The key words are EMOTION, SOCIAL appreciation, desire of overcoming one's own LIMITS, affectivity and LOVE, SYMPATHY and SOLIDARITY, ETHICS, harmony, BEAUTY, eagerness for INFINITY.

EMOTIONS, viscerally lived and shared below the level of consciousness, are elaborated by portions of the cortex that do not give them *words*, but apply to them a true and full logic, though implicit, non-rational, nonverbal: the emotional logics, the 'intelligence of the heart'.

The regions that elaborate emotions are strictly interconnected with the 'anticipation' and 'reward' circuits just described, both directly and through the cognitive and verbal elaboration by other frontal areas that plan behavioral strategies that pursue emotional well-being and gratifications.

The link is tight and twofold: on the one side emotions can easily generate powerful motivational drives; on the other side, these regions elaborate the activities of the 'anticipation' and 'reward' neurons, translating them into emotion: desire, anxiety, satisfaction, pleasure.

Emotions are shared directly, with no need for cognitive elaboration.

These are mechanisms present in animals as well: emotions trigger instinctive behaviors – mimics, bodily postures – that have the function of communicating the emotions to other subjects, so that an animal that detects the presence of a predator rapidly transmits its fear – thanks to its bodily changes – to the whole herd, that can thus escape the danger.

The sub-cortical centers recognize emotion-related mimic responses (in a fundamentally instinctive and unconscious way) and reproduce in the subject who sees them the same emotions that have generated them.

It is not necessary to have a particularly touchy soul to feel joy in front of joy and sadness in front of tears...

From here comes the ability to recognize whether other people accept and appreciate us, and our behavior. This is an extremely strong need for humans: it begins with the total dependence of the infant on the mother and the need to establish a symbiotic relation with her in the first months of life, it grows with the need to be accepted and protected by the parents, the family, and later by the group of peers.

Mirror neurons let us feel other people's emotions; this is particularly true as regards people who are close to us, emotionally, affectively, who occupy a privileged position in our emotional life, in our memory, in our experience.

This attributes a powerful motivational valence to affection and LOVE, and in general contributes to translate social consensus and appreciation into a powerful motivational drive. The tendency to identification also translates into the capacity –once again with no need for a particularly noble soul – of loading with motivational value the needs, the emotions, the dreams of the others, of transforming solidarity into a further important factor of our motivational equilibrium.

The capacity to evaluate what makes us be accepted and appreciated regulates the activity of the serotonergic projections that from the nuclei of the raphe reach the various areas of the cortex and sustain the regulation of aggressiveness, the balance between our needs and what we feel to be the social demands and the principles of justice, the exam of reality and our cognitive and behavioral flexibility.

All these functions of serotonin fight the instinctual selfish and defensive reactions in favor of a more complex elaboration of our behavior, that strongly weighs the possibility of being accepted, sought, appreciated, loved; meanwhile, also of being proud of ourselves, and loved by ourselves as well.

The price for this quest for love, and the counterpart of solidarity and peace of conscience, is, as we mentioned, the anxiety serotonin can produce, when we take care and feel responsible, and the possible depression, if we fail.

* * *

Hamlet and women

Indeed, what wears us out is responsibility, is taking care.

The artist talks to everybody. Literates, poets and heroes have certainly thought that the Bard mostly talked to their heart, directly and precisely.

But perhaps even more – possibly without even wanting it – he talked to the soul of the woman, of each and any woman, mother, housewife, lover, simply woman. The woman who can build a world around herself, for herself and her beloved, and loves it and takes care of it.

The woman who cannot neglect her world, cannot let it degrade.

The woman who asks 'but why can he walk about with no worry among piles of dirty dishes, abandoned laundry, the cover of the W-C always wide open to show the horrid hole to the fetid world down there?', 'and why cannot I, why must I take charge of it, and take care of it?'.

Wouldn't it be much better, at least once, to suffer the slings and arrows of outrageous fortune, instead of taking arms against a sea of troubles – and unmade beds and perfidious bacteria - and by opposing end them? or, maybe, to sleep, perchance to dream...

Maybe this is why Hamlet is so cherished by women.

He is a tender, poor boy, awkward enough to drive his beloved Ophelia mad, so much he loves her, so much this makes him act stupid.

Bewildered, but HE CARES. He looks around, 'something's rotten in (the state of) Denmark', 'the time is out of joint', everything seems to tell him not to care, just mind your own business, if the world is crooked that is not your fault, it is not up to you to clean it up and polish and straighten it, reorder it and put it back to work...

Oh, nay, not him!

'To be or not to be', why should that be my business, why me?
But I cannot just stand here, and look, without doing anything, I wish I
could stay in bed and sleep, and wake up the next morning and the world
has reset on its own and everything is well, without me being the one who
must run and do things...

And perhaps Hamlet is a hero, precisely in this feminine facet of his.
The first hero in history who is not guided by a goddess, endowed with
unshakable certainties, subdued to honor codes and proud of his destiny.

No, he is an orphan.

Orphan of his father. Of gods. Of certainties.

He has the defects of a man, naive, messy, inconclusive; and in his thinking
it over, and taking care, instead of going on along his own way, sure of the
rules they taught him, as any other old hero would do, he is absolutely
disastrous: he becomes capable of candidly pulverizing, as a steam roller,
the soul of anybody who might love him.

Sure, as a partner he may not be the best choice – he can drive you crazy in
a moment... but which woman could ever resist to a guy like that, who can
make her suffer quite a bit, not because he's evil, no, just a little stupid,
with a big warning signal on his forehead
'CAUTION!! I don't know what I'm doing, I might hurt you hard!'...

And he is tender, in addition... HE CARES.

* * *

Thus, vegetative and physiological needs are there to guide our behavior; also running away from pain and discomfort, looking for gratifications and pleasure; but emotions as well, ours and others', and social appreciation, and affects and love, and solidarity.

All this, translated into the activity of neurons that signal the possibility of success in any one of these domains – and generate anticipation. All this translated also into the activation of pathways that elicit PLEASURE, in its strictest sense (physical, if you wish, but I really do not know of anybody who could clearly tell the difference between a physical pleasure and an emotional one, or affective, ethical, esthetic: maybe the pleasure should be defined exactly as what all these forms of wellbeing have in common...).

And everything transformed into motivational drives, in the end, capable of inducing the elaboration of appropriate behavioral strategies and starting their execution.

It is evident, though, that in the end it is not a question of choosing a pair of shoes, of simply selecting the best one among many possible behaviors – in the sense that it is pushed by a sum of motivational forces (in favor and against) that is greater than for the others. No, the problem is to compare and try and reconcile, to renounce, to compose complex strategies, delicate balances, in a mutable picture, while each new perspective, each novel way of considering elements and relationships, casts a new light, and ever-changing shades, on the whole matter.

* * *

What moves us? The urge of need, desires, fears and dreams, and then projects and rationality...

But rationality is manifold, eager, intricate, captious, gray and never satisfied. Like a mischievous sea, stormy at times, unpredictable streams, mutable winds.

It would be nice to have somebody near us, perhaps not to tell us what to do, but at least to share the burden and responsibility – somebody who at least looked at us, held our hand, smiled at us, someone who didn't leave us alone.

Eventually, what we should wish for is an invincible tide, a strong wind, stable, a sturdy motor down there, the ability of regulating the sails, keeping the helm steady...

Eventually, what we should wish is a strong positive motivation, that may put any other desire, doubt, uncertainty to sleep...

Eventually, what we should wish is simply passion – the need, the absolute desire, Achilles' wrath, Abraham's faith, and Agamemnon's, in the absurd will of the gods, Karenina's love – a passion that can shut down reason and take possession of acts.

Sometimes, like Hamlet, we happen to desire folly – rather than pretending he's fool, sometimes he seems to desperately desire it, – the folly of 'taking arms' and fighting without hesitation, or being able to put an end to all of it.

Folly, that frightens and fascinates, because it kills the reason, but along with it, responsibility as well:
'incapable of understanding and acting', thus NOT responsible.

Driven by something other than reason...
FREE from reason? Free from responsibility? Free from conflict

XIV
NARRATING THE WORLD – Space and Time

Neurologically, we are visual beings.

A great part of neuronal circuits work along this paradigm: extracting information, relations, interpretations from myriads of data examined simultaneously, recognizing schemes, orders, positions, hierarchies... SPACE.

It is not at all strange that what we can do best is to extract elements and relations from a cohort of data: larger-smaller, near-far, front-back, unity-multiplicity, order, regularity, relevance. Even numbers – most of us see them in a line, 1 to the left, 10 a little to the right, a billion down there, almost outside the brain, and a thousand billion, and infinity, far away, you can hardly see them, turning your eyes far to the right.

This way of ordering things is the one most congenial to us. And we end up applying to TIME as well. In our brain TIME initially only consists of in capturing before-after relations, perceiving the unity of a sequence, measuring durations through the time necessary to perform a movement or a procedure, to say a word – keep the pace, twenty-one, twenty-two, twenty-three...

We build for ourselves an ordered and infinite *time*, made like *space*, a time that has nothing to do with our representation of ourselves and reality, not even in our memory.

The line of time in our life is a chronology that we must rebuild with an effort every time we need it, by mapping the events on the appropriate coordinates: the date; this, yes, during my third high-school year; that, when my son was two-years old; that, when my sister got married.

Curiously enough, we order the same way, positioned in space, the *intensity* of our moments, experiences, emotions: this, close hereby, is more important than that, down there, and what we care about more looks nearer, larger. In the same way we order depth, along an axis that goes from what appears to be clear out there, and objective and real and material, to what is more ours and personal, to what we ourselves barely feel, or to what even appears so deeply buried in our soul that we can only occasionally perceive it in a vague and confuse way...

Sometimes the axes are overturned; intriguingly, that does not even bother us so much: in Plato's myth of the cavern, we in there, in the dark, things outside, but they themselves only shadows of a true but remote reality; from matter to truth, farther and farther from us.

According to Kant, instead, reality out there, the senses to feel it, the modes of intellect to read it, and truth, pure, within us...

* * *

Relativity

This continuous work to frame experience along axes, in spatial frameworks, is tiring.

No datum can be used as it appears, we have to re-elaborate it and 'locate' it along the axes of space, and time, affective relevance, good and evil...

Maybe this is why special relativity theory is easier than general relativity, and much more popular – nobody ever talks about the latter.

Because it appears that it is merely a problem of accepting that space and time are relative, and that funny things happen in fancy domains, such as that of velocities close to that of light: time gets stretched and can be turned over as a glove, and things appear smaller (well, actually, they BECOME smaller, but it is hard to feel the difference).

Finally, what is the big deal? one would say, what need was there for

Einstein at all? A tower, from far away, is as high as a finger. And we can only perceive time through our neuronal activity; it dilates, contracts, runs forth and back; it jumps, slave of our thought that unfolds our life and folds it back again; it flies and stops; only clocks tell us that time is a nice straight, continuous line that runs regular... and we have learnt to trust clocks. But the soul, deep inside, is happier with relativity than with atomic clocks.

Now, in the face of relativity one struggles to understand. Crawling, one manages in focusing the fundamental aspects and remains with the strange sensation that a great tour has been done to demonstrate something that no one of us would have been able to formalize mathematically, but was already absolutely clear to each of us, because one feels it inside: time and space are relative and the soul wallows in this.

Einstein arrives and demonstrates that this is also true for Physics, which instead had appeared so rigid and inflexible and certain of itself...

Hey, Albert, welcome among us, and good for Physics!

General relativity instead upsets us. Even neglecting that one has to massage his brain quite a bit to understand something of it.

The fact that infinity is limited looks more like a mystical intuition – a rather annoying one, indeed –than science. And black holes seem like unpleasant dreams. Ogres are almost more amiable.

Who can follow all the mathematics gets to the end and says 'gosh, it is true!' and is upset, provided that, although they can mathematize, they have retained a trace of soul. The others tend to say 'okay, let it be like that way, however I do not care, it does not change my life a bit'.

I mean, if one gets convinced by the theory of general relativity, one comes out a bit frustrated, because they have to accept that this universe, infinite as it may be, is limited, a cage you cannot escape from (and just note that although you might have never left your house at the periphery of Town Creek, AL, you will be equally disturbed if they tell you there is some place you CANNOT GO); one must accept the idea that if in a black hole there is another entire universe (because black holes are not empty, are they?), we shall never be able to see it, unless we manage in getting close to it… and get sucked in it forever.

* * *

Genes or experience

Dimensions, measures, directions. In biology, directions are essential. It is sufficient to imagine the complexity of the development of an organism.

The solution of the amateur geneticist:
'it is simple, everything is written in DNA'.

Written in DNA? Come on! then it is the same as being written in destiny.
That would not explain anything, either, but at least it would not require tons of paper, or disks, or miles of molecules.

And it would be much more romantic.

Because in an organism there are thousands of billions of cells, all with the same DNA, as different from each other as a fly can be from a hippopotamus. Then, let us assume that in the library of the nucleus there are all the recipes to make each one of these single cells; what happens next? Every time a cell divides in the embryo, each one of the daughter cells fishes out a number to know which recipe it must use and what its future, its destiny will be?

Now, take the fertilized egg cell. It divides in two, then in four, in eight... Who decides which ones of these cells will contribute to form the placenta and which will make the embryo itself? and among the latter, when they reach a certain number, who is to decide which ones will take care of the bottom and which of the top (technicians would say what defines the caudal-rostral axis)? and which will end up in the front and which in the back (for refined readers, what will define the dorsal-ventral axis)? and then who will tell the cells that they have ended up on the right or on the left (this remains right and left even for the most sophisticated readers), since we can do with a single heart, or one liver only?

I realize one may consider a severe pathological sign the fact itself of asking these questions, instead of simply saying 'ah! the mysteries of life...'

But the answer is there: it is GRADIENTS. 'See, here he is with the words that only he knows', everybody stands up, someone has an urgent date, someone else remembers that they have their spaghetti boiling in the kitchen, and someone feels a sudden dizziness and must lay down a moment...

No, it is simple. And we already discussed this. Because of the asymmetric position of the nucleus, the cellular organelles and the microtubules, that constitute what is commonly called 'cytoskeleton', a graded shade of concentration (gradient) is generated for some substances, from one end to the other of the cell.

When the cell divides, these substances will be found at different concentrations in the two daughter cells and will be able to determine their diverse fates. In the embryo of vertebrates, for example, a gradient in the concentration of retinoic acid is observed along the caudal-cranial axis, already at primordial stages: since numerous genes have control regions that are sensitive to retinoic acid, the latter not only defines the major developmental axis, but also determines differences in the degrees of activation of various genes in cells that are positioned at different levels along such axis.

It is not hard to imagine that the activation of different genes will determine differential synthesis of a number of proteins, which may in turn switch on or off other genes, and so on, thereby infinitely amplifying any very slight difference, and translating it into largely different pictures of gene activation, and protein production, in distinct cells; the result is the production of very different cells, tissues and organs in the various parts of the organism.

It is not worth detailing these mechanisms here. What must be noticed, however, is the impressive combinatorial growth of possible differences, generated not only and not so much by the enormous number of genes that can be turned on or off in any cell (by the way, the number of genes in human DNA is not impressive, probably just some 30000 of them), but rather by the much greater number of signals contained in DNA, that permit a fine regulation of the expression of each gene (production of the protein it codes for), according to the concentration of many other proteins, soluble factors and signals that reach the cell from outside.

Thus, it is not necessary that everything be written somewhere.

It would be crazy to write down, for each cell that will comprise the adult organism, which genes it will have to activate and to what extent – 1000 chromosomes would probably not be enough, and we only have 48 – or, for each of the 300 billion nervous cells, which thousands of other neurons it must contact, and in which particular position of its complicated tree of cellular processes it must receive synapses from each of the thousands of neurons that must contact it.

This is a fascinating example of interaction between what is written – in DNA – and the small, innumerable differences in the surrounding biochemical and cellular environment – some of them graded, other so sensitive to establish a net bifurcation, yes or not.

Such differences exponentially multiply the possibilities of choice, but in the meantime guide an ordered development, precisely because they are not random differences, but they are generated by the previous steps of development itself.

It is an interaction between the WRITTEN *information and the* READING *system; but the* READING SYSTEM CHANGES *due to this interaction. The reading system is an array of proteins, and reading* DNA *produces new ones. New, different reading systems are generated, capable of extracting new indications from the same written information, to generate other different readers, and so on and so forth for a thousand times, until in my skull a neuron is produced that seems identical to that of a mouse, while it seems to share nothing with a leukocyte of mine, though both contain my same sacred, unique, personal and irreproducible DNA.*

This is pure biology.
Still, it is reminiscent of the psychological debate about genetic versus environmental influences on the development of the individual.

It reminds me of those who dare imagine that everything is written in genes.

Or those who, in facing the observation that twins grown up together can have different stories and preferences, need to assume that there be a written destiny, somewhere in the stars, or in the soul, or some daimon or god who – hidden or well visible, helped or contrasted by the world and by fortune – have their own design to pursue and realize.

As if the extraordinary, complex and versatile, sensitive and mutable reading system, that is constituted by body, brain and mind in their forming and changing, had no relevance at all, and required external help to read the information in DNA in an original way, to grow and change, to re-read every day, every moment, not only its own DNA, but all its previous history as well, in an ever new way, and to extract from the egg cell – which after all contains instructions that are quite precise biologically, but rather vague with respect to the choices of life – one's own personal destiny.

* * *

The skin of the soul

Gradients and asymmetries are essential in determining the lines of development of the organism.

And the first and fundamental distinction among cells is between epithelial and non-epithelial cells, because epithelial cells are asymmetric, polarized.

The whole organism is polarized, not only and not so much from the head to the feet, but rather from outside to inside, and from sensations to responses, and from the external world to the depth of the soul. And there, to mark polarizations, and separate different milieus, epithelial cells: skin, mucous membranes, and neurons.

The skin envelopes the body.
Mucous membranes envelope it with respect to 'internal' cavities.
Endothelia separate vessels from the spaces of tissues and organs.

And finally, the other polarized cells, also epithelial, the nervous cells, that derive from the ectoderm (look what a word!), from the most external layer of the embryo, that separates it from – or connects it to? – the world.

At a certain phase of development, the ectoderm forms a furrow, which penetrates in some depth and then closes forming a tube (the neural tube), constituted by epithelial cells, that are by now detached from the external covering of the embryo.

These are the cells that will become neurons, and it seems they enclose something, and separate the organism from something else, that remains inside.

It is easy to remain enchanted.

In discovering that the nervous system is born this way, and a thin tube continues to travel along the spinal cord in the adult, and generates small pouches in the skull – the cerebral ventricles – in the midst of the brain, one may wonder: each nervous cell is polarized... could it not be then that the nervous system is a kind of skin, that separates the organism from something else – from spirit, perhaps? – contained in the neural tube...

In pseudo-scientific elaborations of early 'neuroscientists', this system of liquids in the brain was hypothesized to constitute the site of the 'animal spirits', the site of 'spirit', in opposition with previous interpretations – how infantile and anti-scientific! – that animal spirits resided in the heart and spread about the organism through the blood.

Actually, polarization of the nervous cells clearly has a different function.

All nervous cells have a portion that receives signals – chemical signals from other neurons or stimuli that arrive from outside as mechanical stimuli (pressure, stretch), electromagnetic waves (light, heat), vibrations (sound) or odorant or tasty molecules.

Thus, a portion receives signals; a large portion of the cell summates such signals and translates and elaborates them; and finally, another portion conveys the signal that results from such elaboration and transmits it to other nervous cells.

An evident input-output polarization, a stimulus-response polarization.

This is so clear, in the organization of the nervous system, that it originated the most classical and diffuse interpretative paradigm of the nervous system – a still dominating view – that considers it a system whose essential function is to generate appropriate responses to the stimuli.

But the complexity of the neuronal network is extraordinary, and even if you look at it as a simple system of production of responses to stimuli, it puts up such a richness and complexity of multifaceted regulation, modulation and control activity that it CREATES a true and fully ABSTRACT dimension, a conceptual, logical, cognitive domain, as a side effect of this elaboration.

In this perspective, a slightly different view emerges for the polarization of the nervous system, and of this 'epidermal' concept of the nervous system: yes, a skin, but a skin that in conducting information all around the body and the brain, creates a separate, immaterial domain, and separates the organism – the biological, material organism – from such sphere of cognitive, logic, conceptual elaboration, and from the sphere of emotions and affectivity.

A skin. Yes. The skin of the soul!

* * *

I have heard someone saying: 'science is the dream of defeating time'. Meaning, perhaps, that through genetics, biotechnology, or god knows which other knack – or philosophical stone – we shall be able to prolong human life... I cannot agree: the dream is and remains infinity, it is not merely pushing the limit a little farther. It is depth, not length. It is the innumerable multiplication of dimensions, of views, of interpretations, of comprehension; it is HARMONY, it is not one more piece of knowledge, a centimeter, one more year of average life.

Already in sensory elaboration, the portions of the cortex that specifically deal with it are not content of merely recording sensations, but look for relations, rules, logical criteria, as if one always had to go further, and look for something more.

And this is much more evident in thought, that continually alternates and interweaves a sequential thread with instantaneous syntheses (images, evocations, memories); it looks for explanation and is distracted by visual intuition; it tries to follow logic and gets diverted by palpable evocation. This way, data, objects, facts and event sequences are transformed into a narration, that escapes the limiting dimensions of space and time, and invades the domains of possible, emotion, desire, commitment, passion, fantasy.

Similarly, the language can play with words and keep them alive, by attributing them meaning, color, sound, emotional value, implications, and cultural, political, historical and ideal references; this way words, and the language itself, keep getting richer, more capable of capturing, representing, keeping alive, *singing* reality and its music, in all its innumerable dimensions.

In this way of functioning, one may see the signs of all the complex, fascinating relation that the soul creates between consciousness and affects, logos and passion, good, beauty and righteousness.

* * *

Space arises from the analysis of the relations among elements simultaneously present in experience. It is generated in the brain, in that region that recognizes relations: above/below, larger/smaller, near/far, but also of uniqueness/multiplicity, distance, periodicity, and order, number and cardinality, unity and collectiveness, hierarchy and ordinality, direction, symmetry...

The paradox of space (what remains there when nothing remains) evaporates. Space is no longer a container, but a network of possible relations, not an ontological entity, that abstractly or *materially* exists *per se*, but a LOGICAL entity that exists in an equally real way in the logics of spatial links that our brain elaborates.

These relations do exist even with no contents, like in Kant's intellect.
They are 'in the senses' (broadly speaking) like in Herder's anti-criticism.
But with no need for them to have been *before that* in the experimental datum.
Here Kant wins, and his poetry.

The relations are in the neuronal organization that is capable of recognizing them; that often finds them even where they are not – just think how easy it is to deceive the eye. The most curious aspect perhaps is that Herder was partly right too (I cannot be too hard on a materialist): if a relation is not there, in any experimental datum, it is unlikely that we find an organism with a brain that has produced and preserved neuronal circuital organizations suitable to recognize such relation: it would be wasted neurons, and after so many millennia it would be curious if evolution had not privileged organisms that have found a better use for those neurons...

Stupid as this last observation may appear, it is worth noting that a Kantian intellect that transcends the experimental datum, by imposing relations and categories a priori that do not have any material basis in reality, would not be the maximum of cleverness; on the other side, a sensory system that is only capable of recognizing, a posteriori, relations that are there (before) in experientable reality must anyway be predisposed to recognize them...

It is like the egg and the hen dilemma, as long as you consider an immaterial intellect on one side and a material reality on the other: if nobody has made it so that they are in agreement from the start, we are destined to arbitrarily interpret reality, without really understanding anything.

But if they are in agreement, who organized such agreement?
Or, was it necessary that someone organized such agreement?

Amusingly enough, the evolutional drive, which will necessarily favor the organism that is capable of recognizing a relation that objectively exists in reality, and is relevant for survival, would be sufficient to account for how and why the neuronal circuits have evolved in such a way to elaborate reality through detecting relations and applying schemes that are actually coherent with the objective structure and organization of reality itself.

Here is how the agreement between reality and intellect arose, here is who did it. With no need for somebody who can cross the barrier between matter and spirit...

After all, this is not so bad as a truth criterion. If after billions of years, at the most advanced edge of evolution, we recognize in reality objects, relations, rules and laws, we can be reasonably sure that we are not wrong by much.

Provided that we are clearly warned about where the limit – not irrelevant – of this approach is.

Warning! Warning!
Anything that is irrelevant for survival is not covered by this warranty!

If one sees the sun rising in the morning and going down in the evening, and deduces that it must go around the Earth, he lives just as well. And a brain capable of perceiving astrophysics with no computations and mediations is absolutely no use (for survival, I mean, no offense, my esteemed astrophysicists).

This may also be a quite trivial observation. But if one dedicates a bit of attention to it, maybe this explains why we have never understood anything about space and time, or about infinity, or matter and energy, and why it has been so difficult to believe Einstein when he upset everything in front of us, showing that there is nothing absolute in space and time, the universe is bent and limited though it may be infinite, and matter is nothing but coagulated energy; and why it has remained impossible to intuitively understand all this.

* * *

Okay, space is in the links and relationships that we can recognize among elements that simultaneously come to our observation; space lets us manipulate abstract relations – multiplicity, order, hierarchy, numbers – that apparently have little to do with space. But, if SPACE is somehow there, where is TIME?

Is time a relationship, too, a way of interpreting reality by our brain rather than a reality in itself, a pre-existent entity?

In more than one way it is so. In relativistic terms time only is a relation of simultaneity or antecedence that turns out different and relative, depending on position, velocity and particularly accelerations of the implied systems.

But also in our brain, time is only a generalization of relationships that we can recognize. Time arises in recognizing successions (before, after, delay) and in many ways from the application of a spatial conception – which is so congenial to our brain – to the temporal order (sequence).

On the other side, in its measurability time arises from the awareness and timing of movements: just think how we can wait 10 seconds, 'a hundred one... a hundred two... a hundred three... ...', we have learnt to count loudly and employing about a second for each number...

∗ ∗ ∗

A nice book comes to my mind: "Problems of psychic development" (not sure whether it is available in English), by Leontjev, a scientist of the Soviet neuropsychological school, scholar of Vigotsji.
His claim was somewhat Marxist, very soviet: what distinguishes humans from animals is the capacity of producing.

In that movie masterpiece, "2001, a Space Odyssey", Kubrick invented the capturing scene of the monkey that, holding a bone, discovers it can be used as an instrument to do something that could not be done without it, and in an overwhelming crescendo of incredible music lets us imagine that something epochal just happened, that Man had just become possible.

Extraordinary poetry and evocation.

But monkeys can still learn to use an instrument, and they do not turn into humans, if you forgive the stupid joke.

Many evolutionists believe that the true difference in not about finding how to use an object as an instrument to do something that would otherwise be impossible, but rather in the capacity to build such an instrument: solving the problem theoretically, understanding what kind of instrument is needed in practice and look for, modify or create the needed instrument.

But this way we actually get back to that depressing view of the gray neurologists of Russian revolution: man = productive animal.

Still, I (and Leontjev) believe that what has really revolutionized evolution, what has made the inconceivable step of making Man possible,

is a capability that appears in mammals not even particularly evolved,
and grows and becomes ever more preeminent in primates;
in humans it overcomes some critical threshold that transforms it into
a totally novel potentiality.
It is not the capacity of producing, but something that comes earlier:
it is the capacity of PLAYING.

The point is that in order to play one needs time and unused neurons.
Because playing is an activity WITH NO PURPOSE,
or better that has its own purpose in itself, in the activity it implies,
and to dedicate you to it you must not be too busy in surviving.

But most of all, why should you ever dedicate your time to it,
instead of sleeping, or letting the time go by, your gaze lost in infinity?
Why play, instead of relaxing?

The most reasonable answer is "because neurons never rest",
and if there is no need that pushes they work the same,
they invent some purpose to follow and some problem to solve,
and they solve them, for the sake of doing it.
It may be true that "necessity is the mother of invention",
but to become Human you must not be too busy in surviving:
being able to use instruments is not enough.

To invent them and build them you must have time and neurons in excess,
to try, imagine, simulate, conceive without an aim, to discover
new relations, coincidences, possibilities; to dedicate yourself to activities
that have their sole objective and aim in themselves, in doing them.

You must have time and neurons in excess, to PLAY.
So, it is true that Man is a productive animal, but it is so because
producing, doing, solving problems, inventing, are not needs to survive,
but they are needs of the brain, which cannot stand still.

Why should work ever be the source of stress?
There are people who trash themselves with gymnastics and get gratified,
there are those who build self-made furniture
and it costs them more than buying it, but they do it for fun…
They call them hobbies, but they are not nicer, per se, than many jobs.

The industrial society generates various problems:
there is a conflict between one's personal and social identity,
people are forced to do jobs in which the brain is useless, is not involved,
and the job loses all ludic dimensions, all aspects of play.

A crack insinuates into our imagination: I do not feel the ME *as a person,
as an individual who thinks and desires and loves, and the* ME *who works,
as one and the same person; the job does not fulfill the need of the brain
to be active, and I feel it as alienating;
working has no longer its aim in the activity it implies,
and not even in its result,
it is merely selling one's own time and skills.,*

*The fracture between the person and their job role,
and alienation, contribute to the modern anguish,
to the conflict denounced by Schopenhauer between vital
will and rationality that reads reality.
"Forced" execution of activities that do not engage the brain deprives
working of all ludic components: if I do something for the pleasure of doing
it, it gives me gratification, and if it has at least a gratifying objective
even the unpleasant aspects and effort become a postponed gratification, an
indirect objective, not very remote.
But if the activity is a duty, it is forced by need,
by urge (the need of money, of being appreciated, socially recognized)
there is no more gratification, only a momentary relief, possibly,
from need and discomfort, which however remain in the background
as a basal condition and generate the hormonal, pathophysiological and
psychological picture of stress: a distortion of motivational dynamics,
based on the activation of the amygdala by the coping systems,
to face a persistent discomfort, instead of a positive hedonic evaluation,
driven by creativity, imagination, desire.*

*A second fracture of the Ego is born: an occupation that is unable to engage
our neurons and a motivational framework where* NEED *supersedes desire,
in addition to the conflict between the working* ME *and the* ME *as a person.*

*Not to mention the biggest problem for today's youngsters:
not even finding a job, alienating as it could be.*

*Another problem, not a small one, comes about, if to be human
you need to have spare neurons and time: neurons, we do have in excess;
but what about* TIME?

*We have been celebrating the centennial of Futurism. Enthusiasm for the
machines and the novel exciting dimension of speed: expanding time,
contracting space. Even condemning the implicit or explicit delusion of
omnipotence of the early '900s and its political consequences, one must
acknowledge a certain fascination to that enthusiasm for speed.*

*Because that myth has marked the whole XX Century, it has enchanted
and pervaded collective imagination: stretching time, contracting space.
Indeed, accelerating production processes, and trains, airplanes, cars
upset the relation between space and time.
Speed: space shrinks and there seems to be more time for everything,
distances get shorter, radio, cinema, tv, make remote events seem close.*

*Some fifty years after, many stupid epigones, cartoonists and us children
were hoping that the process would go on for ever:
vertical towns, flying cars, space flights and teletransportation.
We did not realize that something else was happening:
the fight against space was over; the desecration of the Moon marked
the end of an epoch. It seems that space had nothing more to give to us.
So, no more shrinking space – over a certain limit it is no longer
convenient: just eliminate it.
Space is no longer the enemy:* TIME *is the enemy now.*

*Automation accelerates production, computers solve problems
that nobody would have had the time to solve in their whole life,
but above all, electronics change the rules of the game:
with television and telecommunication, the hours saved by jets
and high-velocity trains become irrelevant,
as compared to the possibility of seeing everywhere, of being everywhere.
The power of electronics! It does have its own times,
but in moving information it does not even know what "distance" is,
because its signals travel at the speed of light.*

*Einstein discovered that time gets longer, and space shrinks,
as the speed of light is approached, and mass grows to infinity,
to the point of giving matter to the nothing.
Few understand the theory of relativity but everybody lives it on their skin:
a world gradually deprived of distances, of space, by materializing words,
images, people from far away.*

*Space vanishes, at the speed of light, and time gets misty.
Reality itself gets misty, because whatever Einstein may have said
our brain frames the world in space and time.
It deforms them, it dilates or contracts them, but it needs them,
to understand.*

One no longer needs to go anywhere. You can communicate, know, see.
And it is no longer what looked like a miracle, the tv that tells us:
today each of us can be where and with whom they wish.
But the body does not feel it.
The smell is missing, the warmth, the emotion.
You cannot hold hands, caress the face, you cannot hug…

A new, violent fracture of imagination.

Because virtual reality may well ignore space,
and its time may well stretch to infinity, but the time of the soul,
the time of life, of doing, of loving, that time has not changed at all.

There are spots where we feel at ease in this virtual reality that has
dismantled space and time. But in other spots we still feel the heart
beating, and the seconds ticking of a time that lengthens in the wait,
a time that is never enough for all that we want to do…

A time that is never enough! Why is it never enough?

In thinking about the world of farmers, and the old times,
it seems that there was no room for stress, there.
Still, there certainly were sources of suffering, anxiety and tension,
and things that could go wrong, and frustrations and fears.

Perhaps it is that farmers' job used to be a non-alienated job:
identifying of the private, social and public sphere was somewhat easier,
the ME who works could be the same ME who lives, suffers, enjoys, loves.
In a sense, the product and the value of ones work were tangible,
in front of you, the activity had a well-defined objective, concrete, desirable.

But a stronger reason probably is that farmers' time is cadenced — there is
no hurry: "there is a time to plant and a time to harvest".
In time, nothing more than what can fit in it.

For us it is not like this: we work
less — theoretically, at least; no
longer sixteen, twenty hours a day;
only eight, and short workweeks,
vacations, a lot of "free time",
time of which we are supposed to be
the MASTERS.
FREE time? MASTERS? Or possibly slaves?

The key factor is the society of consumables.

In the modern market, the need of a continuous expansion of demand and consumes asks for a multiplication of the hedonic aims for the consumer, and bombs the imagination with an inexhaustible proliferation of objects to desire. Marketing and publicity display a blasting power in deeply manipulating the whole structure of imagination and the mechanisms of anticipation of gratification. Above all, they illude us about an apparent compatibility of all gratificational objectives.

This way a virtual world is created, symbolized by the overcrowding, simultaneity, reconcilability, atemporality of innumerable objectives, projects, chores. And a heavy muddle in the scale of desirability: the only unifying constant is money and success. But this way the vicious circle of work alienation gets worsened: an activity that has nothing to do with the reason one does it – under the motivational and hedonic point of view – and is totally aimed at indirect and instrumental objectives, getting money, reaching success, at least being accepted by the others.

This increases the pressure, the request of performance.

And the fracture in the imagination gets deeper:
in front of this dilated time, in which everything should fit,
because one can instantaneously have and do everything,
a real world marked by duration, incompatibility, need to postpone,
a finite number of things that can be done and acquired.

It is a fracture that pervades the whole life,
and at the workplace is exasperated by external pressures,
by the invincible pull of money's omnipotence,
and by the need of being accepted and appreciated.

A tension, a discomfort, an anguish for which the only cure can be
in restructuring the imagination.
A renovation in which time must play a major role, a reform aimed at
reunifying the spirit, by becoming again the MASTERS OF OUR TIME.
A renovation of imagination that must reconcile the time, torn apart
by work – with the rhythms of virtual reality, social pressure competition –
and personal life, which cannot do without time.

The real and direct objectives of work must be recognized,
the need for success and social affirmation reduced,
the most true and deep vital needs rediscovered;
one's scale of values revised and governing
the organization of work, of life, or at least of one's relation with life.

The ways and the activities to pursue what is important must be creatively search for and invented; the gratificational investment must turn toward other vital domains, that leave space (TIME!) to emotion, play, fantasy, creative commitment. Not to what can be bought – and one needs to work more to buy it – but what can be invented, done, tried, lived.

What could make us again, from slaves, MASTERS OF OUR TIME.

* * *

Perhaps we should agree first that time is two distinct things:
- a before–after relationship, which is necessary to define an event, a fact, an episode, a process – for its existence itself
- an – unnecessary – alignment in an ordered, non-arbitrary, sequence

But then one realizes that OUR TIME, the time of our life, the time that appears to be a fundamental dimension of our history, is something else. Our time is the time of memory, and memory does not possess the second kind of time, the aligned sequence: it has to be built on top of it every single time. Memory (episodic memory) is a film-library full of innumerable clips – each continuous in itself, sure, but isolated – and contiguity and continuity are generated by the cognitive, emotional, operative perspective, in an arbitrary and capricious way, with no respect for space or time as physical dimensions.

Each event is located on the time axis through association with a date, a phase of our life, another relevant event. But the entire sequence, the succession, of the time of our life – interior, affective life, working, social, political life – simply is not there. It must be rebuilt with a – rather maniacal – operation of reordering. An operation that some very orderly people may do every evening, by reordering events and memories after dish washing and housekeeping, after dusting all books, arranging them according to their height – or their title, or author, or publication year – and putting them back on the shelves.

Those who – like me – are more messy, will instead understand and share the bewildering sensation that grabs one when, in looking back at themselves, only see a mess of memories, near here the most dreadful or the most beautiful ones, perhaps far back in time, but pressing to be remembered, and there in the background events that may be recent but do not call for attention and begin to be forgotten.

And lots of holes and abysses that one can only fill with great effort by recalling with obsessive meticulousness labile traces of events that we have never been interested in remembering.

* * *

Like memory, the WORD – abstraction of the entity, the event, its relationships – shares this freedom from physical dimensions, to the point that it represents the quintessence of negation of space, time, causality, necessity, thanks to its capability of joining what is far apart, of instantaneously evoking images and memories of events that are remote or near in the past, present, future; its capability of stating absurd links and neglecting undeniable relationships...

Still, the word remains the most powerful instrument to create and assert space, time, causality, necessity, be they real, objective, true, or arbitrary, or foolish.

* * *

The nostalgia of what could have been – what WE could have been – steals from us the time we have lived, we live, we shall live.
It forces us to a 'today' somewhere else, with no return.

But the noise and clamor cannot stop the music – inside, – the music that tells us about other times and dreams, and possible lives.

To infinity, and beyond!

Because there exists a time of life and of the soul. It is a time that expands and contracts, evaporates and vanishes, or stops, explodes and leaves behind emptiness and languor (like when the rushing airplane chases the sound, the vibrations it tosses in front of itself, and runs until it reaches and overcomes them in the unacceptably meaningless bang of sound barrier breaking).

Or a time that dances, calm, elegant and harmonious. While a tyrannical and incoercible, monotonous cadence, along a narrow, rigorous, inflexible rail, empties and fills the time of the soul, fights, steals it and gives it back, colors it and sings it, clouds it and silences it.

Sometimes it seems that the soul is fractured by a deep abyss – somebody knows, or thinks they know, who stole the ground, the flesh, the love (the time?) that is missing, many do not have the least idea.

An abyss so deep that we do not even imagine the others may fill it, but we hope somebody might possibly just coat it somehow, conceal its mouth. And the less that somebody is fit to do it and the larger and empty is the cavity of the soul, under there, the more we get attached to them and love them – fictitious, absurd and unhappy loves; and the more we are afraid of losing them, and having to face once more that vacuum, that nothing, that disappointment, that pain.

*Perhaps, the abyss is just time, the time we lost, or was stolen or wasted –
it makes no difference. It cannot be filled, or replaced, either.*

*But if it is true that we are such stuff as dreams are made on, maybe that
time perhaps can be, possibly, regained. By finding again, out of ourselves,
the signs of our own time, the time we lived and the stolen time, and the
eternal absolute meaning of this exhausting, uninterrupted boiling,
smiling and suffering.*

*Maybe, it is not abysses, it is just pieces of ourselves that have stopped
(possibly irrevocably – we know it – with no remedy) in one or another
moment of our life. Blocked. Their time is empty; we tried to fill it back
with joys, affects, friendships, loves; but it is interrupted music, that clips
of songs and refrains – dear and suggestive as they may be – cannot
replace, even less they can revive.*

*The times of the soul, of our history, run like many threads, along brief or
long tracts of our life. Long enough, sometimes. Sometimes, not at all.*

*Nostalgia, regret. Threads that might be possibly tied again, or cannot.
Jealous symbols that do not want to surrender their greatest value.
Implicit conditioning that no words can resolve.
Ties that prevent regret from evaporating into yearnings.*

*Sweet and bitter times, passionate, sublime or tormenting, map our life.
Perhaps the most painful gaps are where these times stop abruptly,
unexpectedly, instead of thinning, evaporating gradually,
giving us the possibility of adapting to their vanishing.*

* * *

Space and time. On one side, their intersection, the intuition of a
moment; on the other side, their pathways, narration and thought.

Thought, even when it is sustained by interior language and guided
along a logical thread, is never a march, a chronicle; it is more of a
narration. A poetical tale that follows a path but can evoke images at
any moment and get lost along other paths.

It is like exploring an old town. You have a path to follow, you are
enchanted by a prospect you were looking for, and then an unexpected
game of shapes and colors hits you, novel symmetries, suggestions,
inviting trails, and while you are supposed to be admiring a palace for
its magnificence you find yourself meandering into a passage that
enwraps you in its mystery, or you end up in a disconcerting open
space, or in a garden that welcomes you, amorous and embracing.

It is particularly so when thought tries to explore emotional life: glances, intuitions, emotions seem to arise from elsewhere, inside; you examine them, you deploy them and follow them, you spell them out and explain, and this brings you somewhere else, to other glances, other emotions you have lived or dreamt of; you try to figure them out, but the logics of that other "elsewhere" inside you follow other paths and elicit intuitions and emotions that again chase one-another meandering away.

Thought as an uncertain and manifold walk... but the whole brain, from sensory elaboration to movement, is soaked in this contradiction.

The organization of neuronal networks elaborates sensory information in a parallel way, by preserving its mode of presenting itself as a complex, multiple, unitary and instantaneous set of data, on one side, but also extracting relations and schemes from it, to translate a cohort of independent elements into a system of relations and properties (from the dots that constitute an image to its conceptual representation).

Neurologically, we are visual beings, and we are very clever with SPACE, very clever in transforming an image into a complex, living reality. Our brain 'applies' space to anything that can be simultaneously perceived. But aside to this this parallel elaboration, other refined neuronal systems elaborate data in a sequential way. If we look at a picture, the gaze moves along profiles, scans the elements that have been detected, IN TIME, and its path is recorded, as if it were a charcoal sketch that is added to the image to help interpreting it and understanding it. In addition, the large portion of the brain that guides movements is busy drawing, programming and performing complex sequences, coordinated and well temporized. These processes contribute to perceiving and handling successions, intervals, to inventing and navigating TIME.

So, the same way as we navigate the image, and violate its unity by transforming it into a narration, and detect processes in its changing with time, conversely we can perceive the sound, which is a pure SEQUENCE of vibrations, in an unitary way, and violate its incoercible movement by transforming it into a unitary harmony, a melodic phrase, as if they were stable and persistent images.

We perceive the sounds through sensory cells of the cochlea, the so-called hair cells. The ear does perceive pressure variations, but what is analyzed in the brain is 'patterns of variation' (sounds) and how these combine to yield an impression, a color, an image (harmony); their sequence itself in time (melody) is perceived as a unitary assembly, a melodic phrase that evokes emotion, intuition, and binds to the next one in this continuous threading of images and pathways.

Those who have seen Walt Dysney's 'Fantasy' surely remember those representations of a violin tone, slim, trembling and strangled like the pulled-out neck of a chicken, and a trombone tone that instead flows down like honey and broadens fatty and soft... Once more, multiplicity: sound has a shape, even a color. It is not by chance that we use the same word to indicate the 'tone' of a sound and a 'tone' of color. And sound has an emotion.

Well, just play a C minor chord, and then a C+ minor chord, and listen to them with your eyes closed. It might be different to you, but C minor gives to me a thoughtful impression, from which C+ minor brings me to a kind of hesitation, or surprise, veiled by query, curiosity, uncertainty (note that this is the tone of Beethoven's moonlight sonata)...

* * *

It is nice, listening to the dialogue among notes and sounds, that melt together every moment into an instant of complex, integrated experience, and flow intermingling into dribbles that seem independent but together sketch a collective path. Music can guide the ear (the brain) to foresee the next note, and emotion consists in the pleasurable surprise for every unexpected turn in the melody, an acceleration of hesitation in rhythm, a crescendo or diminuendo: you may know the piece very well, but when that bit comes, that change of tone, that chord, your ear cannot but get surprised and emotion cannot but arise once more. The same way, the wrong note surprises you, badly; and a strange mixture of discomfort, surprise a pleasurable curiosity comes out of a well-studied dissonance.

It is not strange that the child likes the carol that always comes back the same, how the child likes the story told always the same way: it gives them reassurance and safety.

Prediction errors, surprises, emotional stimuli, are even too numerous all day long, for them, and the look for some peace and reassurance...

* * *

All this makes it possible to recognize equilibrium and order features in the sequence of sounds (harmony and melody) and to enjoy anticipation and surprise in listening to music. Once more, all this talks about the complexity and multiplicity of interior experience.

But this, physiologically and trivially, makes it possible to recognize complex sounds (or sequences) to which a value of danger is associated, or of warning, attraction, repulsion; to recognize verbal sounds that express and communicate emotions; to recognize phonemes that must be analyzed and combined to identify words in the framework of language's symbolic system.

This intertwining between compound momentary picture and a path in time profoundly imbibes the organization of motor systems too: a large fraction – in terms of weight – of what we have in our head and the great majority of neurons are located in two structures that have a fundamental role in movement: the cerebellum and basal ganglia.

The cerebellum is a control system that precisely defines at any moment the timing and intensity of the activation of each muscle that participates to a movement (note that to simply push forward a hand muscles of the shoulder, arm and forearm need to be activate in a coordinated way); also, by comparing the position of muscles and joints at any moment with the motor orders output by the brain, it corrects the movements so that they reflect 'the program'.

On the other hand, the basal ganglia verify each motor command and control which muscles in the body may help or interfere with this command, or with the next one, already programmed in the brain; they return all this information to the cortex in terms of inhibitory modulation and thus make it possible to perform acts and sequences of movements in a fluid and harmonic way.

These two systems are perhaps the most important 'generators' of **time** in our brain, **time** as a succession - one instant after the other - and as a process, a continuous flow of events. As usual, these systems are not used for one function only (movement): this capacity of producing perfect and fluid sequences helps to efficiently and automatically reproduce cognitive sequences (poems learnt by heart), guides mind wandering, and offers to all the elaboration modules in the brain the suggestion and perception of time as a line along which to align a temporal sequence and as a measure of intervals.

All this can be abstracted and generalized to yield the temporal axis itself, along which any episode, sequence, story, can be mapped. In generating this operational conception of **time** in our brain, these systems are flanked by two other types of systems: nuclei and circuits that possess timed or pacemaker activity (many such neurons operate at various levels in the nervous system, for example the groups of neurons in breathing centers, that regulate periodicity of respiratory activity); and the complex game of hormones that originates seasonal and circadian variations – during the 24-hours cycle, also based on light/dark cycle, and feeding and sleeping habits.

* * *

The interlacing and integration of the two modality – parallel and serial, that originate and mold the internal SPACE and TIME – permeates all higher functions: thought, language, feelings and imaginative activity proceed this way, merging the presentation of complex instantaneous pictures (intuitions, images, emotions) with sequential elaboration (analysis, research, explanation).

This dialogue between the two processing modalities – parallel, iconic, evocative on one side and sequential, analytic, explicative on the other side – is particularly evident in language: a THREAD that runs in the words (trying to follow a precise pathway) and a simultaneous, continuous generation of meanings (not necessarily univocal and often capable of evocation and visual remembrance).

The capacity of symbolically elaborating reality donates us, with language, a system that not only describes and analyzes, but that can also associate music to meanings, and rhythm, evocation, emotion, intensity, and knows how to do it; a system that can describe life and NARRATE it in its innumerable dimensions. This continuous reciprocal chasing and intersecting of speech with intuitions and evocations in fact becomes narration, sometimes poetry, and transforms information into a tale. And, borrowing a nice sentence from Alessandro Baricco: 'the tale, not information, makes you the owner of your history'.

A fascinating analogy exists among an image that can capture us, an engaging music, and a well written story, or poem. If one wants to reproduce a vision, they must be able to recreate the general picture, in its *visibility*, with precision and *exactness* for the perceived details and relationships – there is no room for approximation, it is only possible to knowingly and intentionally violate exactness, wickedly, as Picasso did in his portraits of women with disassembled, violated faces…

But in the meantime, it is necessary that the image suggest the pathways and the appropriate TIMES to travel it, and that it offer MULTIPLE elements, relationships, possible readings, perhaps unexpected ones, so that a margin of freedom and *lightness* remains.

In the same way music requires a harmony made of *exact* sounds – not necessarily in agreement, possibly even in dissonance – and a melody that fuses together the chords that follow one-another into a unitary, *visible* perception, but also a rhythm made of *precise times* for the melodic path, and the counterpoint of parallel or contrasting, *multiple* melodies, that intersect each other and bring us to a dimension of incorporeal *lightness*.

EXACTNESS, VISIBILITY, RAPIDITY, MULTIPLICITY, LIGHTNESS...
But this same thing is so clear in language! a thread that runs in words and a continuous generation of meanings, a sequence that is music and a meaning that can be seen...

In the end we shall have to admit that Calvino, in his American Lectures, in listing those five things as the ones that he would put in his backpack to face the new millennium – if he were to get there – and in compiling this way the most appropriate recipe book for good literature, also identified the fundamental features that guide perception, interpretation, reading of reality by our brain, and the fundamental properties and habits of language and of thought itself...

* * *

Almost done with the first draft of these meditations, once more I stumble on Calvino. The end of 'If on a winter's night a traveler...'. In a few pages he writes all that I have been trying to write up to here. What follows is theft in a strict sense, plagiarism and bootlegging. Only minimal changes.

> *'His gaze wanders in the air. But his eyes are not unfocused: an intense fixity accompanies the movements of the blue irises.*
> *Here and there your gazes meet. Suddenly he speaks to you, or better he kind of speaks in the vacuum, though he certainly addresses you:*
>
> *– Do not be surprised if you see me continually wandering with my eyes. This is actually my way of <u>thinking</u>, and only this way <u>thought</u> is fruitful to me. If a <u>question</u> truly interests me, I cannot follow it for more than a few <u>moments</u> before my mind, having captured an <u>association</u> that the text proposes, or a feeling, a question, an image, starts off and bounces from thought to thought, from image to image, along a path of reasoning and fantasies that I feel the need of following to the end, departing from the <u>problem</u> until it is out of sight. The stimulus of the <u>question</u> is indispensable to me, and of a substantial <u>question</u>, although I cannot <u>face</u> more than a few <u>aspects</u> for each <u>problem</u>. But those few <u>aspects</u> already enclose to me entire universes, that I cannot exhaust.*
>
> *– I understand you well – intervenes another, raising his waxy face and flushed eyes from the pages of his book – <u>thought</u> is a discontinuous and fragmentary operation. Or, better, the object of <u>thought</u> is a punctuate and intersperse matter. In the overwhelming extension of reality our attention distinguishes minimal segments, connections among <u>elements</u>, metaphors, <u>relationships</u>, logical links, <u>organizational</u> peculiarities that reveal an extremely concentrated density of meaning.*

It is like the elementary particles that comprise the nucleus of a composition, around which everything else turns. Or, like the void at the bottom of an eddy, that aspires and swallows the streams. And precisely through these clefts, through barely perceptible flashes, the truth that reality can carry manifests itself, the ultimate substance.
Myths and mysteries consist of impalpable fragments like pollen that sticks to the legs of butterflies; only he who has understood this can expect revelations and illuminations. This is why my attention, contrary to what you were saying, sir, cannot abandon the real details, *not even for a moment. I must not get distracted if I do not want to overlook some precious hints. Each time I encounter one of these clots of meaning I must keep digging around to see whether the nugget extends into a vein. This is why my study has no end: I read and reread each time looking for confirmation of a new discovery in the folds of perceptions.*

— I, too, feel the need to reexamine *what I have already* thought, *— says a third reader, — but at each reading it seems to me I am reading a new book for the first time. May it be that I keep changing and I see new things that I had not perceived before? Or is* thought *a construction that is formed by putting together a large number of variables and cannot repeat itself twice along the same drawing?*
Each time I try and relive the emotion of a previous intuition, I get different and unexpected impressions, and I cannot find again the old ones. At times It seems to me that between one time and the next there is a progress: in the sense of penetrating more deeply in the spirit of reality, *for example, or increasing the critical detachment.*
At other times I feel as if I preserved the memories of the impressions *of the same* reality *next to each other, enthusiastic or cold and hostile, dispersed in time with no perspective, with no line connecting them.*
My conclusion is that thought is an operation with no object; or that its true object is itself. Reality *is just an accessory support, or even a pretext.*

A fourth one says: — If you want to insist on subjectivity of memory *I may agree with you, but not in the centrifugal sense that you attribute to it. Each new* experience *I* have *becomes part of that comprehensive and unitary book that the sum of* my memories *constitute.*
This is not an effortless process: to compose that general book, each particular experience *must transform, establish connections with the* memories *that I* built *previously, become their corollary or development or confutation, or comment, or text of reference.*

I have been attending this library for years and exploring it volume after volume, shelf after shelf, but I could demonstrate to you that I have been but proceeding with the reading of one and the same book.

— For me, too, all <u>experiences</u> I <u>live</u> lead to a single <u>story</u>, — says a fifth one looking out from behind a pile of freshly bound volumes, — but it is a <u>story</u> that goes back in time, and barely emerges from my memories.
There is a story that comes before all other stories for me, a story of which all <u>experiences</u> I <u>have</u> seem to bear an echo that vanishes at once.
In my reading I do not search but that book I read in my infancy, but what I remember of it is too little to find it again.

A sixth one, who was standing and exploring the shelf with his nose up, comes near the table. — The moment that counts most for me is the one that precedes <u>intuition</u>.
Sometimes it is a <u>hint</u> that is sufficient to elicit in me the desire for an <u>experience</u> that may not be <u>possible</u>.
Sometimes it is the <u>atmosphere that comes about</u>, the first <u>perceptions</u>... I mean: if a little is enough for you to trigger imagination, I need even less: the promise of a <u>discovery</u>.

— In my opinion what counts is the end, — says the seventh one — but the true, ultimate end, hidden in the dark, the arrival point which <u>reality</u> wants to bring you to. In <u>thinking</u>, I too search for glimmers, — he says nodding to the man with flushed eyes, — but my gaze digs among the <u>details</u> to try and catch sight of what is materializing far there, in the spaces that extend beyond the words 'the end'.

It is time you too say what you think. — Sirs, I must premise that in <u>life</u> I like to read only what is written there; and to link the details with all the ensemble; and to consider certain readings as definitive; and I like keeping an <u>experience</u> separated from the others, each of them for what it has of different and new; and above all I like the <u>ideas</u> that can be <u>followed</u> from the beginning to the end. But in the last period everything has been going wrong for me: it seems to me that only stories that remain suspended and get lost in their way have remained in this world. ...'

* * *

I only changed the underlined words and dropped three or four words. Calvino was talking about readers: books, read, reading. As I modified it, it talks about thought, memories, life, discoveries. But the difference is really slight.

In this vision there is a great modernity. Forget hermeneutics, that cares about the relationship of the author with the text. The book – life – is there to be read, its value is in what you can read in it (out of it), in how you can make it a part of yourself. Sure, there is subjectivity, each one underscores a way of looking at it, but nobody says no, nobody negates the admissibility, and the value, of a perspective different from their own, because everybody realizes that reading – and thought, experience, memory – is never unique and unambiguous, because reading is all Calvino says is in it, and much more.

Among readers, in talking about books, nobody is offended by this exasperated relativism, by this subjectivity, concentrated on the act of reading, irrespective of the value of the book and its author. Literary men and critics would not dare talking like this.

But in front of the great book of life – I knew I would find the occasion to use this expression... – are not we readers, all of us?

Let us leave to hermeneutics the analysis of the texts, and of all references and relationships of the author with each written word; let us leave to philosophers and theologians the analysis of what is 'absolutely' real and true, and of the relationships of each element of nature with its anonymous Author. And let us care instead of how reality enters in us, of what remains in us of each moment of our life, and of how we transform all this into our own history, which is not a list of elements, situations, facts, but a tale about how we have lived, and we live them.

Understanding one's own role often is the best way, possibly the only way, to understand what we are facing.

We are readers, each of us with our own tastes, in a library where reality is made of books, written for us. The metaphor is not crazy, neither is it little scientific.

The problem is not to be deceived by words. Because in revising the evolution and development of higher functions in the brain one cannot avoid the simple conclusion that we are made – our brain is made – to read the book of nature. Reality is written for us, because we are precisely made to read it.

This may appear as an optimistic statement, since it is so easy to deceive our senses – think of optical illusions, for example – and to misinterpret complex natural processes. Still, we have been capable to understand physical principles that govern microscopic worlds that we cannot even see; to clarify that space and time are not what they appear to be;

that the entire structure of space and time is upset by high speeds, accelerations and gravity; to understand that infinity need not be unlimited; to realize that the limit between matter and energy is not an ontological barrier, but rather they can convert into each-other.

This indicates that our brain is designed to look for explanations about all the information it can input: not only data that our sensory systems gather from the external world, but also any logical consequence of that, and more and more information that we can indirectly obtain by developing investigation devices and instruments...

Never satisfied, moved by a force that we may call 'thirst for knowledge', or we should more simply relate to the functioning principle of all brain structures: NAVIGATE information in trying to coagulate unitary visions, navigate among unitary visions in trying to coalesce a more general vision, then do it again and try and conciliate the different results...

Reality is written for us, because we are precisely made to read it.

Reality is a hyper-complex system, the intersection of innumerable levels of organization and complexity, each subsystem governed by distinct sets of rules, and basically (I would dare say 'ontologically') affected by the uncertainty principle.

Reality cannot be comprehended with a single approach, a single criterion; to grasp it in its essence *it is necessary to simultaneously interpret it in a thousand ways and to conciliate the results, accepting that a margin of uncertainty will remain,* and several readings will simultaneously hold, and will have to be accepted, even though they may partly conflict with each other.

And this is exactly the way our brain works, not a single reading but looking for harmonies, harmonies of harmonies, meta-harmonies, despite uncertainties and deceivability of our senses, guided by a fundamental principle that I like to call 'aesthetic'.

Curiously enough, if this multiplicity of readings and levels, with all the inconsistencies that may follow, is guided by a common principle (the search for harmony at each and every level), then this line of though does not bring us towards 'relativism', but rather to the idea that different interpretations are admissible at each level, but convergences and compromises are possible in the name of the COMMON principle (looking for harmony), and shared syntheses can generally be attained at higher levels of complexity.

* * *

So, along these axes – exactness, visibility, rapidity, multiplicity, lightness – a writer can gradually transform a chronicle into a narration, and from here, through creativity and artistic sensibility, legend and myth can be generated; in the same way thought and interior life depart from the elements and the sequences of experience, transforming perception into intuition and reasoning, thinking, and then fantasy and dream. Because intuition is not made of details but rather of meaning, atmosphere, emotion, and its substance are relations (the totality, multiplicity, complexity, the many levels, the structure of relations) rather than the elements. To get hold of the intuition one must examine (travel) its many aspects. It is a process that from the raw reality of the datum arrives to the interpretation and the rule, but from there it further proceeds toward other possible rules, toward other readings, toward freedom.

Most of all, we cannot stop. If elements and relationships, and knowledge, are not sufficient to derive a rigorous interpretation, then nobody stops there, anyway: a possible reading will be looked for and generated by legend, by myth, or fantasy.

This is the outlook of children who, voracious of information and interpretations, understand what they can, and for the rest accept any interpretation, any reading that somebody else can offer them or they can find by themselves.

Lewis Carroll in his Alice in Wonderland captures the essence itself of thought, of the speech as a journey in a stranger, unknown country, new and unexplored. You are in the hands of a world that calls for your glance and proposes and demands ever different perspectives.

Alice has no discomfort in the face of any reading, even the most absurd and paradoxical; she is the true, pluralistic and open-minded investigator of the world. But she is a child, naive, simply free of 'diverting', of wandering (among the wonders of her world...)

But when you are an adult, when you KNOW, when the counts add up correctly and you feel you do understand, it seems you must stop. Stop changing angles and accepting different readings.

Still, trying novel glances, freeing oneself from the limits of a canonical interpretation, noticing other and unexpected relationships, looking for new perspectives... all this remains quite attractive.

Keeping to what has remained in us of the children we used to be. Wandering in other dimensions in search of higher harmonies, not mere knowledge, but comprehending, taking inside, feel, live...

Yes, Alice is a child and is free to simply wander.

But if you know, you still are free, and if you let yourself be surprised, and wonder, this turns into poetry.

Perhaps the most intriguing aspect of OUR time – our interior time, the time of the thought, which does not stop at the first reading but always runs further and, curious, has itself deviated and recaptured, is that it differs from any other sequence of events.

A sequence of events, though it may be irreversible, can be retraced backwards, its time reversed; the path of the thought, instead, which is marked by a non-causal time, by an arbitrary before-after, evocative, curious, the path of thought cannot be tracked back... ('how did I get to this idea? to this image, this memory? how did I end up thinking of this?). No. It evaporates, so often unrepeatable, like dreams at dawn.

It is clear that thought does not elaborate on a still matter, but rather on a multitude of (subconscious) threads of associations, that continually propose more or less sensible or absurd readings of reality and of oneself.

Curiously enough, it is when thought stumbles on an unpredictable result of this bubbling interpretative turmoil that a truly original intuition (or at least an unexpected intuition, perceived as original) occurs.

Creativity, fantasy, solutions to problems and revolutionary discoveries that one could never tell where they popped up from.

* * *

Talking about hair cells

The first time I talked her about hair cells in the inner ear – which we call ciliate cells, in Italy, a name reminiscent of 'ciglia', our word for eyelashes – she first of all objected that if Nature were minimally concerned for consistency it would have put ciliate cells in the eye rather than in the ear, but as we know, nobody is perfect, and some errors may be forgiven also to Nature. Actually – I like playing the teacher – the cilium is useful in the ear because it can vibrate in response to sounds, so that the cell gets excited and thus informs the appropriate neurons that it has perceived the sound. Conversely, nothing vibrates in the eye...

Along the spiral of the cochlea – in the inner ear – the sounds proceed and only reach a certain point: those at higher frequencies – high tones – stop early whereas low tones – low frequencies – are capable of transmitting a vibration to the membrane that runs along the cochlea up to the top;

(ça va sans dire, would a good housewife say, who well knows that in making the bed the sheet must be moved with wide and slow oscillations, otherwise it will not swing to the end; and a proficient hooligan, or a political activist, would say the same, because they know that small flags can be swung fast, but big ones ask for calm, steady hand and wide, slow movements).

Thus, each hair cell, depending on where it is located along the spiral of the cochlea, 'hears' better one or the other sound, and thus preferentially recognizes a vibration at a precise frequency, its preferred particular tone.

But like neurons, hair cells also are generous, hard-working and dispassionate, they do not care suffering, when the cilium moves too strongly and electrolytes – deadly calcium in particular – flow in and out of the cell; they are dispassionate to the point of dying if the stimulation is too intense.

This way, hair cells die at the discotheque.

There is a sad and curious aspect, in all this: what kills each particular cell is not any sound whatsoever, no, for each one of them, it is precisely its own preferred sound, the one it has been designed for, its beloved tone, the one it is destined to, its twin tone...

'God! – she cried out – its one and only love... LOVE AND DEATH!...'

... Eros and Thanatos ...

XV

HARMONY – The soul

During the last decades we have conquered an incredible amount of information on the functioning and organization of the nervous cells, the nervous system and the brain, which demands that we turn to a new scientific outlook, higher and more ambitious. Many are the aspects of our life – perception, idea of self, feelings, ethical and ideal motivations, the need to overcome the limits of the body and of time, the need of harmony, beauty, infinity – that make us think of a soul. For each of these instances we today recognize mechanisms, circuitries, processes and modes, in the brain, that can generate and outline them.

But to understand these new perspectives it is necessary to practice in looking at every aspect of reality and every knowledge process from inside and from outside, by appreciating that each approach and each logic has its limitations, but one must not repudiate it in looking further, beyond such limits.

Thus a few key words capture our attention:

- MULTIPLICITY – not one way only, more than one approach, many mechanisms, a thousand possibilities, infinite readings
- META – something that is reminiscent of the 'dialectics' of idealists and Kant's transcendentalism: being able to exit, to go further, seeing each single system per se, but also its logic, from outside, in relation with other logics, in wider systems
- BEAUTY – the enchant of perceiving unifying aspects, higher syntheses, the flavor of harmonies among different multiplicities, METAs and logics, the synthesis of many glances and perspectives: consistency and *coherence in the multiplicity*

The innumerable modes, paths and hierarchies in the neuronal circuits host a thousand visions and reading levels, prefiguring the 'meta'. And if multiplicity is the manner of the soul, META is its flavor; it lets you think about beyond, about OTHER and MORE, it suggests that the limit is not a barrier, but a border to overcome.

The search for harmonic syntheses, for glimpses of wider horizons, guides the noblest cerebral regions, turns them toward beauty, and thus feeds the soul. Because the essence itself of the soul, of what makes us think of a soul, is but beauty, the harmony that suggests ever new equilibriums, aspirations and dreams, creativity, freedom.

These are the key words that bring to the soul: because suffering, as also an animal can do, is not enough, palpitations are not enough.

The soul cannot be there only, in viscera, instinct and spontaneous gestures, one must *feel* their own suffering and desiring, and their own dreaming and being happy, one must know a thousand views, and enjoy the enchant of harmony, of synthesis, of going beyond, the flavor of infinity.

* * *

Still, once more one would say: ok, the brain up to where you wish, but the soul begins where the brain ends.

The problem is that we might well give up. After millennia of philosophy, preoccupied about what IS and what just seems to be, about what part of reality reaches the soul and what the soul already knows on its own, about how true is what is out there and how true is what moves and cries inside here, perhaps we might finally raise a white flag.

But I think that too much news have piled up during the last century, and they are far from having been digested, not only by the layman, but even by Culture with the capital C. And not even by Science, which did discover them. Matter, energy, form. Knowableness. Mathematics and logic. Space, time. Infinity. Truth. The XX century has destroyed everything. Most of all, it has demolished – and nobody seems to have noticed – limits and borders.

During that century science has written the most revolutionary pages. From Gödel, who demolished uniqueness, totality and coherence of mathematics, to Einstein, who unveiled the ontological inconsistency of space and time, the limitedness of infinity, to Popper, who denied value of absolute truth to the undeniable, founding science on disprovability. Revolutionary pages, because they definitely abolished the right for anybody to impose a view, a reading, as the only one, undeniable.

All this demands that the border between science and philosophy be moved: the fracture is no longer between what is directly knowable (object of science) and interpretation (object of philosophy). Relativistic physics imposes a vision of time and space that does not assume for them ontological reality and fixity. The antinomy matter-energy has vanished in the idea that they are the same stuff, convertible into each other. Such vision, the only one compatible with experimental data, is the most advanced TRUTH, until proven otherwise: interpretation is part of this TRUTH as much as the experimental data is, because the latter, without interpretation, does not say anything. Experimental results do not say anything because they do not concern our everyday experience, but something absolutely else: they concern the knowledge of the world and matter, but knowledge is not made of data but of interpretations.

By the same token, General Relativity demolishes the concept of an infinite and unlimited universe, by clarifying how the gravitational field bends the space-time (*clarifying?!*) in such a way that space turns out to be under all aspects infinite though it might be limited. The curvature of space-time does not tell anything to us, either, does not concern our life more than black holes do, but it does concern the knowledge of the world and its dynamics, a knowledge that is an interpretative picture and not a bunch of data.

More. Quantum physics reveals that there is a limit to the measurability of physical quantities, such as the velocity and position of elementary particles. But the point is that not only it is not possible to measure the position and velocity of a particle because one cannot build a sufficiently rapid and precise instrument. No, this is true, but the crucial point is not this one. The question is that IT CANNOT BE DONE, IT IS NOT POSSIBLE; not even with the ideal instrument, the most absolutely precise one, because a particle DOES NOT POSSESS precise velocity and position, but possesses a velocity which is the more definite, the less definite is its position, and vice-versa. Intrinsically. Physically. Ineluctably.

Indeterminacy. A limit to knowledgeableness. Something like the mysteries of religion, of faith. Indeed, it even goes beyond that, because it is not something which is precluded to OUR capacity of understanding, to the limits of our human mind and our logic; no, the fact is that it is NOT POSSIBLE TO KNOW it, it does NOT EXIST as a measurement. Maybe, it simply means that we should dismantle, after our obsolete concepts of space and time, and infinity, also the concepts of position and velocity. Once more, the question does not affect us, the data don't concern us.

But philosophy, the conception of the world, of reason, of knowableness of reality, should come out a little shaken, shouldn't it?

Even more. The mathematics of nonlinear systems, chaos, with its recognized and stated impossibility of foreseeing the development of a chaotic system, even though nothing is subjected to hazard, even though the rules of each change in the system are precise and perfectly known. Causal systems, deterministic, precise, systems that can be described in every detail, and that one should therefore be capable of 'understanding'. Still, their development is determined in such a subtle and delicate way by imperceptible differences in any one of their parameters, that no prevision is reliable, whatever be the care and precision with which we measure each single parameter: and it is fascinating how the indeterminacy principle hammers us, precisely at this point, in warranting us that such precision can never be absolute.

This should cheer up stockbrokers and meteorologists. Here, there is even some kind of vague relevance to our everyday life, but once more the crucial point regards the conception of the world, the applicability of the principle of causality, the idea of knowableness...

Perhaps the most upsetting one is Gödel's demonstration that a mathematical or logical system, simultaneously complete and coherent, CANNOT EXIST. Either it has a limited field of applicability, and it can be coherent, or it must accept contradictions and incoherence within itself, which is not particularly nice for a system that aims at being defined 'mathematical' (almost a synonym of 'perfect'). And philosophy must face all this as well, as concerns both knowableness and coherence...

In the face of all these upheavals – philosophical even more than scientific – Popper has traced the new definition of SCIENCE and (though he did not say it) the new measure of TRUTH. *Scientific truth does not exist.* It is a process of approaching by approximation. A statement has scientific value if there is a way of verifying it (and therefore of showing it is false) through an experimental approach. Furthermore, its value of truth is in any case provisional, until some experimental evidence turns out to contradict it and requires it to be reexamined, in the frame of a novel interpretation that be able to reconcile and account for the new data as well. A provisional and never resting truth. Nothing is GIVEN a priori, no axioms, no a priori concept; each piece of knowledge – TRUTH – actually is *interpretation,* and what separates scientific knowledge – TRUTH – from nonscientific knowledge is that the first one is amenable to some kind of experimental verification (and confutation).

In front of this revolution, some new rules must be defined for the game.
- We must admit that even the most solid scientific truth might not hold outside a certain domain of physics.
- Certainly, there is a domain of reality – of physics and not only of metaphysics – that trespasses the limits of knowableness.
- Science is not a collection of answers but a way to ask questions, the particular way of asking them that makes it possible to verify (better, confute) the answers.
- overall, SCIENCE is the capacity of INTERPRETING data in a clear, precise and CONFUTABLE way.
- The field of interest of science is not limited to nature. Through physics, mathematics, neurobiology, many aspects can be faced that up to now have been considered exclusive domain of philosophy: matter, reality, truth, thought, emotions, affectivity, human behavior, ethics, aesthetics.

- To face these themes science must keep on with the unprejudiced and courageous attitude with which it has been able to demolish concepts 'inborn in human reason' such as time, space, infinity and matter.
- Each TRUTH is provisional, and only has scientific dignity if it is based on experimental observations, known mechanisms and processes, and on their interpretation, without using any assumption that cannot be verified or confuted in some manner.

Under many aspects, all this brings us back to a science that is more ancient and elevated, a process of gathering information and verifying it in the framework of a strictly philosophical elaboration (knowing and understanding). This should be seriously considered by those who have tried and managed to empty scientific culture of its value and meaning, by opposing a (liberal-humanistic) Culture on one side, aimed at the study of reality and Man in order TO KNOW, and a science on the other side, meant as the study of reality in order to CONTROL and MODIFY it.

A science more and more strictly confined to technology, with no breath, no passion, no poetry.

Science has a lot to say. Indeed, the border between science and philosophy has moved much beyond the classical limit between physics and metaphysics. It has moved to elevated concepts such as space, time and infinity, structure of matter, relation between matter and energy, knowableness, the mechanisms of affectivity, of human behavior, of ideality itself. In addition, a habit to different rules persists: philosophy is permitted to rely on indemonstrable – and un-disprovable – axioms, whose value of TRUTH lies on their logical necessity, on how much they are perceived as UNDENIABLE in the depth of the soul (like space, and time, and matter, perhaps?); conversely, axioms are precluded to science, as are those fields of philosophy where no contribution can come from things that can be studied. For all the rest, certainly many taboo questions remain, on which a scientific approach does not enable us to say anything, but many questions can be asked, and many answers can be looked for.

This way, however, the relationship between science and philosophy is redrawn in a curiously paradoxical way: the most solid, coherent and reliable criterion of TRUTH is a property of science – provisional truth, until the contrary is proved true (which is always possible), and continually evolving – as opposed to an axiomatic truth sustained by axioms which, by the way, have been pulverized one after the other.

* * *

Then, let's dispense with limits and axioms, and try to proceed further, change our outlook, multiply our gazes, reconcile different perspectives.

Perception and interpretation of reality, in the brain.

In the brain, regions that crystallize concrete and abstract 'concepts' into patterns of neuronal activity, and regions that, by elaborating sounds and sophisticated phonetic behaviors, associate words to the concepts and build the symbolic system of language; all this in the brain. And cerebral areas that elaborate space, and time, and numbers and hierarchies and complex relationships, and contribute an impressive power to the capacity of symbolic manipulation of information.

In the brain, many cerebral areas intrinsically capable of examining, simultaneously AND sequentially, multiple and different pieces of information, and of navigating among them to build complex and continuously evolving interpretations.

In the brain, also, the regions of higher elaboration, that translate this same working modality (wandering around to navigate information) into a spotlight that examines reality and oneself, by reading and narrating them, thereby generating a CONSCIOUSNESS of oneself and of the world. Consciousness that can be translated into an explicit tale, an interior language that guides thought.

In the brain, an implicit elaboration of emotions and feelings and, by means of conscious narration, the capacity of reading and interpreting them, and telling them. In the brain, finally, a capacity of choice that is not calculus, but a continuous evaluation and re-evaluation, in search of more and more complex, more and more elevated harmonies. And a force that pushes us to look for such harmony, the pleasure of beauty, that generates esthetics and ethics.

What is missing here? Passion, commitment, fantasy, love, happiness? Blue, need of infinity? Something worth more than life itself? What else?

* * *

Life is the organization criterion of living organisms, the way they persist, by keeping constant, or slowly evolving, certain features of theirs, in a continuous interaction with the external environment. Life is a dynamic, unstable equilibrium, re-created at every moment, thanks to interactions that destabilize it: a static appearance of a system in which nothing is stable. It is a continuous assertion by self-denying, a way of self-protecting and persisting by affirming itself as something different from what it used to be just a moment before.

Memory, our history, our ME, can be described in the exact same way: the continuous product of how we have been living all that has happened to us, a product that asserts itself in the way it lives each new experience, and in the meantime imperceptibly changes because of the marks that each new experience leaves. An outlook on life (a ME) that does not exist without a life to live (it is impressive how much this annihilates the idea of a 'soul' as something abstractly separated from the ME that is living), an outlook on life that asserts itself in living and continuously changes in this asserting itself.

Life thus ASSERTS and SUSTAINS itself by and in changing: we are made of a *part* that tries to SURVIVE by defending itself, and another *part* that tries to LIVE, change, grow, looking outwards, because without interaction and change it cannot even survive.

Physically. Psychologically. Affectively. Still, to survive one defends oneself, and builds walls and barriers, and defines, limits oneself.

What pushes us to defend the unstable equilibrium that we have been able to put together at each moment?

Conversely, what forces us to put it at risk, sometimes to consciously, intentionally demolish it, to proceed further on, to explore life?

Well, in order to live, one has to survive, has one not? and to resist. But surviving is not enough. Something else is needed...

* * *

The central nervous system endows the animal with the capacity not only to react to stimuli, but also to build a model of reality, of the organism itself, of their interactions; and the capacity to orient its behavior based on sophisticated evaluations not only of vegetative needs but also of somehow less easily describable motivational drives.

In front of this, BIOLOGY is not enough. This way meta-biology arises, which PHYSICS cannot describe, which has its own rules, forces and dynamics, and invades the field of immaterial, of knowledge, of a cybernetic that is not automatic, but capable of anticipation, of finalized action.

The impressive development of the cerebral cortex in humans transcends the trivial task of producing responses to stimuli, even the most refined ones: in the cortex innumerable interpretations of reality pullulate, each one arises and evolves by re-elaborating the information that reaches it, according to its own specific modalities, angles and contexts.

Each interpretation is re-read and integrated with the others, but each one is complex in itself and in many regards autonomous, each one is like a dynamic image of a particular aspect of oneself or of the world, and each one is born, grows and develops like a meta-organism, endowed with its own life, though confined in the immateriality of formal, abstract representation.

The encounter of a thousand readings molds the concepts, builds a multiple, complex, varied view of reality (and of oneself), made of metaphors, capable of abstract manipulation and – here is the new, extraordinary jump! – of symbolic activity: a language made of sounds and acts that do not imitate, mimic, represent reality – as it is the case for animal languages – but get combined in an abstract SYMBOLIC system, within which each sound combination assumes an arbitrarily attributed meaning, different in different languages, to yield an instrument of amazing power, not only to describe and model, but to investigate in depth and understand. Here, higher, explicit consciousness blossoms, an outlook conscious of oneself and of the world: synthesis of multiplicity and interpretation of reality.

This way the regulation of behavior becomes careful and delicate, in the varied interaction among vegetative, hedonic, social-cultural and ideal motivational drives; a clear and real possibility of choice materializes, finalized behavior – strictly speaking – appears.

Once more the domain changes, and the language: biology is no longer sufficient, neither is cybernetics, the fields are invaded of epistemology, ethics, freedom; we are evading towards the soul.

Each new dimension asks for new glances. Each new jump asks for a new formal description, because the rules that used to guide simpler systems keep working down there but are no longer relevant here. In order to describe and understand the overall dynamics new specific necessities dominate now, and new interactions, higher ones, that in simpler systems could not even be thought of. From this impressive development of cognitive, cybernetic, behavioral power of the brain something arises, almost as a *collateral effect*: an unexpected and fascinating mixture of interpretative power, emotions and motivations, memory and desire, joy and pain, and consciousness of one's own understanding and feeling, blues and happiness, love, passion and will, curiosity and fear, wonder and disdain, enthusiasm and commitment.

A mixture that constitutes a new LEVEL of life, interior and superior, but not secluded; rather, capable of impinging on reality and the world, in a new and different way, pursuing designs and aims, desires and ideals.

A new dimension of life blossoms from this mixture of outlooks, ideals and fantasies, and the need for OTHER, for infinity, in time and space, the need to overcome one's own limits, to know and find oneself in eternity and infinity... A curious collateral effect, for which it is difficult to find a name that be nicer and more appropriate than SOUL.

* * *

Closed languages, empty music

Why so many of us do not understand mathematics? because it is a language that talks to itself. You can apply it to anything you wish, but it is MATHEMATICS only in the moment you recognize that it is not WHAT you have applied it to, but something ELSE, something abstract, ethereal, impalpable, closed in itself.

The society of welfare, centered on consumes and care of your body and health, of everydayness, teaches you to close your horizon on yourself. Try and sign up for an internet chat, you must choose the topics you are interested in, and you generally find a dozen or so of them, movies, arts, sport... A topic that is always there is 'body care', an interest, an encounter moment!...

It is progress.

No disciplines – it is not a problem of mathematics alone – proceeds beyond a certain point without creating a language of its own, auto-referential. The discipline of well-being is almost there, it is building people that are languages and music that fold back on themselves, like certain obscure musical currents that transform music into an abstract and auto-referential reasoning, like grammars that rigorously mull over relations among empty words.

Take care of yourself!
Was not it 'know yourself'? Old times... Now, it is of no use anymore.

Except that it turns out that depression is nothing but screwing into one's own problem(s), excluding emotions other than pain for one's own emotions, and thoughts other than sad re-examinations of one's own thoughts...

Perhaps it is not so strange that those who are so careful in caring about themselves, forgetting the world, the pain of the others, the wish of building, the need of expressing oneself in action and commitment, so often end up falling into it, into depression.

* * *

In this view behavior is no longer driven by knowledge, utility, rationality alone. It is pervaded by something else, by infinity, affects, ideals and dreams, by the soul.

The best choice, absolutely speaking, cannot be made at the table, by attributing specific scores to each motivational drive, according to a system of precise and fixed criteria, as you would program a commercial or managerial strategy. Precisely because there is no single criterion, or fixed number of criteria, that can guide in this evaluation.

Absolutely speaking, the best choice is the one that manages in reconciling in the best way the maximum number of criteria, that appears to remain valid when you change your perspective, in the face of mutability, with time, of the forces that push toward one or the other hypothesis... Absolutely speaking, there is no best choice. It is different for each of us, and changes with our needs, our affects, our sensitivity to somebody else's needs... and it changes with time, with our history.

This is not a hymn to relativism: the best choice we are talking about is the best one in utilitarian terms, for the sake of pursuit of pleasure and escape from pain. The ETHICALLY best choice is another story. Still, if in *pleasure* we include social and ethical drives, and in *pain* we include other people's suffering, the 'best' choice becomes much more like an ethical choice, much less variable and less sensitive to momentary changes in mood, capricious desires, illusions...

To reach such a 'best' choice the most appropriate criterion is to search for harmony, for a principle that finds unifying aspects, balance (though uncertain and mutable) and conciliation, to follow a thread that gives a sense to the whole of it, justifying the renounces and valorizing the conquests. There is a warning: there is no universal scale of importance of the many aspects that may be involved in an ethical choice; many values have changed in time and differ amongst different cultures.

Still, a principle can be pinned down to define which the most appropriate word is 'beauty' (which also depends on culture).

BEAUTY, yes. Beauty as the possibility of a unifying view, that without renouncing the multiplicity of perspectives can give a sense, a reading criterion.

Be it a conciliatory reading, or an exasperated one, be it calm or passionate, linear or contradictory, holy or painful... whatever, one or the other, provided that one does not pretend that the contrasts are not there, but rather considers and composes them, and the 'sense' is not lost in other possible readings...

Beauty may be a vague and imprecise word, each of us may apply it differently to different objects, events, people, ideas. But if a criterion of 'beauty' exists, in art as in life, it lies in the harmonic synthesis of multiplicities, be it smooth and round, or sharp and edgy. Curiously enough, the sensitivity to beauty may differ, and the judgment, but the mechanism that triggers our sense of beauty is the same: your seeing/feeling beauty, or not, in front of something, depends on your seeing/feeling multiplicity (the interplay of colors, sounds, shapes, impressions, emotions, ideas, dreams) and/or your perceiving a form or some kind of synthesis, of harmony.

I think this is something deeply related to the attitude of Hinduism towards truth: there are many ways to the truth, and you should try and find your own, but though the ways are numerous and different, the truth is not. Each one of us has their sensitivity, is capable of noticing and capturing different details and connections, but the operating modes of our brains are consistent, and when we manage in perceiving the underlying harmony we are bound to converge on the same deep essence and truth.

I think we are pretty distant from 'relativism'...

Following this line of thought we once again encounter the META, its trickiness and charm: the question is to resolve a varied and mutable conflict among motivational drives that cannot be merely added up or contrasted to see who wins. Each of these forces is by itself capable of driving a behavior, if it is not adequately counteracted or inhibited. They are not requests that are presented to a higher decision-making center, which takes note of whatever is happening down there, makes its computations and, precisely, DECIDES.

Higher criteria must solve the balances, but these criteria will not remain out of and above the conflict: the criteria (external and superior) must themselves enter the conflict as forces that play the match with all the others.

According to Thomas Aquinas, *"three things are necessary for the salvation of man: to know what he ought to believe; to know what he ought to desire; and to know what he ought to do."* But often the three conflict with each other. Thus, the NEED for a harmonic and mutable synthesis and a critical and esthetic analysis of the motivational conflict must become itself a motivational force, that can strengthen or weaken, orient and frame the choices in an overall strategy, and finally set out the behavioral responses.

* * *

The non-opposed

The charm of evil. It would seem that if beauty – harmony – characterizes the ethical gesture, then evil should be ugly, shouldn't it?

Well, first of all, the contrary of BEAUTIFUL – sublime that captivates – is certainly not ugly, which can move and amaze, but it rather is DULL.

And the contrary of an ethical gesture is not a wicked gesture, which may be equally difficult, intense and in some cases pleasant.
Rather, it is an automatic gesture, routinely or insensate.

The scale is intensity. Beauty vs. ugliness is only a bifurcation.

Sublimity, still, sits on the branch of beauty, a higher harmony in qualitative terms, and in terms of dimensions and infinities.

Similarly, the ethics of good is qualitatively higher because, given a similar intensity of gratification, and perception of power and absoluteness,
it can invade with harmony some more infinities:
sociality as well, and sharing, smiles and hugs and love.

* * *

So, down there in the deep regions of the brain there are neurons that can translate external stimuli and internal needs into violent impulses that trigger incontrollable expectations and indispensable gratifications.

These are the neuronal bases of what we call motivational drives, some of them physiologic, vegetative, others emotional and affective.

The hypothalamus urges with physiological needs and homeostasis; the amygdala detects threats, dangers, chances, and arouses the cortex; the midbrain dopaminergic systems signal opportunity and achievement of pleasure, serotonergic systems push us toward social acceptability.

The massive projections that from the cortical structures impinge onto these regions make it so that motivational drives, expectations and pleasure linked to social appreciation and self-image are as strong as physiological ones in guiding our behavior.

So, it is not strange that the need to evaluate, understand, judge, appreciate, act and look for synthesis, harmony and love gets transformed through a similar mechanism into fundamental needs, profoundly perceived as essential as food and water are, and warmth and love.

Here, specifically on this point, experimental data is still lacking.

No 'neurons of beauty' have been described yet.

There is no precise description of the pathways that, from the multimodal associative areas of the cortex, and from prefrontal regions that elaborate, simulate and compare behaviors, their difficulties and their consequences, descend to activate the 'centers of pleasure', down in the VTA and ventral striatum, and rise back towards the limbic cortex to generate the subsequent emotional experience. Neurons and pathways have not been identified, but it is difficult to deny that an affective pleasure does exist, and an esthetic pleasure (a languor for intensity, active equilibrium, infinity), an ethical pleasure (this may be the fundamental essence of Kant's categorical imperative), and the pleasure of discovery, of wonder and understanding, of solving problems and conflicts.

True, profound pleasures, 'physical' pleasures, once again pleasures with no adjectives... forms of pleasure, and that is all.

So let us try and survive for some more years or decades, waiting for neurons and nervous pathways to be identified, but in the meanwhile accept that detection of harmony, conciliation of conflicts, the conquest of a unifying view and recognition of beauty, by the areas of multimodal integration and cognitive elaboration in the cortex, MUST travel and arrive as positive signals to the limbic systems that elaborate the emotional coloring of experience, and reach down to the deep areas that trigger gratification responses, and involve 'anticipation' and 'reward' neurons, and the whole deep HEDONIC circuitry, visceral and corporeal (Freud's pulsional ES, possibly, as the source of subconscious drives).

Then, if wonder and understanding, beauty, harmony and conflict conciliation can neurologically produce PLEASURE, this closes the circle, solders and completes the interaction and cross dialogue between deep hedonic structures and cognitive activity. It does it through the crossroad (the 'limb') of limbic cortex, that can perceive the hedonic and motivational valence of cognitive elaboration and translate it into emotional and affective coloring, and in the meantime can analyze hedonic drives and emotions according to a complex logic and translate them into an 'emotional experience' that can be cognitively and consciously (rationally, for those who manage...) elaborated by other regions of the cerebral cortex.

In the first years of the XXI century, functional MRI reports started to appear indicating that the reward pathway – the set of structures that are involved in producing physical pleasure – is activated when we perform an ethical act.

Much ado, in the community of dull journalists and commentators: "the scientists themselves were astonished!" (*really?* I would bet this is exactly what they expected); "but if we prove pleasure in doing good, then morality is unexpectedly present in the brain"; "but then the concept itself of moral responsibility vanishes!"… "If you consider also Damasio's experiments that tells that people with a damaged ventromedial prefrontal cortex – like the famous Phineas Gage – have problems in evaluating ethical questions and controlling their behavior, the picture becomes even more upsetting!".

Really? Didn't Kant himself say, centuries back, that the moral act is pleasurable in itself? He was talking of the *intellect*, not of the brain, but where is the big difference? Did anybody really believe that when we act, moved by ethical, social, affective motivations, we suffer?

* * *

Evolution

And if evolution had a meaning, a dominant directive?

It goes blindly, any path is good to produce and multiply life, because this makes ever new methods and ways possible to exploit the available energy.

It does not abandon the old paths; it may shut them down if it turns out they can no longer compete but, as far as possible and acceptable, it keeps all tactics open: that is 'biodiversity', the thousands of different solutions for each problem.

But in this search for ever new solutions Nature sometimes encounters 'qualitative leaps', new solutions that are essentially more complex, that permit greater malleability, and a multiplicity of strategies by one and the same organism.

Complexity adjoins multiplicity: Evolution does not abandon simple solutions, but in addition to multiplying them it is also capable of adding to them more and more complex solutions; so complex that they begin to spill out of the problematic of mere survival in the world as it is and start and then to represent the world, and then to interpret it, to modify it, and understand it, until they overflow into looking at self, and understanding and developing a consciousness.

Is this an intelligent design?

Who knows, but to explain it THE FORCE *is enough.*

The energy blocked in the chemical molecules, in the matter.
Energy that thanks to living beings can be freed out into entropy.

The energy of the sun, that the plants know how to include into precious molecules, such as glucose, to give life to all animals, energy that on its own would only warm up the Earth, little by little, without having the strength to break – as living organisms can do – molecules that maintain their balance like very complicated card towers, and do not free the chemical energy they enclose, like hydro-electrical basins that, were the dam to fissure, would happily pour billions of tons of water downhill, killing and sweeping out everything in a delirium of destruction, disorder, entropy.

The FORCE is enough. The force of entropy. The force of life.

Each new organism, that has developed a new capacity of freeing out the energy entrapped in some chemical compound, in coal, in petrol, in molecules, in the nucleus of uranium, has on its side, to help it survive, grow, multiply, the insatiable thirst for energy of Universe's entropy.

This is enough to confirm, preserve and consolidate every step Evolution manages in finding new sources of energy, new ways of using it and dispersing it, in its blind wanderings among genetic mutations and recombinations, towards more complex systems that be capable of finding new solutions to survive. At least as long as – let us put a bit of cosmic pessimism in it – there is some free energy left.

If a brain manages in generating a 'drive for beauty', the way of transforming the perception of harmony, of synthesis of complexity, into a motivational drive, this certainly is a gift that Entropy cannot refuse, a gift from Evolution, the promise of ever new solutions, ever more numerous paths to provide more energy to Universal Disorder.

But if the universal force is Entropy, the thirst for disorder, the self-destructive ambition of blocked energy, and if complexity and multiplicity are the directions along which evolution proceeds – spreading out as oil, not running straight as a train... – if this is the direction – complexity and multiplicity, solutions that depart from merely facing the problem, and explore implications and colors, and atmospheres and higher harmonies – well then it is clear that man is not the end-point.

Evolution certainly has already taken another step: woman...

Historic analyses, explorations of myths and unconscious, neuroanatomical studies and psycho-aptitude tests have proposed all possible theories about the differences between man and woman, more or less fascinating and humiliating or exalting for one or the other gender.

The solid data that have a scientific appearance essentially are the following:

In the average (in the AVERAGE!) the woman has a greater capacity of relating her emotional experience and rational activity, a greater verbal ability, a greater attention to details, and to corporeal expressions of emotions and feelings.
Consequently, she analyzes and expresses her EMOTIONAL experience with greater ease and in general has a greater capacity in CONCILIATING different approaches, aspects, viewpoints and criteria into a multifaceted, multiple and intrinsically deeper and more malleable view of reality (of the world, of herself, of the other, of the relationships).

In the average (in the AVERAGE!!!) the man has a greater capacity of abstraction and generalization, proceeds more easily in a THEORETICAL way and through general principles, and even in practical activities tends to follow guiding criteria and more precise RULES.
He theorizes emotional experience as well, his own and other people's, rather than attentively perceiving it and communicating it; he faces each problem with the approach that he considers as the most specifically adequate (and which is not necessarily so) and in conclusion has a greater difficulty in reconciling a multiplicity of tasks and life domains.

If one considers that these characteristics have detectable substrates in the anatomical and functional differences of the various cerebral areas in the two sexes, which are partly congenital and partly generated by the different hormonal picture, it is amusing to propose an interpretative (causal-evolutional) hypothesis.

In mammals, preservation of the species imposes distinct and different tasks to the male and the female:

♀ *in general, the female is not always available for pairing, and in general she has no problem in finding a male to that purpose; procreation for the female is instead a relevant and demanding task*

♂ *the male is always available for coupling, and in order to propagate his genes he must compete with other males; procreation is not a difficult or demanding task per se, mating might rather be so!*

♀ *the female propagates her genes with success if she conducts to proper term her pregnancy and can take care of and protect her offspring until self-sufficiency: this requires attention to danger and safety signals, caring about environment and taking care of others (the offspring) like of herself*

♂ the male propagates his genes with success if he can adapt to the game of partner selection by the female (he sings, runs, fights, dances with his horns better than the others do) and if he can defend the pregnant female and his offspring from other males: his task mainly is to fight and compete, using strength in the one case, ability in following the rules in the other.

♂ How would you design the brain of a male?
- competitive
- capable of internalizing the rules of the game and skillfully following them
- capable at any moment of forgetting everything else and fully dedicating himself to fighting or competing, along the acquired rules
- interested in possibly changing the world rather than adapting, but …
- … one thing at a time, please!

♀ How would you design the brain of a female?
- attentive
- more interested in detecting every possible signal than in theorizing
- capable of understanding the need of the baby – and consequently of others in general – from every single detail of their behavior
- interested in building a micro-environment suitable to herself and her offspring, rather than in changing the world
- necessarily capable of considering several aspects, simultaneously

Now, just add intelligence, and you end up with a man capable of theorizing on anything, and fighting and realizing great enterprises, but not of thinking of two things at a time.

And a woman who understands what goes on around her (and in the soul of her man) and complains that he does not understand her.

These differences may help to make more demanding, and pleasant, looking for the right pace to dance together: you can duet with two guitars, or two trumpets, or drums, but perhaps with different instruments it is more amusing, and it is possible to play better – music, and life as well.

And perhaps it is not so strange that in this game the woman is more careful and talented, because she perceives better the music of the soul, she can do without explaining it – and without misunderstanding it! – when it is not necessary and can follow it and live it and spread it all around.

Good fighters and players, on one side.

Attention, care and multiplicity on the other.

Then Gandhi comes about, and Einstein and Byron, or Mrs. Tatcher and other women in politics, who like to shout and imitate the assertiveness of men, and only consider the last aspect that has been noticed...
and one tends to be confused, doesn't one?

* * *

We have talked of sensory elaboration, and underscored how such elaboration proceeds by navigating among parallel elaborations: each group of neurons in charge of detecting the presence of specific elements, relationships, links, or of cruising through images, sounds, situations, to spot sequences and time-courses to be treated as new significant elements and relationships.

The INTERPRETATION of sensory information follows the same modalities: higher elaboration centers simultaneously examine this bunch of data (they are no longer external stimuli, but recognized elements, relationships, sequences) and navigate among them, moving the focus now on this and now on another set of data, while imagination revives memories and emotions that resonate with the current activity, to enrich it with personal references and affective color in giving them a subjective and private meaning. Further on, 'multimodal' regions perform a similar analysis on the combination of these results of elaboration of images, sounds, odors, tastes, somatic and visceral sensations, emotions: once more the data are combined, to recognize objects and concepts, abstract relations, interpretative categories: unity-multiplicity, cause-effect, enumerability, order, hierarchies... but paths as well become more complex, pausing now on one aspect and then on another, now on a possible relation and then on another one.

This activity of the multimodal cortical regions, that like simpler areas proceed through cruising the information in search of resonance and a synthetic analysis, transforms the processing of internal and external sensations into a narration, a TALE, that assumes the features of CONSCIOUS knowledge of the world and of oneself.

A knowledge that is neither a static picture nor an ordered sequential description: it is not a speech that proceeds straight on, but a cross-contamination of several sequential logic paths with *illuminations, intuitions, evocative* interpretations, that produce deviations, flashbacks and re-examinations, changes of perspective and RE-READINGS.

This is the way thought proceeds too, and motivational conflicts develop.

This interior tale, in its wanderings, sometimes berths to ensemble visions that merge many readings, and draws a logic and emotional path that can be repeated without stumbling into acute contradictions.

When this happens – whether one is looking for a solution to a problem, or evaluating an ethical dilemma, or simply fantasizing – one feels something like a lightening of a tension, an experience of wellbeing and discovery, a feeling of pleasure, in a strict sense.

Thanks to the power and versatility of language, this is also the way verbal thought proceeds, and conscious formation and verbalization of behavioral choices and strategies.

This extraordinary power of language makes an almost autonomous entity out of it, capable of its own life. Sentences, even single words, said at the right moment in the right way, can sometimes grasp and communicate this same pleasure of multiple harmony, of conciliation and unifying fusion of many readings. This occurs when everything fits: the meaning, the rhythm of words and the music, everything their sound evokes, and the images – the other words – that they recall through assonance or semantic vicinity, and the memories they awaken with the emotions associated to them... when all this fastens together and fits. Then from the simple ordered positioning of characters, one next to the other, poetry is born, which no longer merely talks to reason, but rather to the soul, to the part of us that recognizes, or thinks it recognizes, or anyway looks for, the sense of things, not simply their meaning but what justifies them and gives them value and transposes them into a dimension of infinity and absoluteness.

That part of us that gets excited by beauty, in whatever form it can be found.

* * *

The word

The WORD is representation, but also description, interpretation, explanation, comprehension, it is communication, question, answer, it is compliance, self-assertion, thought, and it is dream, gesture and act...

The word relates us to the world – it describes, interprets, deforms misjudges and imagines. It colors the world with pain and joy. And it relates us to ourselves – it unveils, recounts us and dreams of us, and lets us express ourselves, imagine, propose, negate ourselves, love, hate, lose ourselves...

The word is a toy to look at, to explore and discover, or to handle with no aim, no reason. It can be combined like Lego bricks, to give shape to an idea, yes, but just for fun as well, with no plans, perhaps to find ourselves giving life to a dream that we had not even dreamt of.

The word is gemstone, noble metal or vulgar, wood, paper, nails, junk and garbage. It is matter for refined jewels, ingenious machines and perfect mechanisms; for useless and beautiful devices, improbable balances of shapes and colors, metaphors of objects, acts, sensations; and for useless and light jots that help our glance to fly off.

The word is fused brass that transforms the vacuum of abstract concepts, of immaterial simulacra, into the hard and heavy, compact and inarguable reality of stone.

The word is a profound caries that can subtly corrode, rot, empty, void and kill treasures and values, without touching the brilliant and fake enamel.

The word is fire that transforms objects, obstacles, shelters and certainties into evanescent spirals of colored smoke.

The word is fire that can neutralize, but can instead temper, the most sharpened blade.

The word is a lukewarm and soft cataplasm that covers fresh, burning sores and ancient ones that press, pulse and gnaw.
And it soothes.
It heals, perhaps.

The word is magic, that gives a meaning to what it touches, and substance, and weight, and reality.

But it can steal the meaning as well, and the value, and life.

The word is a forceps that can coagulate sneaking lumps from the depth of the soul and throw them live and bleeding onto the operating table, so that we can see them, fight them, accept them.

The word is a sharpened blade to dissect.

The word is a speck of a dream to guess and narrate.

The word is an embroidered veil to transfigure and play.

An embroidered and colored veil that lets you see what it wants, and hides or reveals, and interweaves clashing images and composes dissonances and solves conflicts – and anguishes and ghosts and fears – in a smile.

The word is a wonderful domain of life. Superior, because it is free.

It allows playing and searching, passion and discovery, fantasy and action, project and joy.

But the word is a means as well. And there, we are no longer alone.
It is three of us: the word, you talking and the listener.

But its splendid power of following and protecting and reassuring you, while in the meantime it shakes you and opens unexpected horizons, is easily lost if there is no communion of feelings, emotions, expectations, desires, attitudes. And of codes, and implications. Because without that, without empathy, it is difficult – impossible? – to tame the word, to force it to be a means but still retain all its charm and power.

It is sad that today the most beautiful feature of the language, of words – the possibility that the word flourishes, develops, weaves and enriches to soak up a soul and display it, shining of its brilliance and embracing us in the emotion which it has got hold of – this wonderful possibility is less and less used by poets, to guide our soul out of everyday concerns and troubles towards wider spaces and more intense horizons, worth discovering, and sweeter joys and more awful pains, worth experiencing.

It is less and less used by poets, and evermore by dream merchants. Those who know, with the help of the huge communication instruments, how to inject into the word (the logo) the thought, the image of a lifestyle, and to impose products as an implicit necessity, in order to reach the dream they show us. And on the other side of the screen, a society of credulous targets, taught to believe in dreams, but most of all to believe that dreams can be BOUGHT, a bit at a time...

The problem is not that we do not want any more words, hell, no!

We want them, beautiful, rich, pulpy, aromatic and thick, heavy, profound, moving.

But we want words that will really tell us what they contain, and do not dry up in the sun, by evaporating like a jellyfish with its wonderful colors, shrinking to a shapeless spit, leaving only the clot of the empty characters that compose them...

The word is a link, the strongest link.

For the things we care of, we want a word, we want a NAME – a proper name – because a NAME makes them ours and real and complete, in and out of ourselves.

Better not to give a NAME to what scares us, better not to use it for what discomforts us, for what we do not love, for what we can face better if a halo of uncertainty lets us withdraw, back away while pushing it away in the rarefied space of ghosts, dreams, desires, a space from which a NAME would call it back here, aside, inside us.

VI

BLUES AND HAPPINESS – To be or to survive

Weren't we supposed to talk about the soul?!

Everybody will be disappointed, by now: we have talked of motivation, and we have ended up on emotions and affect, pleasure of beauty, esthetics, ethics...

Indeed, we are not much out of target, are we? when we think of the soul, in the end – unless we simply see it as an immaterial small cloud, detached from the body, from life, pain, pleasure, memory and desires, dreams and commitment – we refer to something that is somehow 'above', but strictly linked to the body, and holds the threads, and suffers and loves and desires and wants and commits itself and judges and decides; and enjoys all that is beautiful and all that is right. And pleads infinity.

We are not off topic, then. But even neglecting theological aspects, something important is still missing in what we said up to now: infinity.

That incoercible plea to overcome the limits of the body, of material reality, of life, and reach for other worlds, farther away and – this may be the right word – more INTENSE.

So, let us talk about that. About intensity. And infinity.

* * *

Eating, drinking, sleeping, healing and being loved give pleasure. Still, thirst, hunger, fatigue, pain and desire of love are contradictory feelings, sometimes absolutely unpleasant, but sometimes stimulating and somehow pleasant: at times they are pure discomfort, but they can also become impatience, desire, languor, nostalgia.

And something very similar seems to occur with harmony, beauty, good and right, intensity, infinity.

The stomach can be full, the body rested, healthy, beloved people nearby. Still, sometimes a kind of nostalgia gets you, a languor that asks for music, and wonder and infinity...

Perhaps it is just the blues.

You get up in the morning and you do not even know what the problem is, but some kind of melancholy oppresses you. Maybe it is tiredness, or the spring that is coming... Women are specialists in this, you can tease them, hug them, try to understand them, just leave them alone...

263

Probably, that does not make much of a difference, the blues is not so bad, it is a kind of perverse pleasure. When I was a child, an old lady who had her beach umbrella and chair next to ours used to complain, because television programs were not as good as they used to be: 'they no longer broadcast good comedies, those nice old comedies that make you cry a lot…'.

What trick is there, in the blues, in "saudade", in effort and exhaustion, in being moved, what is there that veils discomfort with ineffable pleasure and sweetness, and transfigures it into a strange form of enjoyment?

It may be nothing but old Aristotle's story of catharsis: the drama guides you among strong emotions for which there is no real substance, just simulation, and you enact all physiological, visceral-somatic and cognitive responses to such emotions, and that makes you feel better, because when everything is finished you will have discharged all your tension, nervousness, uncertainty, discomfort through fear, anguish and tears, and all causes for such emotional performance have vanished with the final applause.

But perhaps crying and suffering – when there is no real reason to cry and suffer – is not so terrible, it may even be a subtle form of pleasure… feeling one's own sensations, the contraction of the stomach, a knot in the throat, the heart gone crazy, that pressure in the eyes, feeling the intensity of one's own emotions.

Ask a fan whether it is worth suffering so hard when their team goes down… But the joy of victory, further multiplied by sharing it with thousands of people, pays back well for that. Just think of the emotion when, everybody standing up, the national hymn is played to celebrate the victory of an athlete: be it admiration, pride, collective identification, be it the mere sharing of a strong feeling, well, it is a moment of happiness, in the intensity of emotions; it may rapidly vanish, but for a moment the emotion is so strong to erase everything else.

Are these transient experiences only? It may be so, but what is love, then, other than a curious coincidence of emotional and rational states that can *ADD SUCH INTENSITY* to any experience with the beloved one – be it a honeymoon or a simple shopping tour, an evening with friends or the mere thought of the partner on one's way back home?

Thus, one may think that happiness is simply not missing anything, not having any desires, because one has whatever one needs or, following Epicure, one has learnt not to desire…

But maybe happiness also requires finding some answers to that wish for intensity, in any form in which intensity may come and be deeply perceived: intensity as an answer to that feeling that something was taken away from us and is anyway missing, even when everything is fine...

* * *

This brings us back to what we discussed about life, and limits.

Life *asserts* and *sustains* itself by changing: we are made by a part that tries to survive, defending and protecting itself, and a part that tries to LIVE. To survive one shields and guards, and builds barriers, definitions, limits; but to live one must abandon any defense, and face the world, naked, with no protection and no fear of changing.

A force that retains and holds you back, a force that pushes you forward. The need to rest and the longing for trouble. Two forces, and two ways of being 'happy': blessed quiet and intense moments.

This is wonderfully rendered by Angeles Mastretta in her 'Lovesick', in the two prophecies that Aunt Milagros wishes to newborn Emilia: the traditional one

> *'Little baby, you who sleep under the glance of God, I wish to you that you never lose it, that patience be your best ally in life, that you may know the pleasure of generosity and the peace of those who do not expect anything, that you understand your pains and be able to accompany those of the others. I wish you will possess a limpid glance, a careful tongue, a tolerant nose, a hearing incapable of recalling intrigues, precise and moderate tears. I wish you shall believe in eternal life and possess the quiet that faith concedes'*

and her own wish

> *'Little girl, my gifts are folly, courage, ambition and restlessness. Fortune of loves and delirium of solitude. The taste for comets, for water and for men. I wish for you intelligence and ingeniousness. A curious glance, a remembering nose, a mouth that can smile and curse with divine precision, legs that do not get old, a weep capable of restoring your pride. I wish you will have the sense of time the stars have, the perseverance of ants, the doubt of temples. I wish you will have faith in diviners, in the voice of the dead, in the mouth of swashbucklers, in the peace of men that forget their own destiny, in the force of your remembrances and in the future as a promise that contains all that has not happened to you yet. Amen.'*

* * *

Apart from a naive plea for a dull and ill-defined 'happiness', each of us desires, consciously or not, a sufficiently solid well-being, that one would not dare call *happiness*, and in the meanwhile something else – much closer to what each of us think of as *happiness*: INTENSITY, exclusive feeling and absolute privilege of the human being.

About three quarters of the male population is moved by the harmony and INTENSITY of the athletic gesture. Everybody is moved by the INTENSITY of the impossible mission and of the heroic act.

Not everybody, happily, is moved by the INTENSITY of power and oppression (generally felt as strength rather than injustice), but that happens, too.

And one can be moved by combinations of words that can grasp and capture, for a moment, the *intensity* and ineffability of life.

Money, fortune, all that the world and others give us, and the philosophy of enjoying small things, and being able to content oneself, orient toward a blessed-quiet type of happiness.

But restlessness, independence from what they give us, the challenge to BE, to DO, are the prices to pay for intensity. And this is the essence of life, which must be able to protect itself, but in the meanwhile must expose and negate itself in every moment, in search of new and more complex equilibriums.

Maybe happiness can really be defined: it is harmony, but also finding the way, in every instant, for increasingly fresher harmonies, a way richer of discovery and passion.

Restless harmony, and passionate.

True, without surviving one cannot live either.

But even where all energies are indispensable to merely survive – in front of starvation, of war – you come across selfless thoughts and love acts, signs of LIFE, of resistance, of intensity.

And when you see our incapacity of living, in welfare and peace, you realize that to build happiness – which is made not only of quiet and well-being but also of passion and intensity – one must not forget, or must reinvent, for humans, in school education, in communication, in work organization and in all other domains, the ability of attributing value to the things that are really worthy, and most of all the capability of enjoying how and what one IS and DOES, rather than what one possesses and obtains.

* * *

In the shell, or capable of passion

Going around in neat and orderly New England in the eighties, tidy little houses with tidy small green backyards and small white corrals and tidy stars-and-stripes flags raised every morning, and fake small churches, and post offices with white columns, and firehouses with those fire trucks that seem phony, chromed golden redded full-optional with bell and hook-and-ladder – and few black people, invisible, unless you look for them, keeping aside at the backdoors of pubs – and people with their satisfied smiles, who seem to say 'here, we have put our world in order; the others... we just do not care'.

Going around in neat and orderly New England it came to my mind how much the ones among us who still have some human tracts need, to remain alive, something outside ourselves, something greater, higher, stronger, something that inspired, overwhelmed and annihilated us, so that we can 'find ourselves'.

Passion, need of greatness, infinity, intensity. An insatiable need for passion, if you are not able to put it to silence in the name of integration into a society of accountants and tax advisers of well-being, pleasure sellers and conjurers.

Ideal, political, social passion, love, as in a stormy sea that one cannot but surrender to, though striving and fighting with ardor and decision.

A force capable of giving a meaning to pain, suffering and fatigue, not only ours but all that is around, that of others, and war, starvation, oppression.

We might certainly avoid and forget all this by retiring in a paradise of well-being.

But the minimum of humanity that has remained attached to our soul precisely consists in not doing that.

* * *

Forces that may give a meaning to life.

Supreme and invincible love comes to the mind, social commitment, political fight, search for the truth (does it exist?); transcending forces and as powerful as a stormy sea and the fury of elements.

In the life of many of us there might be periods that have remained profoundly etched in our memory: war, for some, or great enterprises, fighting for a practical or ideal aim, *common* commitment (a collective dimension is often involved, the multiplication of passions by sharing).

It is epochs in which, for one or the other reason, events have been lived with amplified, exaggerated intensity, and facts, people, impressions from those epochs appear to be more deeply linked to our life, important for its equilibrium and developments. In coming across a note, a photograph, somebody else's words, that refer to one of those periods or episodes, it is often difficult to accept that it really comes from *there*, the inadequate *intensity* kind of strikes us.

The crucial point about intense epochs and experiences is that they need not be positive experiences: wonderful or terrible, they are equally capable of producing nostalgia and tenderness, in remembering.

In Italy, in the sixties and seventies, a great number of the youngsters who got involved in the political dream of building a new, different, perfect society, had matured their view on life in the catholic environment. I imagine this still occurs, though it may involve a lower percentage of today's youth. Social commitment can be encountered as CHARITY, a means of negating oneself in the name of faith and loving God. Then, one discovers the PLEASURE of working hard, fatiguing and suffering *together*, or in any case *socially*, for a noble cause, seeing the results of one's dedication in the eyes of others. And one finds out that it makes no difference whether a god has stated what must be done, whether a paradise is there or not, waiting for those of us that have done what had to be done; one finds out that there is no selflessness, self-negation, that this is not "abnegating", but rather finding oneself; most of all, one discovers that sharing – ideas, commitment, results – multiplies *intensity*, and intensity changes the perception itself of life, the light, the color, the music.

The incredible power of intensity is apparent to each of us when we think of love stories: the intensity that is so profusely added by love to any experience, feeling, thought and dream, to the point of changing the perception itself of life, of reality, of oneself.

Today a journalist asked an 'expert' of love the interesting question: 'but in the end, people get more pleasure or pain from love?'; the other one answered what anybody would have been able to say, pleasure when you are lucky, pain when you are not.

Baloney! no need for experts to say that!

Ask anybody who has loved – no matter what their level of education – and they will tell you: the problem is not pleasure or pain, pleasure can be so great to hurt and pain so sweet to be lovely, the problem is intensity.

Nobody would renounce to the experience of such intensity; be it the pleasure of being together, talking, finding each-other, having sex, enjoying the joys, the smiles, the fortunes of the partner; or be it the pain of getting separated, desiring, longing, dreaming, missing the partner, suffering for his/her troubles and grief.

Not all that may be pleasure, but nobody would deny that it is as close as one can get to happiness.

* * *

But please, let them be true passions, not fake myths disguised as strength and power. Such as runaways, drugs... Which may well be overwhelming, annihilating experiences, capable of redrawing (erasing?) values, passions, dreams and behaviors, of imposing themselves and forcing choices, acts, destinies. Every other need and desire, problem and trouble, trivialized in face of the ABSOLUTE need, the drug. And this submission to something greater and stronger than you is often shrouded with a heroic charm: you find it desperately cried out by the most lucid *addicts* (just read *Trainspotting* to get an idea), and subtly perceived, but clearly, undeniably, by youngsters that are attracted, captivated, as they would be by great, dangerous deeds, or by extreme sports... The total emotion that grasps you by your guts, and nothing else exists anymore.

I believe that the misconception is severe.

Desires have an object, generally a possible or likely one, and are translated into projects, to realize them. The impossible ones become dreams - that in some cases we can coddle, but that cannot usefully guide our life. If we let them guide our life, they are no more desires or dreams, they become passions. Passion is desire, need, indomitable decision, of pursuing what we cannot achieve, or in any case of pursuing objectives obtaining which does not depend on us: they are not in our power, because they are greater than we are; and precisely the greatness, the higher value, the universality, the unapproachable strength is what transforms passion into a plea to transcend ourselves, to express and find ourselves by negating our limits to fly free [eh, clever!, I have just invented sublimation... or had anybody else already thought of this?].

But here is the trick!
The drug is not strong, it is not high, it is not great.

Drug... you just buy it! Where is heroism, myth, in getting lost in chasing something that does make you forget everything else, but is there for you, does not get pursued in vain, no, it just gets bought?

Great as the need might be, what heroic is there in accepting to be slave of something you can have in any moment, two coins are enough, or a car-radio, or the bicycle or choker of some poor guy, whom you even think right to sacrifice on the altar of this god, sold in small envelopes... Drug cannot be *sublimated*. It is robbery and idiocy to vest it with heroism, transcending value, runaway from everyday routine, dream, vital force.

Drugs are certainly not a mere problem of culture, of distorted search of a leading idea. There are dirty interests that push, in addition. And on the other side there are disease, uncertainty, difficulty, malaise, troubles that may help the image of a different life take root, a bleak and desperate life provided it is not daily and trivial. And here comes the fake color of dream, of myth, of superior strength, the names themselves suggest it, heroin – I say, HEROIN!, not simply diacetyl-morphine, which would be its name at the registry... – and acid, and crack, and ecstasy, not bad, as an atmosphere, as a proposal of alterative, of a way out from asphyxiating, deluding routine.

* * *

Often voices surface about chocolate's capability of stimulating specific neuronal receptors in the 'reward system', and at once somebody expresses a certain fear of being drugged by means of chocolate or other perverse instruments, capable of mischievously introducing into our nervous system substances that might stimulate to some extent our gratification centers.
Well, I would pray you all not to panic.

If you wish to avoid that your gratification centers get activated, it is sufficient that, in addition to avoiding exposing yourself to any abuse drug (nicotine, amphetamine, ecstasy, opiates, cocaine, cannabis...) you follow these simple rules:
- avoid assuming any sweet food
- avoid any physical effort
- avoid exchanging gentle words and especially smiles with anybody,
- avoid getting involved in tasks that have even the slightest possibility of success,
- avoid being exposed to information or news that may elicit any interest,
- avoid exposing yourselves to any art masterpieces that are not sufficiently abstruse to prevent any spontaneous appreciation reaction (Manzoni's stools are ok, for example)
- avoid sea, mountains, green lawns, especially when flourished,

*- avoid getting exposed to the sun, if you happen to have the misfortune of
appreciating good weather.*

But ESPECIALLY:
*avoid in any and whatever way any possible kind of sexual activity
and even more especially, avoid doing it with somebody you love.*

*Actually, everybody knows that nothing generates addiction
(tolerance, withdrawal syndrome, physical and psychological dependence)
more than love.*

Think about that, so, and abstain, if you wish to avoid eroto-addiction.

*Everything else can be done, with no risk of addiction.
Word of a pharmacologist.*

*Chi vuol esser lieto sia (Lorenzo il Magnifico): he who wishes to be happy
let him be so (to their own risk and danger).*

* * *

Here is my attempt at translating a short note written by actress Lella
Costa in a small booklet published by Comunità Nuova, a social
association lead by don Gino Rigoldi in Milan; a booklet that collected
opinions of culture and showbiz people about drugs and addiction.
Here is what she says:

*'I am not particularly interested – and even less prepared – to talk about
drugs, a concept that has become rather vague and evanescent, by the way.*

*According to the registry, and in some respects emotionally, I belong to a
generation that played and experimented with that stuff, and gambled, and
often failed. And paid very high prices. I have been sufficiently lucky, or
intelligent, or maybe both, not to get involved. Often, I wonder whether
there has been any merit in this, or only a series of fortunate coincidences.*

*But one thing has always struck me, and still bothers me: the concept of
addiction and dependence. Which does not relate to psychotropic
substances only, and chemical additives and opium – or grape –
derivatives. It is something else and comes from before. I think of
sentimental dependency: certainly, a feminine experience, though perhaps
not only such.*

*I think of (and recall, also) those moments of total panic, paralyzing pain,
actual incapacity of breathing, talking, sleeping – living – when the
beloved person denies himself, walks away, leaves us even only
temporarily.*

And you think 'I can't make it I can't make it I can't make it' and you mistake for love your tachycardia, and neurosis, and that angst that takes your breath away; and all your certainties get pulverized, and you ask, gasping, 'why? why?', why, and how will I survive until tomorrow.

And you wonder where the true, remote cause of this inability to live is buried, deep in you. You ask whom, or what, you have lost, and when, and why; you wish you knew what they did to you, possibly when you were still a child, to undermine so definitely every autonomy, all certainties, any confidence. You wonder why you need so much to be reassured, and at once, without a single moment of delay.

It is time. Time frightens you: empty time, slow, intolerable, horrifying time. Time to fill in, to nullify, to let go by, in any possible way, whatever the cost, whatever the means.

I certainly have no clear ideas, but it seems to me that if we got to fully understand this dependence, this lack; if we managed in smoking out from inside ourselves the memory of what they denied us, or perhaps we simply misinterpreted; if we discovered where that incapability of facing wait and pain comes from; then, maybe, we might begin to discern a way out.

Maybe.'

* * *

Lack, languor, nostalgia, blues...

A languor that has no clear reason, that sometimes we wish we were able to forget, a languor that generates suffering while we might survive peacefully, a languor that pushes to act because it does not tolerate empty time. Perhaps because empty time is only an invention to understand reality, but empty time cannot exist in our soul.

It is possible that in this languor, that is regret and nostalgia of a lost integrity, be the origin of all dependencies. But where does it come from, this lack, this longing, this need for something else? It is not born from something that has been denied to us. Or stolen. No. That languor is our way of feeling the force down there that pushes us to think and act, even when there is nothing to guard from, or to react to.

It may well be the origin of every dependence, but it surely is the origin of any creativity. May that languor be the soul?

That insatiable need for something else is not only a force that moves us, is something we could not do without.

It might not be any different: we are not *programmed* to merely survive.

* * *

From 'The King of Girgenti' (A. Camilleri)

[Zosimo is a farmer who has been proclaimed king of Montelusa (Agrigento) by the 'viddrani' (farmers) who cast out Piedmont's soldiers. The marquis of Boscofino, who tries to maintain a good relationship with him, talks to him]

' - The aristocracy of Montelusa has not taken a party yet: as long as you kill Piedmont soldiers, everything is ok; but when you begin to kill the Spanish, if you ever manage to kill one, you will have them all against you. You are alone. And you have nobody to ask for help, because no other 'viddrano' has been able to do what you are doing. And so, if you make your counts, what are you giving to these people that come after you?

Zosimo looked at him.

He smiled.

– You will never understand what I am giving them.

– I shall try to

– You cannot, because you have never suffered hunger, and black misery. But I shall tell it to you, all the same: I am bestowing them a dream.

The marquis bowed down to the ground. '

* * *

And then, let us bestow some dreams to ourselves as well!

Let us live such dreams, without the gloomy request that they be actually possible, without the greedy request that they last forever. With no regret when they end, or if they vanish as soon as we disclose the fingers just a bit and let the thread slip and flee, thereby freeing the kite that has captured our gaze for so long and has carried us to fly with it.

Let us preserve these dreams when we wake up, as a treasure, because we have lived them, not as a defeat or a loss because they have finished. Let us preserve them as something we have been able to build and live, and we shall be able to build and live again in the future, or maybe right now.

Because dreams, the dreams we bestow to ourselves and other people, give a meaning to life. Not counting calories, not the size of our car, not our weeks to the Maldives.

And once you have learned how to dream, you will never give it up.

Our behavior is moved and driven by the brain, and by those complex circuits that we call motivational circuits: but in humans these are not driven by external stimuli only... What motivates us is not only hunger, thirst, pain, necessity, needs. If it were so, we would be able to react to stimuli, act to silence physiological needs, defend ourselves and those we care of, perhaps, but nothing more.

We have seen how projections from the cerebral cortex regulate deep structures that generate motivational drives so that they produce drives that are not only aimed at satisfying physiological, vegetative, emotional, affective needs, at avoiding discomfort and pursuing pleasure, but also at evoking expectations and pursuing gratifications linked to social appreciation and to rational, cognitive, ethical, and ideal motivations.

This is the origin of such languor that bread cannot satiate,
that languor that asks for music, and wonder and infinity,
that languor that pushes to act because it cannot bear empty time.

It is true that there lies the origin of any form of dependence and addiction.
Because anything that activates those system,
be it a physical or mental pleasure,
be it satisfaction, illumination or love,
or be it alcohol, nicotine or heroine,
well, it knows how to have itself desired, and strongly missed.

But the languor does not come from something that was denied to us; it is our way of perceiving the force down there that moves us.

A force that bustles inside and pushes us to overcome our limits, to look at others, to seek their love, to understand and sympathize, to transcend ourselves and feel as part of a higher reality, that can prevail over the space and time of our life. It is a need to leave, to take off to be intensely we and in the meanwhile something greater, possibly a single grain of sand in a furious storm, but a storm that has an aim, an objective, a reason, a value, a meaning.

And precisely this force, this longing, is what we love to call SOUL.

* * *

For a theory of pleasure

Intensity: perhaps the key to everything is there. Pain, well-being, pleasure: the crucial aspect maybe is intensity, precisely.

And commitment, tirelessness, dedication of neurons. Neuronal circuitries cannot sit there inactive, not possibly, no way.

Just look at the child. Never still, never inactive. A brain designed to learn, to establish and remodel new connections all the time, to fix new information, develop new interpretations, continuously reread reality.

Never a dull moment. A brain made to act, interact with reality and modify it. And mirror neurons, that imitate and push you to simulate and reproduce, to learn.

When children play, they repeat actions that they have seen performed by adults. They repeat them just FOR THE SAKE OF REPEATING them.

The action of an adult rarely has no aim, rarely it has its meaning in itself: much more often it is instrumental, has its aim and value in what it determines and produces (that is the first step of Marx's alienation, by the way, which is completed when the product itself of the action is instrumental, and given away – alienated – in exchange for subsistence).

The child instead reproduces the gesture per se, and the aim is in the action itself, the value is precisely in reproducing. It makes no difference whether the horse is a broomstick, if the steering wheel is a paper dish, it needn't bring you anywhere, it need not turn the wheels, it must simply permit you to BE dad when he drives the car, and to experience the undoubted pleasure he must feel when he drives (otherwise, why should he do it?).

This is something we have not lost in growing up, even though they do whatever they can to sweep it away from us: we are still capable of playing, of wasting an afternoon in building the doghouse instead of buying it – just for the satisfaction of having built it ourselves, and even more for the PLEASANTNESS of doing it; we are still capable of reading a book to wonder, to feel emotions, for the PLEASANTNESS of reading it...
Of participating to a sports match not only to win, but also for the PLEASANTNESS of staying together, of striving and fatiguing and getting excited, and smiling and hugging each other at the end – what a crime it is to transform children's sports teams into armies, with graduates and officers and stand-ins! And what a disgust those fanatic parents that push along this road, and make of their sons' sport a means of self-assertion and indirect aggression...

Something inside pushes us to act, to do, for the sake – for the pleasantness – of doing, to watch for the sake of observing, and to understand, to learn, for the sake – for the pleasantness – of discovery.

A brain incapable of resting, curious, avid of emotions, and productive.

This is a great evolutionary privilege, because it favors learning, developing ever-new approaches and solutions in the face of vital problems; it favors the possibility of surviving in any situation and facing any changes; possibly, of living even better.

As a consequence of this, motivational impulses arise, that keep bombarding with no pauses the centers that push us to act.
But why, what is the sense of all this? The CAUSE is in the organization itself of the nervous system, in neuronal tirelessness. But the AIM? What is the purpose of all this?

The purpose is mixing up, moving and enriching the motivational game. Making it more interesting and beautiful.

It is a kind of vicious (or better virtuous) circle: the continuous rereading activity, in search for new interpretations, perspectives, unifying views, by the brain, is an intrinsic feature of the organization of the cerebral cortex itself, and the success of this activity – surprise, wonder, intuition, comprehension, detection of harmonies – translates into pleasure, and this reinforces and further incites this activity, this tireless research.

Meanwhile, all this enriches the picture of internal drives and makes it more complex, by transforming the conflict among a few trivial physiological needs into a varied, multifaceted and mutable, complex motivational contest. And this in turn is exquisite material for further search of new harmonies, esthetic pleasure and ethic passion.

Somebody might say 'what a lot of wasted time, and efforts'...
But the brain HAS NOTHING ELSE TO DO!
and neurons, no, they will not shut up!

Why complain, then, if this vicious-virtuous circle, this waste of neuronal energy, offers us beauty, pleasure, emotion, and the joy of a simple sign of love?

Thus, physiological necessities, but also affective and social needs, need of communicating; and curiosity that stirs and transcends them, and longing for novelty, desire of doing, craving for harmony and beauty.

If you look at it this way, the picture is not bad: the brain frolics, it plays the game it likes, and thus amuses itself.

Provided that some original drives are there, as forces that revitalize the game. And provided that such drives are not too strong, so strong to spoil the game, so violent to wipe out all the rest.

Well, I got bored with this theory of pleasure: by now everything has become so obvious...

The pleasure of a slight appetite there at the stomach, a bit of exhaustion after an effort, a slightly crisp cool, a warmth that may be just a little excessive, and some stimulating information, some emotion – positive, if possible, but even a bit of anxiety, before the penalty kick, a slight fear, in skiing down the slope – possibly a trace of pain (there are some that like it a lot...), a bit of fright, adrenaline, some commotion (a movie that makes us cry), possibly a nice, old, good blues...

The discomfort when hunger, sleepiness, cold, hot are too strong, when noise confounds you, when emotion sweeps you, anguish, fear, sadness with no hope...

It is not the kind of stimulus; the right intensity is what makes the pleasure. Stronger, it hurts. Even nice things, though in that case even pain and shock become pleasant, in a climax of tension where it seems you are drowning... 'e il naufragar mi è dolce in questo mare'
[and drowning is sweet to me in this sea, Giacomo Leopardi, 'Infinity'].

* * *

A reasonable amount of quietness, to survive. A reasonable amount of intensity to live. Two forces that move us in depth, in an interplay of discomfort (pain) and gratification (pleasure). An interplay of neuronal activities in search of balance and harmony.

It is a game sustained by life, of which it reflects the rules and the mechanisms: self-assertion in changing, and thus growing and building itself. The game is having the courage of choosing, deciding, and discovering oneself different. And sometimes becoming confused, and disoriented, because little by little – possibly without noticing it – we have corroded fundamental pillars of our equilibrium.

With no possibility of going back, because our way of facing life has not been determined by fate, or our genes, or experience; no, the WAY WE HAVE LIVED every single moment of our life has written in our neurons OUR WAY of facing reality, of interpreting and thinking of it, and changing it. And this is US, there is no way of coming back, erasing the brain, resetting the neurons, it is only possible to change some more, possibly with difficulty, to proceed on a new path and build new balances, new certainties, new desires, new dreams.

Sometimes it is difficult to keep pace, and an insatiable yearning arises, for silence, peace, security. But that is not enough.

* * *

Adaptation

Our senses adapt to steady signals, light dazzles us for a few moments only, sudden sounds startle us, do not let us neglect them, disturb us, but if they persist, they seem to vanish, and one no longer even notices them...

The soul itself adapts: we enjoy more a change for the better, and we suffer more for a failure, than for all we have or miss, or we are or do.

The soul, like the eye, sees the difference. It suffers for something missing and is happy for the slightest nothing added.

It gets used fast. And happiness must be rebuilt moment by moment, all the time. All life long.

And if it is so difficult to be happy, perhaps even harder is to judge the pain and unhappiness of other people.

* * *

I cannot understand women.

But maybe, little by little, I am beginning to discern something.

Men are trained to build situations, to fight against nature, things, society, the others, to change the concrete and practical aspects of reality around them and build a space and a role for themselves. Women can build the atmosphere, they fight against themselves not less than against all the rest to help nature, things, society and the others to get in tune, thereby realizing a space and climate where it is worth living.

Thus, for a woman 'to love' means to be there, to grant the presence of her body, her voice, her commitment, her affection, her care. Not imposing them, just assuring them. An atmosphere, music.
The woman offers CARE. *And maybe she expects the same from a man.*

He tries and understand, rather than getting in tune, he loves asking and giving according to his own rhythms, following his own logic.
He offers, and demands, TIME. *Not music, not* CARE.

If tuning cannot be found, you can have devotion, but love grows weedy, meager. Because the relationship needs the lymph, the life, the emotion, the pain and the joy of an entire person, who lives and strives, builds and dreams, not the devotion of a dog who lives of your caresses and of the food your hand gives it.

Because affection is a welcoming house when you come from the gray, humid, cold street. It is an aspirin when you have a headache.

But it is not love.

Love is a new song, wonderful and enrapturing.
You cannot escape its melody;
it stays in your head and sounds, and comes back and cuddles you, and snuggles you. Its words come back to your mind and take you far away. And you cannot keep loving if the song does not bump in your head, like the mirage of a non-existent place, of imprecise and remote sensations, of balances that can perhaps exist, but you do not know where or how.

And you cannot keep loving if there is not at least a part of the other one that keeps eluding you, though you painfully miss it. You are not addicted if you do not feel the 'monkey'.

Affection is the sweetness of something you possess. Love is the suffering for something you want, you need, you possibly miss.

Were we able to live it this way! Granting a presence, but leaving the others their own lives, so that they will never bore us, and we may never possess them. Not because they run away, not because they are not there: simply because they live, and find themselves, evolve and change, and are ever new.

In exchange, having their presence, their love, their interest for what moves WITHIN US, *their desire that we live and grow and* CHANGE, *so that every day they may find something new and unexpected, in us, something to discover, something that eludes them...*

Because every living thing, like fire, requires watchful and continuous care.

You can enjoy the warmth of the fire, and the enchantment of its restless running after itself and reviving, and know that it is still alive under the ashes, but you cannot neglect to revitalize it before the ashes die away.

This is the atmosphere, the true music...

Enjoying the rhythm, enjoying the exalting melody, but being able to enjoy the blues as well. Feeling the need to commit oneself, the suffering of having duties, of not being able to just sit there and look but being able to taste and appreciate its acid and stimulating flavor.

Because reality is made of flesh and blood and emotion. Of music.
And the substance of life is the music that plays inside you and out of you. You must be able to hear it and feel it, with your skin, with your blood, with your heart.

Words can suggest it, but not understand it, live it.
They cannot tell the music.

Often, it appears that we, males, try and understand, and tell, the music of love. You women, instead, just feel it: when a story is born, vacillates, when it needs a shock, new lymph, when it is exhausted... you feel the change of tone, the crescendo, the false note.
We, once we have learnt the refrain, just repeat it, and care about something else, and we are astonished in feeling out of place, of time, of tone, we are surprised when you point this out to us.

Maybe the explanation is that they teach you girls to color the world, while they require that we boys draw it.

Or maybe, let's say it! the question is that you are lucky: difficult as it might be to reach the climax – and we never know whether you are acting, and it is not only machismo, sometimes even for a male it would be nice to know you really liked it, sometimes we do care, we too can love, and wish the beloved person feels fine... – difficult as it might be, I was saying, when you manage it is a happy teamwork of head and skin. How wonderful it is when sentiment, emotion, excitation and pleasure grow together, push one another, and dance and jump about and thread and play with one another.

For us, instead, no: everyone is on its own. It is nice, sure it is so, when the head and feelings go together with our bit of skin down there, it is nice when you get along fine with it, and you play as a team and you win together, but you'd better be careful, because when you find yourself deep in (ouch!, pun not intended), the whole of you, body and soul, yes, sure it is even more wonderful, and you are going to remember it, but it ends that the only result is that you get to the grand finale too early.

The longer the distance between head and penis, the longer the way from the soul to the testicles, or at least the smallest and insignificant the soul itself, the greater the success! well, is this a nice way to learn to love! is this a nice way to learn to live!

And you girls complain that we do not understand the music of life, that we are not capable of living it without the need to try and control it, that we are incapable of using our soul...

* * *

Sometimes the need for a moment of quiet calls. But the yearning for intensity, pleasure, always compels. The need to be in the meantime oneself and something grater.

It is a need that identification with a social group can satisfy – the group of the peers for youngsters, the sports team fan group, the group of voluntary service, or of social and political activity, and the Country, the army, even the Factory for Japanese workers. It is a need that grabs and carries away when mass enthusiasms arise... It is a need that can amplify and multiply a thousand times each drive, need, desire and longing – love, solidarity and sympathy, but also aggressiveness, defense, revenge and resentment – magically transforming it into an irresistible passion.

The sad aspect of this mechanism is that it is not always easy to get tuned about projects, ideal longings and humanitarian impulses, whereas an enemy, or a 'different' person/nation/habit, a limit, a symbol onto which to project the fear, the menace from which to defend, are sufficient to immediately trigger aggregation, ideal sharing and identification with the group, starting off forceful emotions. It is easy to convene, campaign, get passionate AGAINST. More difficult is to convene and get passionate FOR. Perhaps this is also the reason why it is so difficult for democratic forces to aggregate, stimulate and involve the population in great battles for peace, justice, egalitarianism, and it is much easier to win an election because the other party makes some big error or if some misdeed of theirs gets unmasked. Less difficult, instead, to aggregate *against* the poor, unprivileged and socially excluded people as if they were the cause of criminality, *against* the immigrants with their different culture, habits and needs, *against* increases in taxes to enhance public services...

But even if we do not steal psychologists and sociologists their job, and do not rewrite treatises about mass psychology, it should be clear, with all we said up to here, that the origin of this mechanism of amplification of the drives is itself in the physiological interplay of motivational forces with the production of pain, discomfort, well-being and pleasure. The amplification arises from convergence and coincidence of the individual motivational force with the pleasure of sharing, of social appreciation, of affective bonds, of belonging and the protection that comes with it. And the sublime, interior pleasure of harmony among motivational forces adds (superimposes from outside, from above, meta-adds) to all this, the harmony of forces that agree and unify into a multiple and coherent music, varied and ever new, but embracing and reassuring.

However, alone or in the masses, we must find a way to transcend ourselves, in the intensity of a passion, a way to project ourselves towards infinity. Be it dreams, wonder, love, commitment, but a path and a way must be found by each one of us.

Otherwise, we renounce the soul. Otherwise we suffer, we feel mutilated, as if we were in front of a puzzle which lacks some pieces, insoluble; in front of a choice that does not admit any acceptable solution, because different perspectives conflict with each-other, as each one negates some vital need .

It is a need to surmount oneself. To negate oneself, I would say, if I surrendered to my profoundly catholic formation, but this is not true! It is not negating, this is asserting oneself, it is finding oneself, precisely and fully – to finally BE oneself; it is the need of negating momentary pleasures to the body to obtain deeper pleasures, the need of throwing everything on the table, even one's own life sometimes, because there is something that is worth more, but something that is not out of us, something that is worth more and is WITHIN US; not against us, FOR US, to be well, to be happy.

* * *

Elisa, 20-year-old, eventually gave up to an enemy much stronger than her. She lacked one of the defense mechanisms that cells possess to correct DNA replication errors, a defect that opens the way to tumors. She had seen her father go down that same path, before herself, and leaving her. After years of therapies and operations, that seemed to raise some hope, the wicked genes won.

She was a student of mine. I had known her for only a few months, we had rarely talked, mostly at the exam. A stranger, essentially.
But I had known; for months I had seen her in the classroom, attentive, relentless, committed. In spite of the pain, in spite of the drugs.
Sometimes she disappeared, for a recurrency, a cycle of therapy, an admission; then she reappeared, smiling to her friends, willing to learn, to grow, to acquire the tools to take care of others, some day.
It was difficult to look at her without feeling a deep, strong emotion.

I saw her again, a few days before she left us, in the hospital; suffering, strongly worn-out, but what worried her was feeling weak, not having the strength, she looked forward to the day she could come back, she hoped that her fellow students would not forget to record the lectures for her.

A precise emotion mounted, strong, irresistible. It was not pity. Not at all.

There was anger, sure, a sensation of impotence, sadness, pain.

But something else prevailed, something reminiscent of the astonishment that takes you in front of the snowed peaks of the Dolomites, the infinity of the ocean, the raging sea under the rain, an inflamed sunset, a clear night

*brilliant of stars. The emotion that takes you in front of something
beautiful, great, greater than you, greater than anything.*

It is the emotion you feel in reading the stories of heroes.
*The emotion in front of Hector who puts down his
helm and smiles, not to frighten his little son in
hugging him, before facing his last challenge,
against the cruel and invincible Achilles, in spite of
the prayers of the women, who try to dissuade him:
"Oh, you miserable, your own valor will kill you".
Foolish challenge, one could say, because the result
is written already.*

*But possibly the most noble and inevitable one: not withdrawing in front of
an essential, vital duty, impossible as it may be.*
*Because even if you cannot be successful, even if you cannot win, the sole,
true defeat would be to retreat.*

*The emotion in front of judge Paolo Borsellino's words, before being killed
by the mafia: "We are walking dead men…", "It is normal to be afraid, for
every man, the important thing is that fear be accompanied by courage…",
"I fear the end because I see it as a mysterious thing, I do not know what
will happen on the other side. The important thing is that courage wins".*

It may simply be "being moved". One may not cry for pain.
*Or for defeat, or sadness. But tears come up on their own, and the voice
quivers if you try to speak, when astonishment and admiration and grief
get to you, because you got a glance of a world of beauty and valor,
you have imagined a life that is worth living.*

*Looking at Elisa in the classroom, seeing her in the hospital, at the end,
and in front of that pale wood coffin, I asked myself:*

"WHY CAN'T HEROES EVER WIN?"

Possibly, that is exactly BECAUSE THEY ARE HEROES.

*They know what is important, more important than life and death.
And they do not stop, they do not withdraw simply because what is
important sometimes (often?) is impossible.*

*They rarely win, but they are never defeated, because their battle is not
against an enemy, the fate, death. Their battle is FOR something.*

In the end, we are all bound to die,
so the only way to win is to know what is worth,
in our life,
and not to stop fighting for it,
because to stop fighting would mean to get defeated.

Elisa fought to her last breath,
never doubting whether it was worth,
or even possible.

Making projects, committing herself, looking ahead.
Possibly, she did not win, but she certainly was not defeated.

Elisa taught us the way. May we not forget.

* * *

*Like any other animal with a brain, we have neural circuits that produce
the perception of pain and pleasure. We can produce pain by stimulating
specific neurons, and pleasure by stimulating other neurons.*
*What is different is the complexity of the cerebral circuits that can produce
these perceptions based on abstract reasons: suffering in front to what is
wrong, or unjust; proving pleasure when something surprises us, or we
discover something, understand, manage to make sense and capture the
consistency, the harmony; when we are in front of something beautiful,
and right; when we DO something nice, something right.*
*Here another dimension appears, in the human brain: the value of an act,
of a commitment, because it has a SENSE, because it is right.*

*This society, so centered on competing to prevail, on success, on having,
acquiring, deforms and compresses this dimension: it pushes us to focus
our attention on the practical effect of every act, on the prize, success, social
recognition; on the result rather than the motivation of each behavior of
ours. It may be true that "good intensions pave the way to hell", but we
should not misunderstand this motto: it is easy to interpret it as "what
counts is not the motive, but the result of your behavior", while the real
meaning is something else: you can play fantasizing and dreaming about
marvelous projects, and wonderful intentions, but if they do not become
actions and commitment they are useless.*

*Action, commitment. Not results. Behaviors that make sense, coherence,
beauty, an ethical value, in themselves, per se, whatever is the result.*

This is what makes us different from animals which possess less cortex.

Not the fact that we may be cleverer in obtaining results.

The leopard runs faster, the rat survives in much harder environments,
bacteria can escape antibiotics, tumor cells can expel our drugs and change,
to escape from every trick that our formidable scientific progress can
invent. Often, they win. But what they do has no value.
They are not moved by the need for harmony, beauty, justice, sense.

Make sense. It is about time that we rediscover, and never forget, what
distinguishes us, as human beings: the capacity of being evil and wicked –
as the animalists correctly claim – but also of acting in the name of
something that we feel to be right, in defense of something that has value,
and gives a meaning to an action.

Fabrizio de Andre's verses come to my mind:
"Oh God of misericord / You made you Paradise / mainly for those /
who were not happy   / for those who lived   / with a pure conscience /
The hell exists   / only for those who   / are afraid of it".

And I would like to paraphrase them with an equivalent secular paradox:
death exists only for those who are afraid of it.
Because for them death can rob life of its value.
For "those who have lived with a pure conscience", instead,
for those who know what is important, and can pursue it,
whether it is possible or not, without stopping, looking forward,
for those that we call HEROES,
it is clear that much more important than life is to give life a meaning.

And if pain brings us closer, in the attempt to encourage each-other,
the example of the hero brings us even closer, part of a better world;
it gives us energy, gives us meaning.

It was many of us there, to bid goodbye to Elisa.
There was sadness, there was anger, there was pain. And tears.
But not only tears of complaint; mostly tears of emotion, admiration,
turmoil, gratitude, hope.

Because everybody there, relatives, friends, fellow students,
we strongly felt that she had taught us something essential,
something that made us feel close, united and strong.

She taught us that one can keep being committed, looking forward,
whatever happens. She taught us how clear is the way to face the destiny
and the final challenge that NOBODY CAN WIN, how to face it
WITHOUT BEING DEFEATED: one simply has to GIVE A MEANING to life.

Let us hope we never forget.

* * *

Once more we find ourselves wandering among different levels.
Physical and metaphysical pleasures and needs. Motivations and meta-motivations. Individual drives and collective meta-drives...

And once again, each time we trespass a limit and change our perspective, it seems we are talking about something else, whereas our outlook has simply widened and risen higher.

One would like to associate a noun with what makes this change of perspective possible.

One would like to call SOUL that which lets us transform the interplay of motivations into affects, love, solidarity, ideals, and any mission that transcends us as individuals; and to call SOUL the capacity itself of transcending ourselves, of overcoming the limits of our body, needs and pain and angst and fear of death, overcoming the limits of our own life, by invading the soul and the memory of other people, and thus escaping the limits of the few tens of years that we can spend on the Earth.

But such a 'soul' is like 'life'.

A word that seems to give a separate essence to an abstract principle. What distinguishes the living organism from inanimate is a complex set of physical mechanisms that translate into an organization criterion, and transcend themselves into an abstract principle, that we name LIFE.

A form not less real than matter, immanent in the living matter, physical and out of physics. Not supernatural: internal but it goes beyond.

META-physical, precisely, exactly, properly.

What distinguishes humans from other animals is a complex set of neuronal mechanisms that translates into a complex relational and motivational life, soaked with transcendent yearnings and drives towards harmony, beauty, intensity, infinity.

Here as well it is an organizational criterion, that realizes an abstract principle, that we name SOUL.

A form no less real than matter – about the origin and eternity of which one can wonder – but which is in no way diminished when one realizes its full immanence in human neurobiology, physical principle outside physics, biological and outside biology.
Not supernatural: internal and that goes beyond.

META-physical, precisely, and meta-biological.
Exactly and properly such.

* * *

We are ruffles of the nothing

Quantum physics is pure poetry, it plays with the world because it turns it inside out as a glove, with ironic detachment, to show that there is nothing inside it; it scrambles it and presents it back to us paradoxically pulverized and rearranged, according to illogical logics that can only be grasped in their incomprehensibility: matter is coagulated energy, it is tangible reality generated by frantic oscillations of nothing...

Impressive and amusing hypotheses, the truth and reality of which do not change our existence a bit.

Pure cabaret... Quantum physics play an important role, for sophisticated and restless spirits, like mathematics for those who are willing to understand that, yes, it is a matter of balances, calculus and pyramid building criteria, but the real thing is another ball game, it concerns something else, it looks for its coherence in other spaces and dimensions.

It is the same function as that of music, for those who can, in addition to enjoying it inside, define it and capture its essence and matter.

They are all nice games. Because when we hear the sound, the mechanisms of our conscious reasoning force us to look for the object or the phenomenon that has produced it; to be reassured, in the same way as we are reassured, in looking at the spot of lull among windy ruffles and wavelets, if we realize that what appears calm or perturbed is anyway water, and not vacuum, or nothing.

Horror vacui. But if we overcome horror, then the soul, music, mathematics and quantum physics let us perceive the absolute existence of harmonies, logics, energies and processes; the MATERIAL existence, the dynamics and the life of RELATIONSHIPS, not less real themselves than the objects they link.

It is a part of the world that the skin does not feel, the eyes do not see, that makes no noise and has no smell or taste, that one must learn to perceive, to feel, to interpret with suitable cognitive instruments, which we use insufficiently, too little and too awkwardly.

Shall we ever learn?

Maybe this is the next step of evolution, because if we have performed the great step, leaving behind the monkeys, by conquering the coherent consciousness of ourselves in the world, a long way remains in front of us, a lot of consciousness remains to be conquered.

Because too many people think that music is perturbed air and not the perturbations themselves.

Too many wonder how vacuum may be perturbed, while they should be moved by a whole world generated by perturbations of the nothing.

And we still know really little about our ourselves and the world, if it is true that – as the poet said – 'we are such stuff as dreams are made on'.

Then it is about time to stop considering only that which is physically tangible as the object of science.

If quanta are perturbation of the nothing and matter is made up of quanta, in what does the SOUL differ from it, this wonderful reflection, perturbation, this ruffle of the nothing?

* * *

Perhaps not many scientists would agree on all this. Still, I believe that in front of the brain, being content with simple mechanisms does not help to understand a bit.

The convenient view, dominant although unconscious, of a great part of the scientific community is seeing the nervous system as an instrument to produce the right responses to external and internal stimuli. It is convenient, because the mechanisms of each response can be studied and a 'reductionistic', 'deterministic' picture can be assembled to describe behaviors. But for the human brain this is not only profoundly limited, it is also absolutely wrong.

Just think of a tribal society, a very simple social and economic structure: the behaviors of the group are rather well described and foreseen based on the knowledge of the social rules and of the main needs and forces that move the singles. The individual easily finds a synthesis between personal and collective benefit and generally acts in a way coherent with social advantage and well-being.

In a complex, stratified, society, where economic and social dynamics intersect and conflict, trying to explain social phenomena as the result of motivations and longings of the singles has no longer any sense: even if one knew in their minimum details the psychology of the single persons, one would not be able to explain many aspects and distortions of society and economy. A comprehensive approach to economy is needed, and a sociology; you need politics – not politicians but a theory and management of social interactions. And distortions do not arise from a flaw of the singles: the complex system they live in adds its own contributions, at a different level. This is what we refer to as 'meta', here.

The complexity of the brain similarly adds its own contribution to the input-output scheme, to the stimulus reaction paradigm, so that human behavior cannot be understood (and even less can it be predicted) without considering that the simultaneous elaboration of information at many different levels and with many different approaches, perspectives and aims introduces new dimensions: logical, emotional, affective, historical, social, ethical and esthetic aspects that need to be considered with specific intellectual instruments, distinct from the physical and biological paradigms that may be sufficient to understand and explain stimulus-reaction chains.

Though science cannot be considered a lobby, a compact group, I feel that what I have been writing constitutes a diffuse attitude across a good fraction of the scientific community, and in any case reflects the direction along which science is moving: not renouncing to *ask questions* even about uncertain domains such as emotions, dreams, consciousness, creativity.

Many would say, in front of these arguments, that they do not need scientific explanations in these domains, possibly they would prefer that science did not even try and give explanations that have not been asked for, unsolicited answers. But this is a misconception, because science is not the art of giving answers, and even less is it a collection of answers – possibly, it rather is the art of asking the right questions...

I like to spend a few words on science, because it is performed by neurons, and I believe it is itself a part of the soul. Under certain respects science was born – or *reborn* in a modern sense – with Galileo and friends, and as a baby – like any child – essentially requested the *right* of asking questions, and like any child was favorably ready to share any apparently reasonable interpretation, in trying to understand. When it became adult, it shifted attention towards the *answers*: now it wants answers and when it finds one it tends to stick to it.

As of now, the enemy of any new scientific idea is no longer the Church but what somebody likes to call the *scientific community*, which is so fond of any dogma in force. We talked about limits and defense to survive, ignoring that living is changing and putting in doubt everything and oneself...

Today science is mature. And as for any adult who has the courage and the force, it is now necessary not to let anything stop us, and claim the right to ask questions, to try new readings, to *discover, surprise* and *wonder...*

We live in a culture marked by two opposed stereotypes.

The poet-literate, who can appreciate feeling lost in front of Leopardi's hedge and the infinity it excludes, who knows how to peek in with timid and reverent imagination, as if they feared wasting the charm of uncertainty, vagueness, indefiniteness.

And the scientist, who coldly tries to sidestep all hedges to look farther and farther.

The integer man, instead, can fully enjoy the commotion of the hidden and imagined infinity, but can also confidently try and look over, with no fear of losing the infinity, sure instead that they will find a thousand more new hidden infinities, in front of which to get moved, and thousand more obstacles to overcome. Provided one does not lose the capacity to marvel and enjoy the enchant of wonder.

* * *

The soul, thus, is an immanent form in human neurobiology, a biological principle outside biology, meta-biological. Properly and exactly.

Still, with all this, we have not demonstrated anything. We have only seen that almost all aspects that are normally put in relation to a spiritual dimension of life, to a SOUL, can be related to known functions – or in any case to functions that can be investigated – in the nervous system. Many of the statements contained in these pages are scientifically tenable (they agree with all available experimental evidence, are not based on any indemonstrable axiom and are possibly disprovable by appropriate studies) and can thus be considered an acceptable truth – tentative, temporary, until disproven. Many other statements are only working hypotheses; they do not contradict experimental evidence either, but are based on still very meager observations and on a good amount of intuition and arbitrary interpretation; they are WORKING HYPOTHESES, in favor of or against which it is possible to obtain experimental verification and confirmation, and that can be widely extended and re-elaborated based on new observations that may accumulate with time.

Many other questions certainly remain: whether the soul is immortal, whether it comes directly from god, whether it reincarnates after death and whatever else one may wish to ask. On the one hand, these questions regard something extremely evanescent, because if the soul is not what is necessary for emotion, affection, ethicalness, esthetic sense and need for infinity, if it is not interwoven with memory, desires, dreams, ideals and longings, then for it, outside the body, only remains a fleshless gust, rather dull, a puff that cannot feel the heart beating and the viscera twist, cannot cry or laugh, and therefore might well live for the whole eternity, but only a life that is not rewritten all over at any moment, that does not change, that does not LIVE.

It is easy today for us to imagine a robot, capable of learning, building an image of itself, possibly suffering and loving – certainly easier to imagine it, science-fictionally, rather than thinking of how to build it, scientifically. Let us try and imagine it, unrealizable as it may be. Where would its 'ME' be? in the power supply, which gives it electricity and energy, in the immaterial force that keeps it alive? Or maybe in the information, the memories, the learning and experiences that are recorded on its memory chip? Let us switch off the mains, take out the current, and we shall have killed it, but it may still be there, ready to come back if we plug it in again; but if we erase its memory, we shall have destroyed all its *individuality*, we shall have killed it in a much more complete and cruel way.

And as we are in the middle of fantasizing, move its processor to another robot; or take out the soul from a person and move it to the body, and to the brain, of someone else: that soul will read a memory, a way of reasoning, an affectivity, a habit of reacting, an ethic and esthetic attitude, which are written in the host nervous system and are not its own.. its own... of whom?

<u>Acknowledgements</u>

Honestly, I should acknowledge my debts to the authors of most of the books I have read.

However, there are at least four people I must name:

Eric Kandel, Nobel prize for Medicine in 2000 for his studies on the cellular bases of memory, that have given a revolutionary contribution to our understanding of neural plasticity: his textbook has been for me instrumental to understand what I have understood about the neurophysiology of higher functions;

Douglas Hofstadter, to whom I am deeply indebted for his splendid treatise about the META, and switching cognitive domains and ontological realms ('Gödel, Escher and Bach');

Michael S. Gazzaniga, for his wonderful introduction to cognitive neuroscience, which I would prefer to call metaneurophysiology

and

Noam Chomsky, for his illuminating views on the structure of languages, and of natural languages in particular.

I hope none of them will be angry at me for how I may have deformed their original ideas.

* * *

This book is dedicated to my sons,
in the hope I may have left them something worth leaving

INDEX